Political Survival of Small Parties in Europe

NEW COMPARATIVE POLITICS

Series Editor
Michael Laver, New York University

Editorial Board
Ken Benoit, Trinity College, Dublin
Gary Cox, University of California, San Diego
Simon Hix, London School of Economics
John Huber, Columbia University
Herbert Kitschelt, Duke University
G. Bingham Powell, University of Rochester
Kaare Strøm, University of California, San Diego
George Tsebelis, University of Michigan
Leonard Wantchekon, Princeton University

The New Comparative Politics series brings together cutting-edge work on social conflict, political economy, and institutional development. Whatever its substantive focus, each book in the series builds on solid theoretical foundations; uses rigorous empirical analysis; and deals with timely, politically relevant questions.

Curbing Bailouts: Bank Crises and Democratic Accountability in Comparative Perspective
    Guillermo Rosas

The Madisonian Turn: Political Parties and Parliamentary Democracy in Nordic Europe
    Edited by Torbjörn Bergman and Kaare Strøm

Political Survival of Small Parties in Europe
    Jae-Jae Spoon

Veto Power: Institutional Design in the European Union
    Jonathan B. Slapin

Democracy, Dictatorship, and Term Limits
    Alexander Baturo

Democracy, Electoral Systems, and Judicial Empowerment in Developing Countries
    Vineeta Yadav and Bumba Mukherjee

Political Survival of Small Parties in Europe

Jae-Jae Spoon

University of Michigan Press
Ann Arbor

First paperback edition 2015
Copyright © by the University of Michigan 2011
All rights reserved

This book may not be reproduced, in whole or in part, including illustrations, in any form (beyond that copying permitted by Sections 107 and 108 of the U.S. Copyright Law and except by reviewers for the public press), without written permission from the publisher.

Published in the United States of America by the
University of Michigan Press
Manufactured in the United States of America
⊚ Printed on acid-free paper

2018 2017 2016 2015   5 4 3 2

Library of Congress Cataloging-in-Publication Data

Spoon, Jae-Jae Michelle.
   Political survival of small parties in Europe / Jae-Jae Spoon.
     p.   cm. — (New comparative politics)
   Includes bibliographical references and index.
   ISBN 978-0-472-11790-1 (cloth : alk. paper) —
   ISBN 978-0-472-02769-9 (ebk.)
   1. Political parties—Europe. I. Title.
 JN50.S66   2011
 324.2094—dc22
                                      2011014825

ISBN 978-0-472-03630-1 (pbk. : alk. paper)

For CJ

Contents

	Preface	ix
	Acknowledgments	xi
	List of Political Party Names	xiii
CHAPTER 1.	Small Party Survival: Challenges and Solutions	1
CHAPTER 2.	Balancing Preferences: A Theory of Small Party Survival	26
CHAPTER 3.	Preelection Coalitions in France: A Lasting Electoral Strategy?	53
CHAPTER 4.	Focusing Locally and Targeting Nationally in the United Kingdom: Working toward Representation in Westminster	79
CHAPTER 5.	Communicating Credibility: Elected Officials and Media Strategies	109
CHAPTER 6.	The Balancing Act Synthesized: Policy, Electoral, and Communication Strategies	139
	Appendixes	153
	Notes	161
	References	175
	Index	193

Preface

AS THIS BOOK WENT TO PRESS, the United Kingdom was undergoing remarkable political change. In the May 2010 general elections, for only the second time since World War II, no party received a majority of seats in the House of Commons. After five days of negotiations, David Cameron's Conservative Party and Nick Clegg's Liberal Democrats formed a coalition government. Postwar Britain had no precedent for a true coalition government, where the parties would share the cabinet portfolios, as is the norm in many West European countries. Cameron became prime minister, and Clegg was appointed deputy prime minister. Consideration of the party's long-term policy goal of electoral reform was a condition of the Liberal Democrats' agreement to enter into a coalition with either Labour or the Conservatives. Much to the surprise of his own party and political pundits alike, Cameron agreed to a referendum on the alternative vote, even though it would likely hurt the Tories in future elections.

A second event, of no less historic importance, was that the Green Party of England and Wales won its first seat in Westminster. Thirty-seven years after the party's founding, it achieved its ultimate goal of electing a member of Parliament (MP). Despite the first-past-the-post electoral system, co-optation of issues by the larger parties, and strong voter allegiances to those parties, the Greens' long-term strategy of building support in local elections and targeting efforts in national elections enabled it to overcome these hurdles. As in 2005, the party targeted three constituencies for the 2010 general election—Brighton Pavilion, Lewisham Deptford, and Norwich South. The national party funneled funds, volunteers, and other resources to these constituencies. The local parties chose their candidates early and selected candidates who had previously run, who were well-known both inside and outside of Green Party circles, or both. Several years before the election, the Greens selected Caroline Lucas, current leader of the party and member of the European Parliament since 1999, as their candidate in Brighton Pavilion. Through grassroots organizing, astute campaign tactics, and a favorable political environment in which the Labour incumbent was not seeking reelection, Lucas won nearly 31.3 percent of the vote, 10 percent more than the party's Keith Taylor had won in the constituency in 2005, and was elected the Greens' first MP. In their two other targeted constituencies, the Greens won an average of 10.8 percent of the vote, far higher than the 1.8 percent the party averaged in all of the constituencies in which it ran candidates.

The Green Party's win in Brighton Pavilion is evidence of how a small party can survive even in the most unfavorable political and electoral environments. Moreover, the party's strategic behavior and ability to balance its competing preferences of both policy implementation and vote and seat maximization ultimately enabled it to achieve its thirty-year goal. This book shows that despite all of the factors working against them, small parties can and do survive and even succeed, as the Greens' win in the United Kingdom most recently exemplifies.

Acknowledgments

THIS PROJECT IS THE RESULT of years of guidance, assistance, and support from many individuals in Ann Arbor, Iowa City, France, the United Kingdom, and elsewhere. I could not have completed this book without their efforts.

Several faculty at the University of Michigan—Chris Achen, Samuel Eldersveld, Zvi Gitelman, Allen Hicken, Harold Jacobson, Orit Kedar, Ken Kollman, Andy Markovits, and Roy Pierce—introduced me to the excitement of studying politics and becoming a researcher. I especially thank Andy Markovits for his constant encouragement and support.

Ken Kollman has remained a wonderful mentor and friend. He has encouraged me to ask the important questions and has always seen the potential in my work, even when I may not have. I have endeavored to be the same kind of mentor to my own students.

At the University of Iowa, this project has benefited from the efforts of several individuals, including Doug Dion, Sara Mitchell, Ben Read, and Dave Redlawsk, who read over drafts, talked through theoretical and statistical issues with me, and provided general advice and support. I am especially grateful to Chris Jensen and Kelly Kadera, who may at times have regretted having the office across the hall from mine. My heartfelt thanks go to Brenda Longfellow, Tracy Osborn, and Jennifer Sessions, for our weekly meetings that kept me on track and moving forward, even during the most frustrating of times.

Outside of Iowa, I thank Jim Adams, Andrew Appleton, Tim Bale, Sara Binzer Hobolt, Jeff Karp, Bonnie Meguid, and Irfan Nooruddin. Florence Faucher-King and Daniel Boy helped me make initial contact with the British and French Green Parties, respectively. I am indebted to the elected officials, staff, and members of the British and French Greens for opening up their parties to me. I especially thank Martine Billard, Michel Bock, Yves Cochet, Jean Desessard, Jérôme Gleizes, Gilles Lemaire, Serge Malloreau, Nöel Mamère; also Elise Benjamin, Peter Cranie, Darren Johnson, Jean Lambert, Noel Lynch, Richard Mallender, Adrian Ramsay, Chris Rose, and Keith Taylor. Several years of interviews, attending party meetings, nosing around party offices and archives, and reading party documents enabled me to understand the strategic behavior of these parties that laid the foundation for this book.

I am grateful to Mik Laver for pushing me and this project further than I ever could have imagined. It is a better and bigger book than it otherwise would have been. At the University of Michigan Press, I thank Melody Herr for all of her work throughout the review and publication process, Susan Cronin for her editorial assistance, and the two anonymous reviewers for their critiques and suggestions. Of course, all errors remain my own.

Several undergraduate and graduate students provided excellent research assistance at various stages of the project. I thank Zac Greene, Tim Hau, and Jamie Siers for their hard work. Chapter 5 would not have been possible without Alison Gibbons's and Lauren Levitz's commitment and perseverance in reading and coding French and British newspaper articles. Michelle Pritchett did outstanding work on the index.

Material in chapters 2, 3, and 4 was previously published in "The Evolution of New Parties: From Electoral Outsiders to Downsian Players—Evidence from the French Greens," *French Politics* 5.2 (2007): 121–43; and "Holding Their Own: Explaining the Persistence of Green Parties in France and the UK," *Party Politics* 15.5 (2009): 615–34, and is reprinted here with permission of Palgrave and Sage, respectively.

Finally, I am grateful to my family and friends for their continuous support. More than anyone, I thank CJ for his keen editorial eye, great brainstorming abilities, and willingness to spend months away from me while I was doing fieldwork. This project would never have become a book without years of his encouragement, laughter, patience, and confidence. I dedicate this book to him.

Political Party Names

Alliance Ecologiste Indépendant (Independent Ecologist Alliance, France)
Anders Gaan Leven (To Start Living Differently, AGALEV, Belgium)
Association of State Green Parties (ASGP, United States)
Avodah (Labor Party, Israel)
British National Party (BNP, United Kingdom)
Bündnis 90/Die Grünen (Alliance 90/The Greens, Germany)
Casa delle Libertà (House of Freedoms, Italy)
Christlich Demokratische Union Deutschlands (German Christian Democratic Union, CDU, Germany)
Christlich-Soziale Union in Bayern (Christian Social Union in Bavaria, CSU, Germany)
Coligação Democrática Unitária (Democratic Unity Coalition, CDU, Portugal)
Comhaontas Glas (Green Alliance, Ireland)
Confédération Ecologiste (Ecologist Confederation, France)
Conservative Party (United Kingdom)
Conservative Party of Canada (Canada)
Co-operative Party (United Kingdom)
Democratic Party (United States)
Divers Droite (Miscellaneous Right, DVD, France)
Ecolo (Ecologist, Belgium)
Ecologie Aujourd'hui (Ecology Today, France)
Ecologie '78 (Ecology '78, France)
Ecology Party (United Kingdom)
Entente des Ecologistes (Alliance of Ecologists, France)
Esquerra Republicana de Catalunya (Republican Left of Catalonia, ERC, Spain)

Eusko Alkartasuna (Basque Solidarity, EA, Spain)
Fédération de la Gauche Démocrate et Socialiste (Federation of the
    Democratic and Socialist Left, FDGS, France)
Federazione dei Verdi (Federation of the Greens, Italy)
Freiheitliche Partei Österreichs (Austrian Freedom Party, FPÖ, Austria)
Front National (National Front, FN, France)
Génération Ecologie (Generation Ecology, GE, France)
Green Party of British Columbia (Canada)
Green Party of Canada (Canada)
Green Party of England and Wales (United Kingdom)
Green Party of the United States (GPUS, United States)
Greens/Green Party USA (G/GPUSA, United States)
Déi Gréng (The Greens, Luxembourg)
Groen! (Green!, Belgium)
GroenLinks (Green Left, GL, Netherlands)
Die Grünen (The Greens, Austria)
Independent Working Class Association (IWCA, United Kingdom)
Kristdemokraterna (Christian Democrats, Sweden)
Labour Party (United Kingdom)
Lega Nord (Northern League, LN, Italy)
Liberal Democrats (United Kingdom)
Liberal Party of Canada (Canada)
Ligue Communiste Révolutionnaire (Revolutionary Communist League,
    LCR, France)
Lijst Pim Fortuyn (List Pim Fortuyn, Netherlands)
Likud (Israel)
Lutte Ouvrière (Workers' Struggle, LO, France)
Miljöpartiet de Gröna (The Environment Party, the Greens, Sweden)
Mouvement Démocrate (Democratic Movement, MoDem, France)
Mouvement Ecologiste Indépendant (Independent Ecologist Movement,
    MEI, France)
Mouvement des Radicaux de Gauche (Movement of Radicals of the Left,
    MRG, France)
National Front (NF, United Kingdom)
New Democratic Party (NDP, Canada)
Parti Communiste Français (French Communist Party, PCF, France)
Parti de Gauche (Left Party, France)
Parti des Travailleurs (Workers' Party, PT, France)

Parti Ecologiste (Ecologist Party, France)
Parti Radical de Gauche (Radical Party of the Left, PRG, France)
Parti Socialiste (Socialist Party, PS, France)
Partido Socialista (Socialist Party, PS, Portugal)
Partido Social Democrata (Social Democratic Party, PSD, Portugal)
Partit Laburista (Labour Party, PL, Malta)
Partito Comunista Italiano (Italian Communist Party, PCI, Italy)
U Partitu di a Nazione Corsa (Party of the Corsican Nation, PNC, France)
People (United Kingdom)
People's Party (United Kingdom)
Plaid Cymru (Party of Wales, United Kingdom)
Rassamblement pour la République (Rally for the Republic, RPR, France)
Republican Party (United States)
Respect, Equality, Socialism, Peace, Environmentalism, Community, and Trade Unionism (RESPECT, United Kingdom)
Schweizerische Volkspartei (Swiss People's Party, SVP, Switzerland)
Scottish National Party (SNP, United Kingdom)
Sozialdemokratische Partei der Schweiz (Swiss Social Democratic Party, SP, Switzerland)
Sozialdemokratische Partei Deutschlands (German Social Democratic Party, SPD, Germany)
Sozialdemokratische Partei Österreichs (Austrian Social Democratic Party, SPÖ, Austria)
Suomen Sosialidemokraattinen Puolue (Social Democratic Party of Finland, SDP, Finland)
Svenska Folkpartiet (Swedish People's Party, SFP, Finland)
L'Ulivo (The Olive Tree, Italy)
Union Démocratique Bretonne (Breton Democratic Union, UDB, France)
Union pour la Démocratie Française (Union for French Democracy, UDF, France)
Union pour un Mouvement Populaire (Union for a Popular Movement, UMP, France)
United Kingdom Independence Party (UKIP, United Kingdom)
Les Verts (The Greens, France)
Vihreä Liitto (Green League, Finland)
Vlaams Blok/Belang (Flemish Block/Interest, VB, Belgium)

CHAPTER 1

Small Party Survival: Challenges and Solutions

"No to the European Single Tomato." (Campaign by the Greens–European Free Alliance group in the European Parliament to reform food policies across the European Union, 2004)

A poster depicting a white sheep kicking a black sheep off the Swiss flag above the statement "to create security." (Poster for a Schweizerische Volkspartei [Swiss People's Party] initiative to deport foreigners who are criminals, 2007)

"The ecological revolution." (Campaign slogan for Dominique Voynet, French Vert [Green] presidential candidate, 2007)

A poster portraying several individuals who are Chinese, African, Muslim, and Roma standing in line in front of an elderly Caucasian man. It asks "Guess who comes last?" followed by "For your rights on housing, employment, and health care. Vote Lega Nord [Northern League]." (Campaign poster for Italian regional elections, 2005)

"Shout independence, equality, dialogue, peace, Basque language, human rights." (Eusko Alkartasuna [Basque Solidarity] campaign leaflet for Spanish national elections, 2008)

WHEN BRITISH PEOPLE (the forerunner to the Green Party) was formed in 1973, European party systems were still dominated by large, mainstream political parties stretching ideologically from the communist left to the center right. During the 1970s, the communists, social democrats, liberals, conservatives, and Christian democrats together received an average of 86.2 percent of the vote share (Gallagher, Laver, and Mair 2006, 232–48). Parties such as the British Conservative Party, French Rassamblement pour la République (Rally for the Republic, RPR), Sozialdemokratische Partei Deutschlands (German Social Democratic Party), and Partito Comunista Italiano (Italian Communist Party) embodied old politics and materialist issues, which included "economic growth, security, and traditional lifestyles" (Dalton 2008, 82). Conversely, voters at both the right and left ends of the ideological spectrum who were concerned with "new politics" issues such as "individual freedom, social equality, and quality of life" (82) were just starting to organize political parties to run candidates and lists in local and national elections. Many of these parties grew out of social movements, such as the student and rights-oriented groups of the 1960s. The voters, activists, and leaders who formed these parties were frustrated with the existing parties' issue agendas and policy preferences. Among the oldest of these new politics parties were the extreme right French Front National (National Front, FN), founded in 1972, and British People.[1] During the early years, these parties, which Meguid (2005, 2008) classifies as niche parties, initially struggled electorally and received very low vote and seat shares.

Thirty years later, the party landscape has changed significantly. Smaller, more narrowly oriented parties with campaign slogans and messages like those highlighted above are now common across the continent. While the older mainstream parties still dominate electorally and in government, these niche parties, which are focused on new politics issues, have undertaken electoral, communications, and policy strategies that have greatly influenced Western European political systems. The mean electoral volatility between 2000 and 2004, for example, rose to 11.8 from 8.6 in the 1970s (Gallagher, Laver, and Mair 2006, 294; see also Dalton, McAllister, and Wattenberg 2000).[2] In Austria, Ireland, Iceland, Finland, Belgium, France, and Germany, many of these parties, especially those on the left, have been included in governments. In several countries, new parties on both the right and left are achieving vote shares above 5 percent. Among the most successful of these parties are the Austrian Die Grünen (Greens), French FN, Belgian Vlaams Block/Belang (Flemish Block/Interest), and Finnish Vihreä Liitto (Green League).[3]

Figure 1.1 shows the vote and seat share for all Western European niche parties (green, extreme right, and ethnoterritorial or regional) from 1980 to

Small Party Survival

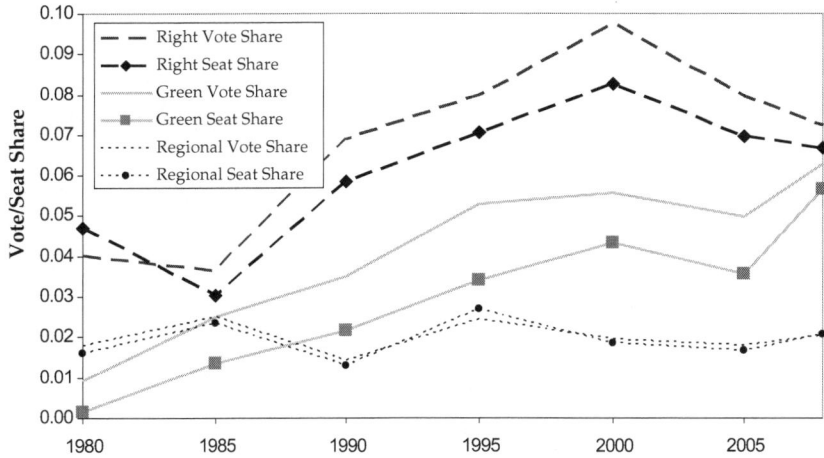

Fig. 1.1. Niche party vote and seat share, 1980–2008. (The countries included are Austria, Belgium, Denmark, Finland, France, Germany, Greece, Iceland, Ireland, Italy, Luxembourg, the Netherlands, Norway, Portugal, Spain, Sweden, Switzerland, and the United Kingdom.)

2008. Each data point represents the average vote and seat share for all parties in the group over the previous five years. The 1985 point, for example, is the average vote and seat share for parties between 1981 and 1985. The 1980 point represents these results from the last election before 1980, and the final data point is the vote and seat share between 2005 and 2008. Both green and extreme right parties have experienced overall increases in both vote and seat share across the countries and parties. The highest average vote and seat share for the extreme right parties occurred between 1996 and 2000 (9.7 percent and 8.3 percent, respectively). For the greens, the 2005–8 period resulted in the highest vote and seat share shares (6.3 percent and 5.7 percent, respectively). The average seat and vote share for regional parties has hovered between 1.5 percent and 2.0 percent for the entire period (and is largely driven by parties in Italy and Spain and the concentration of these parties in specific geographic areas of those countries).

Figure 1.2 provides a different view of the niche party experience during this period. It shows the total number of these parties in parliaments across Western Europe. The data points represent the same periods that are shown in figure 1.1. The results are essentially the inverse of the vote and seat shares, with many more regional parties than extreme right parties in par-

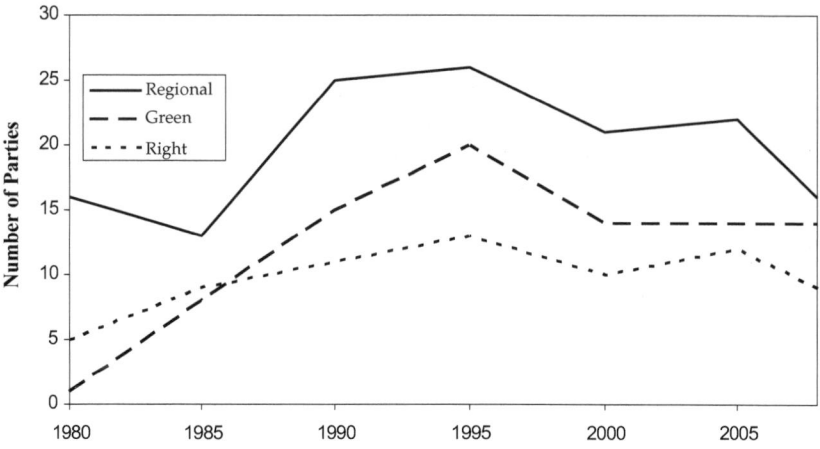

Fig. 1.2. Niche parties in parliament by party family, 1980–2008. (The countries included are Austria, Belgium, Denmark, Finland, France, Germany, Greece, Iceland, Ireland, Italy, Luxembourg, the Netherlands, Norway, Portugal, Spain, Sweden, Switzerland, and the United Kingdom.)

liament. Although most of the regional parties have had only one or two seats, they have had a consistent presence in many European parliaments over the past three decades, especially in Italy and Spain.

Niche parties have had the most success in terms of parliamentary representation and participation in government in countries with proportional representation (PR) systems. As such, these parties have also received the bulk of scholarly attention. But these parties in more restrictive plurality systems cannot be ignored. While they might not have the opportunity to win votes and seats, like their counterparts in PR systems, they, too, are working to be viable, credible parties at various levels of government.

In this book, I show that small parties, of which niche parties are a subset, have not withered, as much of the literature has suggested. Whereas extant theories are largely static and do not allow for a dynamic story of small-party behavior that accounts for party evolution, interaction with larger parties, and political context, I argue that the missing piece of the puzzle is small-party agency. Thus, the parties have survived by being proactive and by balancing the competing goals of vote maximization and policy differentiation. To explore this delicate balancing act, I examine the parties' policy, electoral, and communication strategies.

The chapter will proceed as follows. I first introduce and discuss the concept of small party. Next, I review the extant literture on small party success and failure. I then introduce the balancing model of party competition. In the second half of the chapter, I discuss the research design of the book and provide background information on the French and British Greens, the two parties of particular interest in this study. The final section provides the outline of the book.

DEFINING SMALL PARTIES

Small parties are hard to define. Some descriptions focus on the parties' electoral success in terms of vote and seat shares, while other definitions concentrate on the parties' ideologically extreme or narrow positions. My definition of small parties considers both size and scope. These parties appeal to a subset of the population and do not seek to be catchall parties (Kirchheimer 1966) by broadening their ideological appeal to attract the greatest number of voters. To be included in the small-party category, a party must be small in terms of ideology (that is, must focus on a limited set of issues) or be small in terms of vote and seat share (that is, not among the major players in a party system). Table 1.1 presents the three types of small parties that follow from this definition. Only the lower-right cell, which represents those parties that are large in terms of size and have a wide ideological appeal, are not classified as small parties. The upper-left cell includes most European green parties, which focus on a limited set of issues and typically win between 3 and 8 percent of the vote in national elections. The upper-right cell is comprised of far-right parties, such as the Freiheitliche Partei Österreichs (Austrian Freedom Party, FPÖ), which has consistently won more than 10 percent of the vote since the mid-1990s, reaching a high of 26.9 percent in 1999, and the Schweizerische Volkspartei (Swiss People's

TABLE 1.1. Typology of Small Parties

	Type of Political Actor	
Ideological Scope	Minor	Major
Wide	minor, narrow	major, narrow
Narrow	minor, wide	major, wide (not small party)

Party, SVP), whose vote share has risen from 11.9 percent in 1991 to 28.9 percent in 2007. While parties such as the FPÖ and SVP may at times be major players, they are still ideologically focused on a limited set of issues. The lower-left cell includes those parties that are ideologically part of more traditional party families but have very low vote or seat shares. Examples of these parties are the Swedish center-right Kristdemokraterna (Christian Democrats), which has exceeded 10 percent only once since its founding in 1964, and the British Liberal Democrats, which despite winning 22.1 percent of the vote in 2005 had only 9.6 percent of the seats in the parliament.[4]

The niche parties discussed earlier are a part of the larger group of small parties and generally fulfill both of these criteria, though exceptions occur (those in the upper-right cell). However, the parties that scholars include in the niche category vary. Adams et al. (2006), for example, define niche parties as those that present either an "extreme ideology," such as communism or extreme nationalism, or a "noncentrist niche ideology," such as ecologism (513). Thus, their definition includes parties that are in the communist, green, and nationalist party families. Conversely, Meguid (2005, 2008) adopts a narrower three-part definition that focuses on the new politics dimension of these parties (Inglehart and Rabier 1986; Inglehart 1997; Dalton 2008). First, niche parties do not follow the traditional class-based orientation of politics, which excludes the communist party family. Second, the issues raised by niche parties do not "coincide with existing lines of political division," meaning that they transcend traditional left-right classifications. Finally, niche parties limit their manifestos to focus on a narrow set of policies that are central to their agendas (Meguid 2005, 347–48). Meguid's classification of niche parties thus includes green, radical right, and ethnoterritorial or regional parties. Within the universe of small Western European parties, this study focuses on the parties that can be characterized as new politics parties. Thus, I follow Meguid's categorization of niche parties rather than that of Adams et al. (2006), which includes old politics communist parties.

THE SMALL-PARTY EXPERIENCE: EXPLAINING SUCCESS AND FAILURE

The small-party experience has varied vastly across Western Europe. Some parties have won substantial numbers of seats and have made their way into national governments, while others have stayed in the shadows. However, no direct link exists between type of party and electoral success. The three niche party families—green, radical right, and ethnoterritorial or regional—have had these varying experiences. All three types of parties have been in government in different countries—the German Bündnis 90/Die Grünen (Alliance 90/The Greens), Belgian Ecolo (Ecology) and Groen! (Green!), Finnish Vihreä Lütto (Green League), and Irish Comhaontas Glas (Green Alliance); radical right FPÖ and SVP; and regional or ethnoterritorial Italian Lega Nord (Northern League) and Finnish Svenska Folkpartiet (Swedish People's Party). Within party families, however, a great degree of variation in seat and vote shares has occurred. Vote shares for European green parties in the last ten years, for example, have ranged from well below 1 percent in Norway and the United Kingdom to more than 10 percent in Austria and Luxembourg. For radical right parties during this period, vote shares have varied from less than 1 percent in Sweden to nearly 30 percent in Switzerland.

These results raise the important question of what explains small-party success and failure. Scholars of political parties have provided several different explanations, which can be categorized into three types: systemic, party, and individual. Systemic explanations include the electoral system and other rules and institutions. Party explanations encompass the behavior of large parties toward small parties. Individual explanations focus on explaining voters' decisions.

SYSTEMIC EXPLANATIONS: RULES AND INSTITUTIONS

As Duverger (1954) first demonstrated and others subsequently substantiated (see, for example, Rae 1967; Riker 1982), a strong relationship exists between a country's electoral and party systems. Because of the psychological and mechanical effects associated with electoral rules, a country's electoral system can largely explain the success or failure of small parties. Furthermore, Cox (1997) argues that the maximum number of parties in a given district should be one more than the district magnitude (the M + 1 rule). Ezrow (2010, 75–76) shows that an inverse relationship exists between the disproportionality of the electoral system and both the number of niche parties and their combined vote share in a given country. European electoral systems vary from low-threshold, large-district PR systems (the Netherlands with a threshold of 0.67 and a district magnitude of 150) to single-member-district or plurality majoritarian systems (the United Kingdom and France). Along the continuum are varying thresholds, district magnitudes, and electoral formulas for translating votes to seats. The higher the minimum threshold, the lower the district magnitude; the more favorable the formula is for larger parties, and the less likely it is that a smaller party will gain seats (Taagepera and Shugart 1989). In the United Kingdom, for example, the Liberal Democrats' average vote share in the four most recent national elections prior to 2010 was 18.8 percent, but its seat share never exceeded 9.6 percent (which it won in 2005). Furthermore, beyond the simple PR/plurality distinction, there are mixed systems (Germany and Italy from 1994 to 2006), and two single transferable vote systems (Ireland and Malta).

Small parties typically have had the most success in PR or mixed systems.[5] In Western Europe between 1980 and 2008, for example, a moderate correlation ($r = 0.23$) exists between small-party vote share and the existence of a PR system. Using a 3–5 percent threshold for vote or seat share in national elections and/or government participation as a loose definition of success, all of the parties that qualify as successful are found in countries that have some form of proportional representation.

An exception to this trend is the French Greens' participation in Lionel Jospin's Socialist government from 1997 to 2002. After the first elections in which the two parties participated in preelection coalitions resulted in a win for the left, the Parti Socialiste (Socialist Party, PS) invited the Greens to take part in the government via the post of minister of the environment (held first by Green leader Dominique Voynet and subsequently by Green member of Parliament Yves Cochet). In the 1997 legislative elections, the Greens won 6.8 percent in the first round, which gave them eight deputies following the second round—about 1.2 percent of the Parliament. Thus, the party was included in government not because of its seat or vote share but because of its willingness to work with the Socialists.

Although the mechanisms of plurality make it very hard for small parties to succeed, parties outside the top two have persevered. Several factors help explain this. Survival may be based on institutional arrangements, such as federalism. In their study of the United States, Canada, the United Kingdom, and India, Chhibber and Kollman (1998, 2004) show that Duverger's Law holds only when a strong national government exists. When the national government is weak, regional parties will thrive. Hicken (2009) builds on this idea of centralization in arguing that national party systems are the result of cross-district aggregation or linkage. Voters' and parties' ability (or inability) to coordinate across districts results in fewer (or more) national parties. Survival may also depend on the number of social cleavages in a given society. Several scholars have found that social heterogeneity, as measured by the number of ethnic groups, may mitigate Duverger's Law (Ordeshook and Shvetsova 1994; Amorim Neto and Cox 1997; Cox 1997; Mozaffar, Scarritt, and Galaich 2003; W. R. Clark and M. Golder 2006). Survival may also be related to dissatisfaction with the major parties or stronger ties to a party in a particular geographical area, perhaps as the result of historical context or the concentration of a specific demographic group. Examples include the persistence of the Parti Communiste Français (French Communist Party) in several industrial areas surrounding major cities; the strength of the British Liberal Democrats in parts of Scotland; and the success of the American Independence Party in the American South in 1968.

Beyond the electoral system itself, a host of other rules can affect the likelihood of small-party success. From ballot access rules to party finance and campaign regulations, small parties are often disadvantaged because of their size (Harmel and Robertson 1985; Rosenstone, Behr, and Lazarus 1996). In much of Europe, public funding and time for campaign broadcasts on television, for example, are often allocated in proportion to the number of members of parliament (MPs) a party has or the size of its membership (Farrell and Webb 2000; Norris 2002). In the Netherlands, however, all parties that present lists at the national elections receive the same amount of time on radio and television regardless of size or representation in Parliament (Koole 1996, 519). Small parties are often not invited to debates or are kept off of national commissions that decide the debates' participants, as in the case of the Federal Election Commission (FEC) in the United States (Rosenstone, Behr, and Lazarus 1996). These and other rules can severely disadvantage small parties. Conversely, more favorable rules can create an "opportunity pull" toward new parties (Rüdig 1990; Hug 2001).[6]

PARTY EXPLANATIONS: CATCHALL, CARTEL, AND CO-OPTATION

A second explanation of small party success or failure is major parties' reaction toward them. Postwar Europe has seen the development of many catchall parties whose goal was to maximize votes and seats (Kirchheimer

1966). Parties often work toward this goal by moving their policy positions along the ideological spectrum. In two-party systems, this behavior can leave little room for new parties to develop. However, in multiparty systems, when new issues emerge and the existing parties are not responsive, new parties will develop (Kitschelt 1988). But in both types of systems, catchall parties often co-opt the positions of small parties and consequently take their voters. For example, the U.S. Democratic Party responded when Ralph Nader won 2.7 percent of the popular vote in the 2000 presidential election by focusing on and then shifting its positions on the environment and trade to the left to reintegrate these lost voters into the party (Dao 2000). In addition, the British Conservative Party has sought to improve its image on environmental issues by changing its logo to a stylized tree; using the slogan "Vote Green, Go Blue"; and putting the environment and climate change policy high on its agenda (Glover 2006; www.conservatives.com).[7] New parties emerge only when the existing parties do not respond to new issues (or when their responses are not sufficient for those who care most about the issue) (Downs 1957). These new parties then face the challenge of staking out their ideological space in the party system and of ensuring that they do not get reabsorbed by the larger parties.

Another obstacle for small parties is the development of cartel parties (Katz and Mair 1995). Cartelization happens when the large established parties become increasingly dependent on the state for funding and isolate themselves from voters. The cartel parties often collude against small parties by determining rules for funding, campaigning, and the like. As with catchall party behavior, this collusion can result in the co-optation of these parties. The FEC, for example, comprises representatives from the Democratic and Republican Parties. Because this body decides which candidates will be invited to participate in presidential debates, third-party candidates are typically omitted from the roster.[8] As a result, larger parties find it easier to co-opt third parties' potential voters and issues since the parties are not in the forefront of the public's mind.

INDIVIDUAL-LEVEL EXPLANATIONS: SOCIALIZATION,
PARTISANSHIP, AND VALUES

At the individual level, socialization and partisanship offer a third set of explanations of why small newer parties may not succeed. In the American politics literature, socialization to a two-party system is often provided as a strong explanatory factor for why long-lasting third parties have never taken root. Voters typically do not vote for a third party because they consider it a wasted vote (Rosenstone, Behr, and Lazarus 1996). We also know that where partisanship is strong, voters are most likely to support the party to which they feel closest (Campbell et al. 1960; W. Miller 1991; Lewis-Beck et al. 2008). As partisanship in an electorate wanes, however, voters may begin to turn to other parties, which can take several forms. They may be "flash parties" that emerge and contest candidates or lists in one or two elections before disbanding (Rüdig 1990, 5; Dalton 2008, 190), such as the Dutch List Pim Fortuyn, which participated in local and national elections from 2002 to 2006. Small parties may also be more durable, contesting elections at all levels in as many districts or constituencies as possible. Dalton and Wattenberg (2000) have identified a trend of dealignment, or declining partisanship, across countries in the Organization for Economic Cooperation and Development, which can lead to an increase in support for new politics parties on both the right and the left.

Changing values within the electorate often created the push that voters needed to move toward both forming and supporting new parties (Rüdig 1990; Hug 2001). This push can come from value or demographic changes within a population. Inglehart and others have argued that value changes occurred in many Western European countries beginning in the 1960s. With a societal shift up Maslow's hierarchy of needs from material needs of food, shelter, and employment to postmaterial concerns about quality-of-life issues such as the state of the environment or equality between the sexes came the demand for political actors to address these issues. As those born in the prosperous postwar era came of age, the number of voters with postmaterialist values greatly increased (Inglehart and Rabier 1986; Inglehart 1995, 1997), as did the pressure on the existing party system.[9] This set of transitions is the push factor typically credited with leading to the fragmentation of the party system and to the formation of left-wing new politics parties, often termed New Left parties, in the late 1970s and early 1980s (Dalton, Flanagan, and Beck 1984).

The formation of right-wing new politics parties, called the New Right, is often attributed to an increase in the saliency of new issues stemming from various exogenous changes, such as population change (Ignazi 1992; Kitschelt 1995). For example, the influx of North African immigrants to the urban centers of France induced nationalist feelings and concerns regarding the outcome of such a change in the population composition (Mayer and Perrineau 1996; Perrineau 1998; Mayer 2002). This new issue pushed many on the right, as well as previous Communist Party supporters, toward the creation and subsequent support of the far right FN.

Finally, Kedar (2005, 2009) offers an institutional perspective on when voters will support more extreme parties (often niche parties), which she calls compensatory voting. In multiparty parliamentary systems, voters are forward-thinking and consider the postelection coalitions that may form. In turn, they will vote for more extreme parties with the belief that the postelection coalition formation process will dilute all of the parties' positions. Collectively then, the coalition's positions will more closely approximate the voters' preferred policy preferences than would voting for their most preferred party.

A REVISED THEORY OF PARTY COMPETITION FOR SMALL PARTIES: BALANCING COMPETING GOALS

According to these explanations, the barriers for small parties are quite high, especially when the rules are more restrictive, the large parties are more co-optive, and the electorate's partisan ties are stronger—in other words, the more majoritarian the system. But these theories are largely static in that they do not provide a dynamic story of small-party behavior. Conversely, a dynamic model enables us to understand why some small parties survive despite these hurdles.

I argue that the missing piece of the puzzle is small-party agency. The parties' perseverance is based on their strategic decisions and interactions with the larger parties in the policy, electoral, and communications spheres. This behavior has changed over time and varies with the political context. Moreover, this behavior helps small parties persist despite adverse systemic, partisan, and individual-level factors. Meguid (2008) makes a similar argument about mainstream party strategy to explain niche party success or failure, but her theory places all of the agency in the hands of the mainstream parties. She focuses on mainstream party behavior rather than on the explicit behavior of niche parties and what they are doing to survive despite the often detrimental behavior of the larger parties toward them, especially in the policy realm.

Traditional spatial theories of party competition, such as the Downsian model, do not take policy into consideration. They argue that parties are vote maximizers, seeking to win as many votes as possible. To do so, the parties are willing to move around the ideological spectrum. Indeed, Downs (1957, 28) argues that parties "formulate policies in order to win elections, rather than win elections in order to formulate policies." This idea is further developed by Kirchheimer's (1966) notion of a catchall party. In his conception of parties, ideology also plays a secondary role to winning votes, seats, and office. However, these theories do not help us to understand small-party behavior, especially that of new politics parties that arose in reaction to policy deficiencies in the major parties. These parties do care about policy. In fact, many of these parties formed in reaction to the existing parties' neglect of the issues about which they cared most (Kitschelt 1988).

Kitschelt (1989, 41) describes these new parties as having to choose "from a continuum of options located between polar alternatives represented by a logic of constituency representation and a logic of electoral competition." The notion of constituency representation is based on the ideal of representing the political beliefs of the party's core supporters. Parties that have chosen this strategy have made a commitment to follow a path of ideological purity rather than shifting their positions to increase their popular appeal. A logic of electoral competition, in contrast, seeks to maximize public support through an appeal to all party sympathizers, including those at the margins, even if doing so means adjusting policy programs and strategies. Kitschelt argues that left-libertarian or New Left parties can thus be distinguished from their conventional competitors in that they primarily follow a logic of constituency representation rather than one of electoral competition. Kitschelt recognizes that these new politics parties "show some signs of moving toward a logic of party competition" (281).

Small new politics parties' electoral behavior has moved even closer to that of their major-party counterparts in Europe over the past two decades. They are evolving from policycentric, neither left nor right parties to electoral competitors that care about votes, office, and policy (Strøm 1990; Müller and Strøm 1999). In short, they are beginning to resemble goal-seeking, outcome-oriented Downsian political parties (Sjöblom 1968; Przeworski and Sprague 1986; Schlesinger 1991). They have shifted their outlook from the immediate or short term to the long term. These parties have come to understand that winning today may not be possible but that decisions made today can and will lead to the realization of future goals. Thus, if winning seats in parliament is the small party's eventual goal, it does not make sense to let a larger party subsume the party's key issue positions and then draft and pass legislation, thereby leaving the small party without a purpose. This evolution in party goals can be attributed to discrete changes, such as changes in leadership and dominant factions within the party, and to external stimuli, that include the issue positions of other parties, election results, and entry or exit from parliament (Przeworski and Sprague 1986; Panebianco 1988; Harmel and Janda 1994; Harmel 2002).

More recent literature on party competition has recognized that policy matters for some parties. Meguid (2008), for example, argues that niche party success and failure are driven by mainstream party strategies regarding issue or policy ownership, salience, and position. Niche party success, by her account, depends on whether the mainstream party is adversarial, accommodative, or dismissive toward the niche party's policies. Meguid shows that the nonproximal French Socialist Party's adversarial strategy toward the FN worked to solidify the niche party's ownership of the immigration issue and maintain its salience. At the same time, the Gaullists' divided accommodative strategy on this issue was weaker. These two strategies combined led to the FN's success in the 1980s and 1990s.

Moreover, spatial modelers have long since departed from the Downsian approach and have adopted a policy-seeking framework to understand parties' positioning (see, for example, Wittman 1973, 1983; Hinich and Munger 1997; Adams, Merrill, and Grofman 2005; Adams and Merrill 2006). Adams et al. (2006) find that niche parties are less responsive to shifts in public opinion than are mainstream parties and that where the niche parties moderated their positions, they were more likely to suffer in the next election. The authors conclude that niche parties "can be considered 'prisoners of their ideologies'—they have no real choice other than to cling to the policy ground they have staked out for themselves" (526). But does this necessarily mean that these parties are not also trying to maximize their vote and seat share? While not all parties are the same when it comes to preferences for votes, office, and policy, a complete theory of small-party survival must consider both policy preferences and electoral strategy.

What, then, explains small parties' perseverance? If they cared only about policy, they would either languish at the fringes of the political system or be absorbed by a larger, mainstream party that co-opted their issues. But if they were concerned only with votes, seats, and office, they might stray too far from their ideological foundations and core voters in trying to pull in as many voters as possible and end up unable to differentiate themselves from larger catchall parties. Thus, small parties' survival is based on a careful balancing act in which they must determine how to maximize their vote and seat share without completely sacrificing their policy preferences. In his study of the French, British, Swedish, and German Green parties, Burchell (2002, 163) argues that "the process of transformation within the Greens has reflected a balancing act between the ideological goals and commitments inherent within the Greens' historical roots, and the electoral opportunities and constraints facing the parties."

Building on Burchell's observation, my theory puts this balancing act at the center of small-party behavior. But the parties are not just playing the role of reactive pawns in the electoral game, as he argues: they are proactive strategic agents and recognize that to succeed, they must take matters into their own hands, establishing a way to win votes and seats while avoiding a move too far away from their policy preferences. When successful, this calculation has enabled small parties to survive in plurality systems that would otherwise spell their demise.

Figure 1.3 illustrates how small parties must weigh the competing interests of policy differentiation and vote maximization to survive.[10] This balancing act distinguishes the behavior of the parties both from the pure policy-seeking or constituency-representation model and from the pure vote/seat/office-seeking model of party competition. If a party devotes too much of its efforts to either goal, it will get out of balance, lose its raison d'être, and die.

To demonstrate small parties' strategic behavior, I examine the policy, electoral, and communication strategies through which they balance their competing interests. Policy strategies reflect how the party positions itself on issues in relation to its major-party competitors and include the calculated decision of how differentiated policy preferences should be and on which issues the differentiation should focus. Electoral strategies are those that the party utilizes in election campaigns and include decisions such as whether to work with other parties either formally or informally and whether certain districts should be targeted (and if so, which ones) to maximize vote and seat potential. Finally, communication strategies determine how the party portrays itself to the public through the media and includes decisions about which party elites are used (local, national, or supranational, for example), how proactive to be, on which themes to focus, and

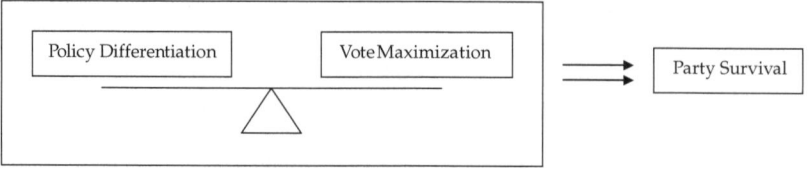

Fig. 1.3. Balancing interests model of small party survival

how to use the tools of the media, such as letters to the editor and opinion pages of newspapers. These decisions affect the party's ability to differentiate its policies while conveying to voters its viability as a party. Together, the strategic decisions in these three areas reflect a party's balance between the competing goals of policy implementation and vote maximization. When successful, these decisions enable the party to survive.

Key Terms

I define *strategic* in the general sense of being outcomes-oriented and considering how choices and decisions will affect larger goals. *Success* is a complex concept, often depending greatly on context and on the actor. Indeed, Harmel and Robertson (1985, 510) argue that "there are many ways that a party may be considered successful without ever winning many votes or any legislative seats." To a large, established party, success may be achieved only when an election is won and the party holds the position of prime minister. But for a newer small party, success may be winning its first seats in parliament or even crossing the threshold to qualify for seats. In her analysis of ethnic parties in India, Chandra (2007, 5), for example, defines success as "the degree to which a party is able to capture the votes of members of its target ethnic category." For small and big parties alike, success may also be the passage and subsequent implementation of a policy.[11] Failure, of course, is often in the eye of the beholder and may vary greatly across parties. Whereas success and failure can be hard to pinpoint, I use *survival*—whether a party exists—as a more straightforward concept. Thus, survival is not tied to success, however defined. After a party forms, if it continues to contest elections fairly regularly, I argue that it is surviving or persevering. A party's *durability* or *survivability* is largely based on the decisions it makes in election campaigns, on policies, and in regard to its interaction with other parties. Part of succeeding, though perhaps not of simply surviving, is the ability to demonstrate to voters credibility as a party. *Credibility* again can vary depending on level of government and role. A voter may consider a party credible to hold councillor positions at the municipal level, for example, but may not have a similar opinion of the party in terms of representation in the national parliament. The party seeks to come across as credible to voters in the particular election being contested. Of course, the more credible the party is, the more likely it is to be viable and to succeed. Like success, *viability* can also have several definitions. Some are formal, such as the threshold for advancement to a runoff round of voting or eligibility for seats, while others are informal, such as simply having the ability to win an election or govern. In her study of indigenous parties in Latin America, Van Cott (2005, 18), for example, describes viability as "the achievement of a sufficient level of consolidation and voter support to continue as a competitor in elections." Whereas credibility and viability are necessary conditions of success, success is not a necessary condition of survival. Finally, *context* is key in assessing a party's strategy as well as its credibility, viability, success, and ultimately survival. Success in a PR system is very different than success in a plurality system, especially for a small party. A party's campaign strategy, for example, may be a consequence of its previous election results as well as the results achieved by other parties. Its policy preferences may also depend on those of other proximal (and non-proximal) parties. As the party system and the preferences of the parties in the system vary, so might the position of a given party. Thus, context is essential to any model of party survival.

RESEARCH DESIGN

To test my theory of small-party survival, I concentrate on the greens as a small-party family that is focused on new politics issues. I use both cross-national data on Western European green parties and in-depth comparative case studies of the strategies of two green parties that have survived in similar electoral systems. The cross-national data on policy positions (Budge et al. 2001; Klingemann et al. 2006) and expert survey data (Laver and Hunt 1992; Benoit and Laver 2006) test the overall balancing thesis and show that green parties have balanced their competing preferences for policy differentiation and vote maximization over time. But these data have their shortcomings. First, not all green parties are included in the data sets. The British Green Party is one such missing party. Second, and perhaps more important, these data do not show how the parties' balancing of their policy- and vote-seeking preferences manifests itself in their electoral and communication strategies. As I demonstrate, it is these strategies that have contributed to the parties' survival.

My goal of understanding how and why small-party strategy and success have varied strongly influenced my selection of cases. To maximize my ability to compare these cases, I follow King, Keohane, and Verba's (1994) suggestion to expand the number of observations by examining the parties' strategies in two contexts (electoral and communication) to determine how they have balanced their competing interests. I analyze each strategy using a mixed-methods multilevel approach, utilizing both qualitative and quantitative analyses, a strategy that is often termed triangulation. Multiple-method triangulation allows for testing the degree of external validity (Jick 1979, 602–4).

I chose to study two parties that have survived because I seek to understand how parties balance their competing interests of policy and votes; thus, I cannot necessarily make conclusions about what leads to survival (to do this would require examination of a party that has not survived). But, as I am more interested in understanding *how* parties balance their competing interests of policy and votes, I have focused on two parties that have survived. Because I consider a party's ability to balance interests as a necessary condition for survival, selecting parties that have survived makes sense.[12] Thus, this project answers many questions but leaves others open for future research.

In this study, I analyze the Green Party of England and Wales and the French Verts (Greens). This is a most similar case design (Przeworski and Teune 1970) in terms of electoral system and party type. First, both the United Kingdom and France use majoritarian electoral systems for national elections. Though France's two-round system differs from the United Kingdom's first-past-the-post (FPTP) system, the decisive round for legislative elections operates in the same way: the candidate with a plurality of the votes cast wins. Although small parties have had their greatest success in multiparty PR systems, these two parties have not disappeared, as Duverger's Law would have predicted, but have survived even under the restrictive electoral rules of the plurality system. Second, the two parties make related appeals to a similar cohort of the electorate—that is, just to the left of the main center-left party.[13] Comparing the strategies of a green party with an extreme right party would be more difficult in that their appeals are aimed at vastly different electorates and voters have vastly differing perceptions of the parties.

BACKGROUND ON PARTIES

The British and French Greens were part of the wave of new politics parties that grew out of the social movements of the 1960s. Although restrictive electoral systems have prevented them from achieving great electoral success, they have altered the political landscape of their countries. Table 1.2 provides an overview of the two parties' elected officials as of 2009. Both parties have survived because of their focus on balancing the competing interests of votes and policy; however, they have had varying degrees of electoral, communication, and policy success.

LES VERTS

In 1974, René Dumont was the first candidate to run for the French presidency on an environmental or ecological party label, winning 1.32 percent of the vote. The Greens did not emerge until ten years later, when the party formed out of the consolidation of several small, disparate ecology parties.[14] It first ran as a unified party in the European elections of June 1984,

TABLE 1.2. Overview of French and British Green Parties in 2009

	Vote Totals	MPs	MEPs	Other Elected Officials
Green Party of England and Wales	1.07% (total vote share in 2005 national elections); 3.4% (in seats contested)	0 (2005)	2 (2009)	100 parish councillors, 120 Principal Authority councillors, 2 members on GLA, 1 Lord (1999–2008)[a]
Les Verts	3.25% (first round of 2007 legislative elections); 1.57% (first round of 2007 presidential election)	4 (2007)	14 (2009)	41 mayors, 18 cantonal councillors, 168 regional councillors, 5 senators

[a]Timothy Beaumont was a life-peer from 1967 to 2008. He left the Liberal Democrats and joined the Green Party in 1999 and was subsequently a Green peer until his death.

when it received 3.4 percent of the vote. Under the leadership of Antoine Waechter, the Greens' official ideological position was "neither left nor right but in front," similar to that of the German Greens, from whom the French party took the slogan. Waechter rejected the entire notion of a left-right spectrum and believed that distinguishing the Greens from the far right was just as important as separating the party from all other more mainstream political parties (Cole and Doherty 1995; O'Neill 1997). He opposed alliances with other parties and stated that "ecology was not available for marriage" (quoted in Burchell 2002, 83). In his 1988 run for the presidency, Waechter won 3.8 percent of the vote. He headed the party from 1986 through 1993, during which time it remained ideologically isolated from mainstream politics, and its national electoral performance was dismal. In the 1989 European elections, however, the party achieved its highest vote share to date—11 percent—which translated into nine seats because of the proportional system in place.

In 1990, one of Waechter's foes within the party, Brice Lalonde, founded a rival green party, Génération Ecologie (Generation Ecology, GE), with the encouragement of Socialist president François Mitterrand. Lalonde was willing to join alliances with other parties and to give up the party's electoral independence if the strategy would result in increased representation in the government. This approach was most evident in the 1988 presidential elections, when Lalonde backed Mitterrand rather than Waechter. Lalonde was subsequently invited to join Michel Rocard's Socialist government as environment minister (Holliday 1994; Cole and Doherty 1995; O'Neill 1997). In the 1992 regional elections, the Greens and GE ran separate lists, but neither fared very well.

By 1993, the two parties temporarily put aside their differences and formed an electoral pact, the Entente des Ecologistes (Alliance of Ecologists). They agreed on a national list of candidates and did not run competing candidates. The Alliance received 7.8 percent of the vote, the highest score ever for an ecology party or list in French parliamentary elections (Holliday 1994; Faucher 1998). After 1993, the Greens and GE parted ways again over ideological differences, and the Greens have become the dominant ecological party. Today, GE considers itself more on the center-right and continues to run candidates in legislative elections, but the party rarely receives more than 1 percent of the vote in any district. In 2007, GE's presidential candidate failed to receive the endorsement of five hundred mayors required to appear on the ballot.

With the coming to power of a center-right government with which they had little in common, the Greens recognized the need for a changed strategy. At the party's November 1993 postelection congress in Lille, the majority of the delegates voted to overturn the party's isolated positioning in favor of "a cautious dialogue with the left" (Szarka 1994, 455; Faucher 1998, 57). After eleven motions, Waechter had lost power. The party's new leader, Dominique Voynet, led the party to its current position, which focuses not only on environmental issues but also on other new politics issues, among them social justice, feminism, the developing world, and a decrease in working hours as a means to create jobs. Her positions on these and other issues placed the Greens to the left of the Socialists. In the 1995 presidential election, Voynet won 3.3 percent of the vote. The pragmatic Voynet further recognized that the only way the Greens could gain representation in parliament and keep the extreme right out of government would be to ally with other parties (Faucher 1998). Beginning in 1996, the party considered seriously the possibility of entering into preelection alliances with the Socialists. The parties first allied for the June 1997 legislative elections, in which the Greens won 4 percent of the vote and seated eight deputies. This was the first time an ecology party in France gained representation in the Assemblée Nationale (National Assembly). Voynet was invited to join the Jospin government as environment minister. The Greens and the PS again entered into a preelection coalition in 2002, when the Greens won 4.5 percent of the vote and placed three deputies in parliament. In the 2007 legislative elections, the Greens did not enter into a formal alliance with the PS, but the Socialists did not run candidates against the three Green incumbents and the PS did not run candidates against Greens in three other districts where either local or department-level agreements had been made. The three incumbents won, and a fourth deputy was elected from one of the other three districts.[15]

In the 2002 presidential elections, Noël Mamère won 5.25 percent of the first-round vote, the highest vote share to date for a Green candidate. However, this result proved paradoxically harmful to the Greens and other left-wing parties. In the first round, 25 percent of the votes on the left went to parties other than the PS. As a result, the Socialist candidate, Jospin, came in third, which meant a second-round runoff between the RPR's Jacques Chirac and the FN's Jean-Marie Le Pen.[16] To ensure that the far right candidate did not advance to the second round in the 2007 presidential election, many non-PS voters on the left voted for the PS candidate.

The Socialists' first-round vote share increased from 16.2 percent in 2002 to 25.9 percent in 2007, while the Greens' vote share decreased to 1.6 percent.

Greens now hold seats at several other levels of government as well as in parliament. At the municipal level, the Greens have entered into alliances with other parties of the left since the mid-1990s. As of 2009, forty-one of the country's nearly thirty-seven thousand municipalities had Green mayors; the party also had five senators and fourteen members of the European Parliament as well as representation in many regional parliaments.[17]

BRITISH GREEN PARTY—GREEN PARTY OF ENGLAND AND WALES

From its inception in 1973 as People, the Green Party of England and Wales identified itself as "neither left nor right," preferring grassroots activism to the more traditional activities of political parties.[18] As in other nascent European green parties, deep divisions existed between the British Greens' antisystem pure ecological faction and those who preferred a more socialist approach to ecologism (O'Neill 1997). Over time, tensions developed between those who saw the Green Party as "a living embodiment of a new lifestyle, and others in the party who preferred a more measured and pragmatic politics." The two groups are often referred to as the decentralists and the electoralists, respectively (O'Neill 1997, 285; Burchell 2002).

Similar to the French Greens, the British Green Party's electoral breakthrough came with the European elections of 1989, when the British party received 14.9 percent of the vote. However, because of the FPTP system used at the time, it did not win any seats in the European Parliament. Following these results, a group within the party, headed by Sara Parkin, Jonathan Porritt, and Jean Lambert, formed the Green 2000 movement, which sought to obtain parliamentary representation by 2000. The electoralist Green 2000 initiative sought to centralize the party organization and to streamline decision making within the party. Disappointing results in the 1992 national elections and increasing internal factionalization led to the effective abandonment of the Green 2000 initiative and to Parkin's resignation as chair of the party executive later that year (O'Neill 1997; Burchell 2002; Carter 2008; Rüdig 2008). Party leaders subsequently reoriented their electoral priorities toward the local level, where representation was more attainable (Burchell 2000, 2002; Carter 2008). The more decentralist 1993 Basis for Renewal program outlined this new focus on electing local councillors through the FPTP system and electing members to bodies that utilize more proportional electoral systems, such as the Greater London Assembly (GLA), which uses a mixed-member proportional system.

At the local level, the party implemented the Target to Win strategy and has directed its efforts toward wards where there were already a strong base of activists and local support (Burchell 2002). The Greens' first district or county councillor was elected in Oxford in May 1993.[19] By 1996, the targeting strategy had resulted in three Green city councillors in Oxford and two councillors on the Oxfordshire County Council.

At the national level, the Greens' steadily improving vote shares have also resulted from a targeting strategy. For the 2005 general election, for example, the Greens stood candidates in 202 constituencies but targeted 3 in particular (the constituencies of Brighton Pavilion, Norwich South, and Lewisham Deptford).[20] The Greens' vote shares have increased considerably in these targeted constituencies. In 1997, the Green candidate in Brighton Pavilion won 5.5 percent of the vote; in 2001, that number rose to 9.4 percent. In 2005, the Green candidate in the constituency, Keith Taylor, received 21.9 percent, the highest vote share ever won by a Green candidate.

The British Greens' twofold strategy has proven successful over the past decade. After the 2009 local and European elections, the party had 100 parish or local councillors, 123 principal authority councillors, 2 of the 25 seats on the GLA, and 2 members of the European Parliament. Its average vote share for the parliamentary seats it has contested rose from 1.3 percent in 1992 to 3.4 percent in 2005. And in 2010, Green candidate Caroline Lucas won the Brighton Pavilion seat, becoming the party's first representative in Westminster.

PLAN OF THE BOOK

The chapters in this book demonstrate how small parties have been able to survive not only in proportional systems, but also in more restrictive electoral environments. Using both cross-national analyses and case studies of the French and British Greens, I show that the parties' ability to balance their competing goals of policy implementation and vote maximization has enabled them to persevere. To do this, I examine three types of strategies: policy, electoral, and communication.

In chapter 2, I develop and test the theoretical argument presented in chapter 1. I specify more fully the balancing thesis and derive expectations about the behavior of small parties as it relates to their policy positions. I then test the theory by comparing the policy positions of the greens with those of the major parties on the left across Western Europe. I use manifestos (Budge et al. 2001; Klingemann et al. 2006) and expert survey data (Laver and Hunt 1992; Benoit and Laver 2006). The findings from the cross-national tests demonstrate that to maximize potential vote share, small parties need to find the optimal point of policy differentiation. If there is too much or too little differentiation, the parties' vote share will be compromised. Examples from the British and French cases show how the policy positions of the greens and socialists change from one election period to the next as the parties react to each other's behavior.

Chapters 3–5 build on the cross-national findings by examining how the parties' balancing of preferences in restrictive plurality systems manifests itself in electoral and communication strategies of the French and British Green parties. In chapters 3–4, I examine the electoral strategy of the French and British Greens. In chapter 3, I analyze the 2002 preelection coalition between the French Greens and Socialists and the Greens' decision following the 2007 presidential elections to not enter into another nationwide coalition in the June 2007 legislative elections. I show that districts were more likely to have alliances in 2002 where both the mainstream right and the extreme right had higher likelihoods of success. In 2007, although the party's strategy did not change, the political context did. To maintain its ideological distinctiveness as a party and its future potential to win votes, the national party chose to run candidates on its own, with the exception of four districts, three of which were those of the incumbent Green MPs. The Greens' electoral strategy in both 2002 and 2007 shows how the party is balancing its preferences within the constraints of the French system.

In chapter 4, I explore the British Greens' twofold strategy of targeting in national elections and focusing on local elections. Through these two strategies, the party has survived in a hostile electoral environment and become a credible and viable party at the local, national, and supranational (European) levels. In addition, the party has balanced its electoral and policy goals with a desire "to do politics differently" internally. Through these strategies, the party has demonstrated its goal of balancing policy differentiation and winning votes and (ultimately) seats.

Chapter 5 compares the French and British Green parties' communication strategies. The parties use their national and supranational elected officials to communicate party credibility, as content analysis of national newspapers shows. Both parties proactively seek the media's coverage, but they focus on different tactics. These strategies enable the parties to balance the dual goals of distinguishing themselves in the party system and attracting voters.

Chapter 6 synthesizes the evidence and discusses extensions of the project. I argue that it has been through the three types of strategies that the parties have achieved the twin goals of policy differentiation and vote maximization, which have led to party survival and will ultimately result in party success. I then explain why the French and British Greens have had differing levels of success and discuss the implications of my findings for small-party survival more generally. Finally, I propose several empirical and theoretical extensions of the study to further test the balancing-interests model of party competition.

CHAPTER 2

Balancing Preferences: A Theory of Small Party Survival

"Put *écologie* in the heart of public policy."
—LES VERTS, LE MONDE CHANGE,
AVEC LES VERTS CHANGEONS LE MONDE, 2007

"Greens place people and the planet's resources at the heart of our policies."
—GREEN PARTY OF ENGLAND AND WALES, *GREEN PARTY MANIFESTO: THE REAL CHOICE FOR REAL CHANGE*, 2005

IF WE FOLLOW THE Downsian definition of parties as groups that exist to control government and only formulate policies to win elections (Downs 1957, 25, 28), then we would expect political parties that do not fulfill these criteria to have disappeared. However, we know that there are small parties from across party families (green, ethnoterritorial, religious, far right) that have survived over long periods of time despite garnering relatively little electoral success. For many of these parties, policy is of the utmost importance. On the left, many of them formed because of the large old politics parties' unresponsiveness to issues raised by a generation of Europeans who had come to political maturity during the volatile 1960s and 1970s (Kitschelt 1988, 1989; Markovits and Gorski 1993). On the right, many of the parties developed in reaction to the issues that the New Left placed on the agenda. My theory of party competition posits that a party's ability to balance competing goals of policy implementation and vote maximization explains its longevity.

The extant literature explains why small parties survive or fail only by exploring factors exogenous to the small party itself, including the population's partisan attachments, large party behavior, and systemic constraints. In this chapter, I explore how the parties and their leaders balance their competing interests; only when they are successful do they survive. When the parties get too out of balance and there is too much policy differentiation or too much emphasis on vote maximization, the party will lose its raison d'être and fade from the party system. Furthermore, a party's ability to balance these competing interests is even more important in a plurality system, where the restrictive rules increase the likelihood of party failure.

TWO TYPES OF SMALL-PARTY LEADERS

We can imagine two pure types of party leaders—the vote maximizer and the policy maximizer. The first type of small-party leader is a true Downsian, motivated only by the prospect of votes and seats. She will follow the behavior of a typical party leader, willing to compromise the party's ideological goals to reach more voters. We can think of this leader as an Aggregator, Hunter, or Predator (Laver 2005, 267). All of these leader types seek vote and seat maximization. The Aggregator sets policy at the mean position of all of the party's supporters. The Hunter searches for support and follows a "win-stay, lose-shift" policy strategy. Finally, the Predator will not move her policy position if her party is the largest; however, if it is not, she will move toward the position of the largest party. The second type of party leader is a policy purist, following Wittman's (1973, 1983) policy-driven expectations for leader motivations. This leader is not willing to compromise the party's ideological goals to win votes or seats. We can think of this leader as a Sticker as defined by Laver (2005, 267)—that is, someone who "never changes policy positions, regardless of the ideal points of voters and the positions of other parties."

For a small party, especially in a plurality system, neither the pure vote-seeking nor the pure policy-seeking approaches will ultimately result in longevity. A pure vote-seeking strategy can lead to two outcomes. First, to win votes, party leaders compromise on the issues about which they care most, move the party too close to a large mainstream party, and thus leave little policy differentiation between their party and the larger party. Strategic voters who care about this issue will vote for the larger party when faced with a small, fairly unsuccessful party and a large party with similar positions. Second, the party could stand its ideological ground and be content to only receive very small vote shares. In both of these vote-maximizing cases, the party will wither.

Pure policy seeking can also lead to two potential outcomes. First, if the party cares only about policy implementation, then its leaders will be satisfied if a larger party subsumes the small party's issues and ensures their eventual implementation. However, the large party may also co-opt the small party's issue but then shift its position on it or minimize the potential change to the status quo, for example. Second, staying true to its pure ideological preferences, the party may have placed itself too far from potential voters—in essence, the same behavior as the second pure vote-seeking scenario. In both situations, the pure policy-seeking strategy also results in the party withering.

Thus, to survive in a plurality system, the small-party leader cannot be either pure type and needs to balance these competing goals. If she were only a vote maximizer, the party would lose its reason for formation and fail. If she were only a policy maximizer, the likelihood of survival would also be quite low. Thus, she must be an adept compromiser, balancing the twin goals of policy differentiation and vote maximization. She must determine how much policy distinction will differentiate her party from other parties but not sacrifice too many votes. Too much distinction and the party will have difficulty attracting voters; not enough distinction, and it will differ little from other parties, another scenario in which attracting voters becomes problematic. Party leaders, therefore, face the challenge of identifying this optimal position, a goal that parties must ultimately accomplish to survive. Balancing is also important for party leaders in proportional representation (PR) systems, but these leaders can be somewhat more policy-focused given the electoral rules.

Similar to the two leader types, there are two pure voter types, the sincere or expressive voter and the strategic voter. The sincere or expressive voter will always vote for her most preferred party regardless of its potential for electoral success (Schuessler 2000, 54). Expressive voters support small parties because they identify themselves as party x voters and seek to attach themselves to a collective of similarly minded individuals. The strategic voter, conversely, is oriented toward short-term outcomes and always seeks to vote in such a way so as to not waste her vote (see, for example, Niemi, Whitten, and Franklin 1992; Cox 1997; Alvarez and Nagler 2000; Blais et al. 2001). In both plurality and PR systems, a small party can survive only when it ensures the support of its sincere or expressive voters as well as attracts more strategic voters who see its long-term potential. Furthermore, parties' strategic decisions are often tied to assumptions about what their voters are likely to do or not do. While the voter side of the story is important for understanding the puzzle of small-party survival and ultimate success, I do not systematically study vote choice in this book.

EXPLAINING PARTIES' POLICY POSITIONS

Most scholars generally follow the Downsian conclusion that parties adopt policy positions that will result in the most votes. For large, mainstream parties in two-party systems, parties typically will center their policy preferences on those of the median voter (Downs 1957). Even in multiparty systems, the left- and rightmost parties can attract voters by shifting their positions toward the center of the ideological spectrum, where there are more voters. But Downs also recognizes that parties in multiparty systems "will strive to distinguish themselves ideologically from each other and maintain the purity of their positions" (126–27). In essence, they will be "marker parties" (Budge 1994). They seek to differentiate themselves from "a neighbouring party with which they are in long-term competition" (461). Furthermore, in his seminal work on European party development, Kirchheimer (1966, 190) posits that as larger parties transform into catchall parties, "a drastic reduction of the party's ideological baggage" will occur. As ideology becomes less important, a party reaches out and attracts more voters from across the spectrum. Kirchheimer argues that this process can result in the disappearance of small parties because as catchall parties change their policy positions to bring in more voters, political competition wanes and small parties may lose their purpose and cease to exist. However, small parties have persisted precisely because they care about both policy and votes. These parties cannot simply shift their policy positions to please the majority of voters, since doing so would sacrifice their distinctiveness and often their raison d'être as a party. They also cannot simply let their issues be absorbed into the big tent of the catchall party or stand firm on their ideological preferences, since doing so again would reduce their reason for existence as a distinct party.

Recent literature has addressed the relationship between policy preferences and potential vote share among small parties. Adams et al. (2006) find that when niche parties moderate their positions, they are typically punished in subsequent elections. Moreover, Ezrow's (2008) research concludes that niche parties with more distinctive and therefore less moderate positions tend to gain votes. Taking a slightly different approach, J. T. Andrews and Money (n.d.) refer to parties as "champions" (those that have been part of a governing coalition) and "challengers" (those that have not). Champion parties are typically mainstream parties, whereas challenger parties are often niche parties, though in some cases they have been part of governing coalitions. Examples of these challengers include the German, Belgian, and Irish Greens; the Finnish Swedish People's Party; and the Italian Northern League. Consistent with Adams et al. (2006) and Ezrow (2008), J. T. Andrews and Money (n.d.) find that champion parties increase their vote share by adopting more centrist positions, whereas challenger parties have more electoral success when they take more extreme positions. To receive enough votes to become part of the government, champion parties need to support more centrist positions. Challenger parties, conversely, find themselves in a more difficult situation. To increase their vote share, they need to differentiate themselves from the champion parties and hence take positions further from the center. But if they differentiate themselves by too much, their potential to participate in government may diminish.

In sum, recent work on niche parties' policy positions demonstrates that if these parties moderate their policy positions, they will be worse off electorally. However, much of the current research on niche parties' policy positions does not include green parties. Adams et al. (2006), for example, include only one green party (the Dutch GroenLinks [Green Left]) in their analysis of thirty-four mainstream and niche parties. J. T. Andrews and Money's (n.d.) analysis uses data through 1989 and focuses on the composition of cabinets in Western Europe and therefore does not include any green parties, as the first green party that participated in government was the Finnish Green League in 1995. Ezrow (2008) includes only niche parties in his study of thirteen parties; four of them are green parties.

THEORY OF POLICY BALANCING

Just as small parties, like the greens, experience negative effects from moderation, they also encounter undesirable consequences from extreme policy positions. Going too far to the left or the right costs them potential votes. Their electoral survival depends on the parties' careful positioning of themselves on the issues. These parties thus need to find the position on a given issue that will distinguish them—but not by too much. All party leaders' decisions are constrained in two ways. First, they need to balance the preferences of their core supporters with a desire to maximize votes. This idea resembles Przeworski and Sprague's (1986) account of why socialist parties had less electoral success than they might have obtained. Even though party leaders reached out to other classes by pursuing a "supraclass" strategy, they did not distance themselves enough from their working-class supporters. Socialist parties' votes stagnated as a consequence of the tension between appealing to new voters and keeping their core voters. Second, leaders must work to satisfy various internal factions—policy-motivated activists and vote-motivated supporters. Aldrich (1983, 1995), G. Miller and Schofield (2003), and Schofield and Sened (2006) argue that parties are not unitary actors and are essentially coalitions of elites, activists, and voters. These authors demonstrate that party behavior and strategy are based on balancing coalition members' demands and preferences.

Building on these constraints, I argue that small parties have two challenges. First, they need to identify the optimal position on an issue—that is, the position that enables the party to maximize its potential vote share. If the party's position either converges on or diverges from that of its mainstream party competitor, it will lose votes. Figure 2.1 illustrates this parabolic relationship. The curve represents vote share. G_1 represents the optimal amount of policy differentiation between the greens and socialists on a given issue in a given country. When the greens' position moves toward either point G_2 or point G_3, vote share decreases. At G_2, the differentiation between the parties' positions is too small; at G_3, the differentiation is too large. At G_2, vote share decreases because more sincere or expressive voters abandon the party as it has sacrificed too much of its policy distinction. At G_3, vote share decreases because more strategic voters abandon the party as too much distinction exists between the greens and the socialists and these voters fear that the party will have difficulty attracting voters. At G_1, both the expressive and strategic voters are satisfied with the greens' policy position relative to that of the socialists and support the party. In other words, the party has optimized its policy position and potential vote share by appealing to the various members of the party's internal coalition.

Second, recognizing the potential to lose votes if the differentiation becomes too large or too small, these parties need to be willing to innovate and change their policy positions to ensure the right amount of differentiation. The British Greens' changing position on devolution illustrates this process. In 2001, the Greens supported extending devolution to the Scot-

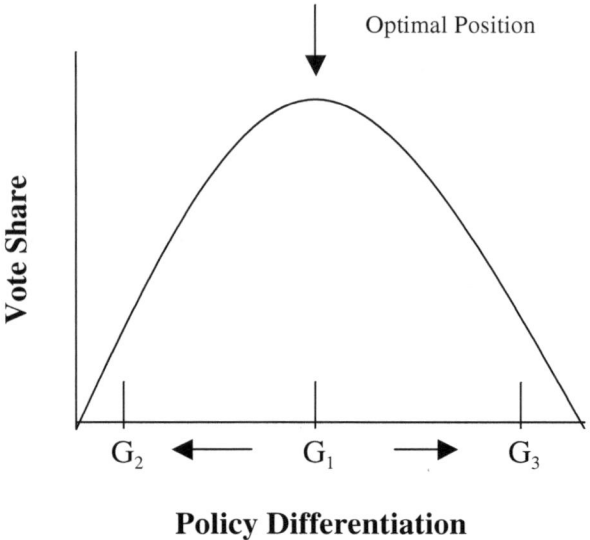

Fig. 2.1. Relationship between policy differentiation and vote share

tish Parliament, Welsh Assembly, and Greater London Authority, "leading to full independence for Scotland and Wales should they approve it by referendum" (Green Party of England and Wales 2001, 15), whereas Labour pledged continued support of directly elected regional governments. By 2005, the Greens moved their position closer to that of Labour's 2001 position, supporting the granting of greater powers to the Scottish and Welsh assemblies if "the citizens of the respective countries so wish" (Green Party of England and Wales 2005, 29). Labour moved its position in 2005 as well, advocating increased devolution to local authorities, a stronger Welsh Assembly, and working with Northern Ireland to reestablish devolved institutions. Thus, although the two parties' positions moved closer to each other, the Greens' position remained distinctive.

In sum, by determining the optimal amount of differentiation, the parties can increase both their potential vote share and their chances of survival. Too little or too much differentiation results in lower vote shares and eventual failure. I derive three specific hypotheses from this theory:

Pure Policy-Differentiation Hypothesis (H2.1): When too much policy differentiation exists between the small party and the ideologically closest large mainstream party, the small party's vote share will decrease.

Pure Vote-Maximization Hypothesis (H2.2): When too little policy differentiation exists between the small party and the ideologically closest large mainstream party, the small party's vote share will decrease.

Balancing-Interests Hypothesis (H2.3): When the optimal amount of policy differentiation exists between the small party and the ideologically closest large mainstream party, the small party's vote share will increase.

Importantly, the optimal amount of policy differentiation is context specific. It can vary across elections in a single country and across countries.

DATA AND METHODS

To test the balancing-interests hypothesis, I compare the positions of the greens with those of each country's largest mainstream left party—typically the socialists or social democrats. Although I am testing the theory on the greens' policy placement vis-à-vis the socialists, this model of small-party survival can explain the survival of other types of small parties.[1] Furthermore, although this test of the thesis is not a direct test of survival (which simply means existence), it assumes that some votes are necessary for survival in a party system. I use party expert survey and party manifestos data for green and socialist parties across Western Europe. I first show how the two party families differ in terms of position and saliency on several issues, both within a given country and over time, and how these differences relate to the greens' vote shares. I then demonstrate that an optimal amount of policy differentiation exists between the two parties, resulting in the greens' highest vote shares (H2.3). I show that both too little and too much differentiation hurts the parties' potential vote share (H2.1 and H2.2).

Among scholars of political parties, the traditional methods of analyzing party policy preferences utilize either the Comparative Manifestos Project (CMP) data (Budge et al. 2001; Klingemann et al. 2006) or expert survey data (the most recent of which is Benoit and Laver 2006). While both are widely used, there is some debate among scholars about the relative merits and problems of each of these data sets. In comparing the various methods, Volkens (2007, 118) concludes that both approaches have their strengths and weaknesses and that they should be used to complement each other.[2] To show the robustness of the relationships between policy differentiation and green vote share, I use relevant data from both the Laver and Hunt

(1992) and Benoit and Laver (2006) expert survey and the Budge et al. (2001) and Klingemann et al. (2006) manifesto data sets for the 1979–2003 period for the large-N analysis of European green and socialist parties.[3] The former two data sets measure party position and salience on different issues; the latter two measure saliency.

Although casual observers may argue that green parties tend to be single-issue parties, scholars have shown that green parties' agendas have focused not only on environmental sustainability but also on social justice, decentralization policies, institutional reform, and a generally cautious outlook toward increasing European centralization (see, for example, Bomberg 1998, 2002; Shull 1999; Bomberg and Carter 2006). To elaborate further on two of these issues, the greens have long supported decentralization and increased local and regional autonomy, a position that has translated into strong support for policies that devolve power to lower levels of government and grassroots democracy (Bomberg 1998; Shull 1999). Furthermore, green parties generally offer strong support for European Union (EU) integration but are weary of the increasingly centralized powers of EU institutions (Bomberg 1998, 2002; Bomberg and Carter 2006).

After reviewing British, French, and other European green party election materials, including campaign leaflets and posters, party election broadcasts, and political speeches since 2000, I concur with these overall assessments that a group of issues emerges as central to the "green agenda." These issues include the environment and energy, transportation, agriculture, decentralization, social justice, institutional reform, and a cautious support of Europe. Many of these issues lie at the core of the postmaterialist new politics issue agenda (Inglehart 1997; Dalton 2008).[4] Indeed, the French Greens refer to this set of issues as *écologie*. Roughly 43 percent of the British Green Party's 2005 manifesto and 38 percent of the French Green Party's 2007 manifesto are devoted to these issues. The comparable figures for the British Labour Party and Parti Socialiste (PS) are 17 percent and 21 percent, respectively. I thus look at the following issues in the expert survey and manifesto data: environment, decentralization, European integration, social justice, and multiculturalism. These issues are conceptualized slightly differently in each data set (see appendix A).

Using these data, I develop two measures for assessing the parties' policy positions. The first is the mean of the green and socialist party families across all countries. The second measures the policy differences between the greens and socialist parties in a given country. Where there is more than one green or socialist party in a country (Belgium, for example, has two green and two socialist parties), each green-socialist dyad's position is included in the analysis. The following equation represents the second measure, which is the mean difference on a given policy dimension.

$$\text{Mean Policy Difference} = \frac{\Sigma |Gi-Si|}{PD} \qquad (1)$$

where Gi is the position of green party i, Si is the position of socialist party i, and PD is the number of party dyads. The mean policy difference is thus the sum of the absolute value of Gi minus Si for all party dyads divided by the total number of party dyads in the data set. The number of party dyads in the Laver and Hunt, Benoit and Laver, and CMP data are 12, 15, and 74, respectively. Based on the balancing-interests hypothesis, the closer to the optimal point that the difference between the green and socialist positions lies, the higher the greens' expected vote share.

Except for France, all of the countries included in the difference of means analyses use some form of proportional representation for their parliamentary elections.[5] The other plurality system in Western Europe, the United Kingdom, is not included in these analyses because the British Green Party is excluded from these data sets.

Expert Survey Data

I first examine Benoit and Laver's (2006) expert survey data, which measure party positions on the environment, decentralization, and European authority, before putting them into historical context with comparisons to the earlier Laver and Hunt (1992) data. The Benoit and Laver data were collected in 2002–3. Party expert scholars were asked to place the parties on a twenty-point scale for each issue dimension. Experts then scored the importance or salience of the specific issue dimension for the party on the same twenty-point scale. Benoit and Laver report the mean of the expert scores for each party on each issue. (See appendix A for the specific wording for each issue dimension and the parties included in each analysis.) Although other key issues such as social justice and multiculturalism appear on the greens' agenda, they were not covered in the party expert surveys. I find that distinct differences exist between the green and socialist parties' issue positions and saliency.

Table 2.1 shows the mean and range for position and saliency for each of these issue areas for the green and socialist parties. The mean saliency value for the fourteen Western European green parties included in the data set on the environment measure is 18.56, and the range is 1.71. Both support for decentralization and opposition to increased EU authority have saliency values around 12 and ranges of just below 7. Some parties, how-

TABLE 2.1. Issue Position and Salience for Green and Socialist Parties, 1988–89 and 2002–3

	Mean	Range	Number of Parties
Benoit and Laver 2006			
Green Parties			
Environment position	2.49	2.73	14
Environment saliency	18.56	1.71	14
Decentralization position	8.23	8.04	14
Decentralization saliency	11.90	6.95	14
EU authority position	9.00	12.10	13
EU authority saliency	12.81	6.86	13
Socialist Parties			
Environment position	9.86	9.23	21
Environment saliency	12.47	6.47	21
Decentralization position	10.39	8.02	21
Decentralization saliency	11.51	6.00	21
EU authority position	7.84	12.24	20
EU authority saliency	13.03	6.77	20
Laver and Hunt 1992			
Green Parties			
Environment position	2.24	6.75	11
Environment saliency	18.56	10.00	11
Decentralization position	4.29	5.36	11
Decentralization saliency	13.35	13.25	11
Socialist Parties			
Environment position	10.19	9.03	20
Environment saliency	12.24	9.50	20
Decentralization position	10.64	10.31	20
Decentralization saliency	10.77	10.50	20

Source: Laver and Hunt 1992; Benoit and Laver 2006.

Note: Each value is out of a maximum of 20. See appendix A for explanation of each policy dimension. Countries included in analysis: Austria, Belgium, Denmark, Finland, France, Germany, Greece, Iceland, Ireland, Italy, Luxembourg, Malta, Netherlands, Norway, Portugal, Spain, Sweden, Switzerland (only Benoit and Laver), and the United Kingdom. Not all countries have a green party nor are all green parties included (e.g., the British Green Party). Experts in Iceland were not asked about joining the EU. Belgium has French and Flemish green and socialist parties.

ever, deviate substantially from these means. On the decentralization dimension, the French Greens and Swedish Miljöpartiet de Gröna (the Environmental Party, the Greens) have values of 14.68 and 15.45, respectively. The Irish and Swedish Greens' emphasis on opposition to increasing EU authority are also higher than the average, with values of 16.96 and 17.06, respectively. In comparison, the twenty-one socialist parties' average saliency on the environment is 12.47, and the range is 6.47.

In terms of the parties' policy positions, clear differences exist on the Benoit and Laver (2006) environment, decentralization, and EU dimensions for the socialist and green parties. The average green party position on the environment is 2.49, compared to 9.86 for the socialists. This finding demonstrates a much stronger preference for environmental protection even at the cost of economic growth, which is how the survey frames this issue. Furthermore, the dispersion on the environmental dimension is much greater for the socialists than for the green parties. The Maltese Partit Laburista's (Labour Party) value is 14.00, compared to the value of 5.43 obtained for the Sozialdemokratische Partei der Schweiz (Swiss Social Democratic Party), for example. On average, the greens are more in favor of decentralization policies than are the socialists, with values of 8.23 and 10.39, respectively. Finally, the greens are slightly more concerned with increasing EU authority than are the socialists, though the green group has a range of 12.10. The Swedish Greens' value is 17.47, while the position of the Italian Federazione dei Verdi (Federation of the Greens) is 5.67.

As table 2.1 also shows, only small changes occurred over time in the different parties' positions. Laver and Hunt (1992) asked experts similar questions on the environment and decentralization in 1988–89.[6] On both environmental position and saliency, the greens and socialists have similar positions in the two expert surveys. However, on the decentralization question, the socialists' position and saliency remain constant, but the greens' position moved further away from a pure decentralist position (from 4.29 to 8.23) and has become slightly less important to the parties (13.35 versus 11.90).

Based on the balancing thesis, we would expect that as the differentiation between the greens and socialists gets larger, the greens' vote share would increase. However, if the differentiation gets too large, then the greens' vote share would start to decrease, as they appear too extreme to those voters who lean toward or sympathize with them. Table 2.2 presents the mean difference for the green-socialist party dyads for both position and salience for each issue. It also reports the minimum and maximum values and standard deviation for the party dyads. The values for both position and salience range from 1 to 20; thus, the maximum difference possible is 19, and the minimum is 0. The two largest differences between the parties are on environmental issue position and saliency, perhaps not unexpected given the green parties' issue focus.

Table 2.2 also shows the correlation between the absolute value of the difference on issue position and saliency for the three issues and the mean green vote share for each party dyad. The greens' vote share is from the national election that was closest to the 2002–3 survey. For both position on the environment and decentralization, a moderate 0.30 correlation exists between the difference in position on the issue and green vote share. This finding demonstrates that as the difference on issue position increases, so does the greens' vote share. However, these are not high correlations. These findings thus show that some distinction between the parties' positions is beneficial for the greens but suggests that there is a tipping point.

Figure 2.2 illustrates the relationship between green vote share and decentralization saliency. On the y-axis is green vote share, and on the x-axis is the difference in policy position for each socialist-green party dyad. The line is a fitted regression curve for an ordinary least squares equation that

TABLE 2.2. Difference in Policy Positions and Salience between Greens and Socialists, 1988–89 and 2002–3

	Mean	Min	Max	S.D.	N	Correlation with Green Vote Share
Benoit and Laver 2006						
Environmental position	7.00	3.57	10.15	1.74	15	0.30
Environmental salience	6.20	3.83	7.64	1.08	15	−0.53
Decentralization position	2.99	0.32	7.64	2.33	15	0.30
Decentralization salience	1.39	0.1	4.13	1.32	15	−0.25
EU authority position	2.97	0.39	8.79	2.64	14[a]	−0.27
EU authority salience	1.6	0.08	5.09	1.61	14	−0.19
Laver and Hunt 1992[b]						
Environmental position	8.80	3.13	11.6	2.41	12	0.24
Environmental salience	7.03	3.94	9.5	2.11	12	−0.54
Decentralization position	6.85	0.68	12.67	3.51	12	0.41
Decentralization salience	3.83	0.86	7.33	1.91	12	0.38

Source: Laver and Hunt 1992; Benoit and Laver 2006.
[a]Iceland not included in the EU data.
[b]EU dimension not included in data.

Balancing Preferences 39

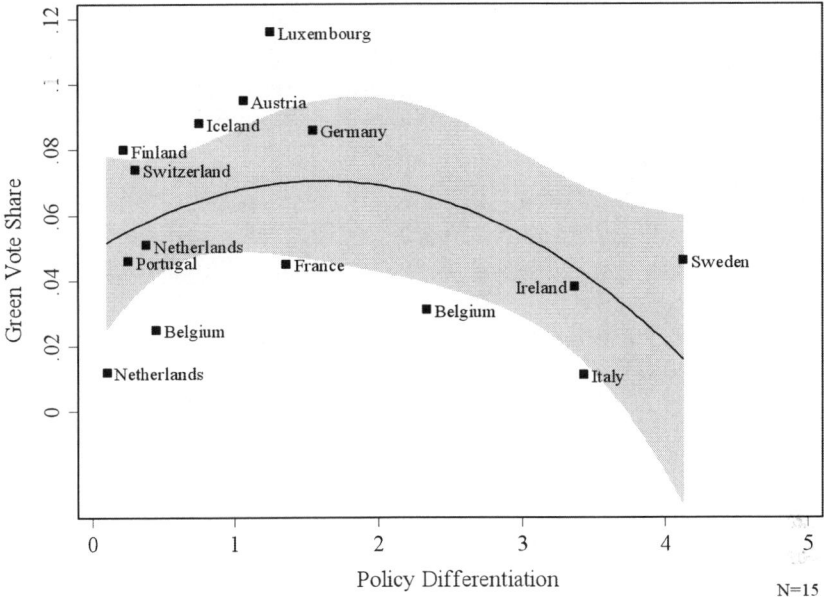

Fig. 2.2. Green-socialist differences on decentralization salience, 90 percent CI. (Data from Benoit and Laver 2006.)

regresses both the difference in decentralization saliency between the two parties and the variable squared on green vote share. The observed value for each party dyad is also included. The shaded area is the 90 percent confidence interval. While there are indeed outliers (France, for example) and a fairly wide confidence interval, this graph suggests the parabolic relationship that I theorize. We can think of the position of Luxembourg's Déi Gréng (The Greens) as the tipping point. Vote shares generally fall off on either side of this level of differentiation of 1.25. Because France is the only non-PR system in the sample, its electoral system may explain its lower vote share even though it is near the optimal point of differentiation. Importantly, this graph includes only fifteen observations at one point in time.

Table 2.2 also illustrates how these differences have evolved over time. On both environmental and decentralization position and salience, the difference between green and socialist parties in a given country has decreased. The largest decrease can be seen in the difference on decentralization position. In the 1992 data, the difference was 6.85; in 2006, that number was 2.99. The correlation between the difference in decentralization position and green vote share in the earlier data is 0.41, which similarly demonstrates that as the difference increases, so does green vote share. However, over the thirteen- to fifteen-year period between surveys, the greens' positions moved closer to those of the socialists but remained distinctive, as the devolution example shows. In addition, the correlation with the difference on decentralization saliency in the earlier period is positive but is negative in the later period. This finding may be explained by the fact that the difference had decreased too much, meaning that voters who cared about this issue found too few differences between the parties' positions. This result illustrates the need for an optimal amount of policy distinction. To increase the number of party dyads in the analysis and show the evolution of policy differentiation over time, I turn to the CMP data.

Manifesto Data

Unlike the party expert survey, the CMP calculates the percentage of a party's election manifesto that is devoted to a given issue area by coding the text. In essence, these data measure the saliency of an issue for a party, as the greater the percentage of the manifesto that a party allocates to a given issue, the more important the party deems that issue. In accordance with the green agenda, I look at the following issue dimensions: environment, antigrowth economics, decentralization, European integration, social justice, and multiculturalism. (See appendix A for the specific wording of each issue dimension and the parties included in each analysis.)

Several scholars have acknowledged the limitations of the CMP data. Laver and Garry (2000, 621), for example, note that not all issues include both positive and negative positions. For some issues, saliency can imply position. The "environment" category (501) is an example of such an issue dimension. There is no corresponding antienvironment category, which would be an additional way to show socialist party movement away from the greens. Thus, a party's emphasis on the environment can be understood as its position on the issue—that is, more coverage on environmental issues means more support for proenvironment policies. Benoit, Laver, and Mikhaylov (2007, 13–14) argue that "seepage" can occur across categories, whereby manifesto sentences could be miscoded or put into more than one category. Of the issue categories I use, they identify multiculturalism (607) as having the potential for seepage into favorable mentions of underprivileged minorities (705) and noneconomic demographic groups (706), such as assistance to women, the elderly, and so forth (Klingemann et al. 2006, 159). Moreover, Klingemann et al. (2006, 115) contend that one way of addressing potential overlap is to combine the issue categories into broader scales. Finally, Benoit, Laver, and Mikhaylov (2007, 2009) propose a modification to the CMP data that corrects for error in the coding of the manifestos by bootstrapping the standard errors of each CMP estimate.[7]

As the CMP project has collected manifestos over a much longer period than the expert surveys, I code several manifestos for each party over time. I examine the 1979–2003 period, selecting 1979 for the start of the analysis because it is the first year the data set includes a green party (the Swiss Greens). I break up this twenty-four-year period into five shorter periods for analysis (1979–83; 1984–89; 1990–94; 1995–99; and 2000–2003), selecting those ranges based on the overall experience of green parties in Europe. The greens' average vote share steadily increased from 2.1 percent in the first period to 6.1 percent in the fifth period (see figure 1.1). In addition to the greens' improving electoral fortunes, these periods illustrate the greens' growth as political parties. For the first five-year period, the parties were just entering into electoral politics. In the second period, many parties were contesting their second national elections and increasing their bases of support. In both of these periods, the green parties were still on the "outside" of left-right politics and trying to find their place in electoral politics. By the third period, the parties were solidifying their issue and ideological agendas and electoral strategies. In the fourth period, they were testing their agendas and strategies as parties on the left of the ideological spectrum, and their electoral performance was increasing. The final period is when the greens saw the most success both at the polls and with the realization and implementation of their policies.

Table 2.3 shows the mean and range for each of these issue dimensions and for the green agenda, which is the sum of the parties' positions on the six different issues for each period. The values are the percentages of the manifesto devoted to the issue area and are thus measures of the issue's salience for the party. Comparing greens and socialists across all periods, the clearest difference is in the percentage of the manifesto that is allocated to the environment. For the entire 1979–2003 period, an average of 19.85

TABLE 2.3. Issue Saliency for Green and Socialist Parties, 1979–2003

	Period 1 (1979–83)	Period 2 (1984–89)	Period 3 (1990–94)	Period 4 (1995–99)	Period 5 (2000–2003)
Green Parties					
European integration	0.53	0.75	0.71	2.82	1.88
	(2.24)	(3.60)	(4.58)	(14.58)	(5.86)
Decentralization	2.82	2.56	2.19	0.96	1.50
	(9.80)	(9.95)	(9.95)	(4.66)	(5.4)
Antigrowth economy	4.89	5.51	3.45	3.59	2.58
	(14.71)	(22.67)	(14.43)	(13.91)	(10.29)
Environment	22.11	20.60	23.40	16.78	16.37
	(46.60)	(50.62)	(43.96)	(43.72)	(37.09)
Social justice	2.08	3.05	4.34	9.36	8.06
	(6.71)	(9.20)	(16.25)	(22.39)	(20.31)
Multiculturalism	7.03	6.51	6.40	7.44	7.69
	(16.58)	(12.50)	(15.94)	(19.66)	(10.98)
Green agenda	39.46	38.98	40.49	40.95	38.09
	(38.33)	(45.59)	(35.74)	(46.36)	(46.80)
Number of parties	7	17	16	18	12
Socialist Parties					
European integration	0.98	1.96	2.67	3.73	2.55
	(4.21)	(9.59)	(10.98)	(18.75)	(7.16)
Decentralization	1.91	2.26	2.30	1.64	1.81
	(8.70)	(7.60)	(10.13)	(5.42)	(7.22)
Antigrowth economy	0.05	0.42	0.55	0.78	0.51
	(1.30)	(8.06)	(2.92)	(4.98)	(3.12)
Environment	4.33	5.43	7.24	5.15	4.99
	(18.40)	(15.90)	(22.44)	(12.65)	(10.08)
Social justice	6.96	7.09	5.74	8.58	5.80
	(20.55)	(18.56)	(15.95)	(28.69)	(22.32)
Multiculturalism	5.93	7.41	6.60	5.49	7.34
	(19.16)	(35.06)	(15.62)	(16.93)	(11.72)
Green agenda	20.15	24.56	25.29	25.28	22.99
	(32.36)	(36.79)	(27.56)	(31.90)	(23.88)
Number of parties	35	35	28	30	22

Source: Budge et al. 2001; and Klingemann et al 2006.

Note: Number in each cell represents the mean for the issue. Range is in parentheses. Countries included in analysis: Austria, Belgium, Denmark, Finland, France, Germany, Greece, Iceland, Ireland, Italy, Luxembourg, Malta, Netherlands, Norway, Portugal, Spain, Sweden, Switzerland, and the United Kingdom.

percent of the green manifestos covered environmental issues, compared to 5.4 percent of socialist manifestos. Large variations exist, especially among green parties. In the 1990–94 period, for example, the range on the environment issue among green parties was 43.96. A total of 44.24 percent of the Italian Greens' 1994 manifesto covered environmental issues, compared to 0.28 percent of the 1991 manifesto of Anders Gaan Leven (To Start Living Differently, AGALEV), the Belgian Flemish Green Party. Over time, the percentage of the greens' manifestos devoted to environmental issues decreased, from an average of 22.1 percent to 16.4 percent, showing the parties' widening issue agenda. In addition, whereas the socialist manifestos' coverage of the social justice issue remained fairly steady over time, the greens devoted more of their manifestos to the issue over the twenty-four-year period, especially from 1995 to 2003. This development could reflect the changing political environment and importance of this issue more generally or influence from the socialist party priorities. A large difference also exists between the two groups of parties with respect to the green agenda scores over time. The average percentage of the green parties' manifestos devoted to the green agenda decreased slightly over time. Conversely, over the entire period, the socialist manifestos' coverage of most of these issues increased, demonstrating the greens' potential influence on policy. As table 2.3 shows, however, the greens' positions are moving more than their socialist counterparts, especially on the environment and social justice dimensions.

In both the expert and CMP data, the saliency is the highest for the environment issue. However, the specific issues are not necessarily measured in the same way in both data sets, so the data are not entirely comparable. Thus, even though the salience measure in the expert survey data may be high, a party will not necessarily have a high percentage of its manifesto devoted to the issue. The French Greens, for example, have an environmental saliency measure of 19.42 (of 20) on their strong support for protection of the environment even at the cost of economic growth in the expert data. Although the CMP data show that 20.7 percent of Les Verts' 2002 manifesto was devoted to issues of the environment (preservation of natural resources, environmental improvement, support for green politics), no text in the manifesto addressed antigrowth economic policies, which is much closer to Benoit and Laver's (2006) environmental dimension. This example highlights the importance of using both the expert and manifesto data in assessing parties' policy positions.

Table 2.4 shows the mean saliency differences between the greens and socialists in each country on each issue and on the aggregate green agenda. The difference on the green agenda for a given party dyad is calculated by totaling the positions on the six issues for a country's green and socialist parties and then taking the absolute value of the difference between the two total scores. Again, the largest differences occur on the issue of the environment in all five periods. An overall decrease took place in the saliency difference between the parties on this issue, mirroring the overall rise in the greens' vote shares.[8] In the first four periods, the correlation with green

TABLE 2.4. Difference in Issue Saliency between Greens and Socialists, 1979–2003

	Mean	Min	Max	S.D.	N	Correlation with Green Vote Share
Period 1 (1979–83)						
European integration	0.93	0	2.53	0.86	7	0.62
Decentralization	1.71	0	4.03	1.57	7	0.48
Antigrowth economy	4.89	0	14.71	6.78	7	−0.29
Environment	14.58	3.66	46.08	15.61	7	−0.55
Social justice	5.68	0.04	10.54	3.40	7	−0.79
Multiculturalism	6.31	0.72	15.16	5.16	7	−0.13
Green agenda	19.81	5.78	48.25	14.15	7	−0.72
Period 2 (1984–89)						
European integration	2.20	0	9.59	2.66	17	−0.04
Decentralization	1.76	0	9.95	2.38	17	−0.18
Antigrowth economy	5.39	0	22.67	7.40	17	−0.21
Environment	15.35	1.3	41.00	12.14	17	−0.30
Social justice	4.03	0	14.50	3.55	17	−0.08
Multiculturalism	7.19	0	33.08	8.70	17	0.09
Green agenda	18.80	0.8	43.57	13.17	17	−0.39
Period 3 (1990–94)						
European integration	1.98	0	5.52	1.46	17	−0.13
Decentralization	1.45	0	8.03	2.11	17	−0.33
Antigrowth economy	3.09	0	14.43	4.14	17	−0.38
Environment	16.05	0.51	42.96	13.27	17	−0.19
Social justice	3.13	0	12.45	3.78	17	−0.04
Multiculturalism	4.19	0.98	8.61	2.19	17	0.50
Green agenda	16.75	1.31	44.44	13.41	17	−0.37
Period 4 (1995–99)						
European integration	2.13	0	6.13	1.81	19	−0.03
Decentralization	0.57	0	2.08	0.63	19	−0.30
Antigrowth economy	3.34	0	13.03	4.35	19	−0.12

Balancing Preferences 45

TABLE 2.4.—*Continued*

	Mean	Min	Max	S.D.	N	Correlation with Green Vote Share
Environment	11.73	0.95	43.31	10.81	19	−0.35
Social justice	3.88	0.37	10.06	3.21	19	−0.29
Multiculturalism	3.73	0.61	10.45	2.60	19	0.30
Green agenda	15.62	2.45	36.20	9.76	19	−0.09
Period 5 (2000–2003)						
European integration	1.51	0	5.12	1.65	14	−0.19
Decentralization	0.64	0	1.82	0.65	14	0.03
Antigrowth economy	2.09	0	10.21	2.85	14	0.07
Environment	10.03	0	27.98	9.58	14	0.34
Social justice	2.17	0	5.63	1.68	14	0.21
Multiculturalism	3.20	0	8.97	2.15	14	−0.09
Green agenda	13.13	0	33.49	9.63	14	0.58
Overall (1979–2003)						
European integration	1.88	0	9.59	1.89	74	−0.02
Decentralization	1.16	0	9.95	1.69	74	−0.28
Antigrowth economy	3.66	0	22.67	5.20	74	−0.26
Environment	13.50	0	46.08	11.90	74	−0.23
Social justice	3.59	0	14.50	3.29	74	−0.20
Multiculturalism	4.78	0	33.08	4.97	74	−0.08
Green agenda	16.50	0	48.25	11.54	74	−0.23

Source: Budge et al. 2001; Klingemann et al. 2006.

Note: Country pairs (green-socialist) are included beginning with the first year the green party is in the data set. The following countries were not included in the analysis because either they do not have a green party or the green party was not included in the data set: Denmark, Greece, Norway, Malta, Portugal, Spain, and the United Kingdom. There are more parties in periods 3–5 in table 2.4 than in table 2.3 because there are two country pairs for the Netherlands, as there are two socialist/social democratic parties—the Labour Party (PvdA) and the Socialist Party (SP). In the 2000–2003 period, there are two additional parties, as there were two sets of Dutch elections and thus two additional country pairs.

vote share is negative. However, in the 2000–2003 period, when the difference on the environment dimension is the lowest, the correlation is 0.34. This finding suggests that as the difference on the saliency of the environment decreases, the greens' vote share increases. The social justice issue follows a similar pattern; moreover, differences between the country pairs on most issue dimensions are at their lowest level in the final period, as is the difference on the overall green agenda. The correlation with the green vote share is now positive for all issue areas except European integration and multiculturalism and is the highest for the overall green agenda. Finally, when the five periods are aggregated, all of the correlations are negative, and those for European integration and multiculturalism are almost nonexistent. This result is driven by the first four periods, which include sixty of the seventy-four country pairs under analysis. The data on the environment dimension and overall green agenda suggest evidence for the parabolic relationship hypothesized in the balancing thesis. To further explore this relationship, I graph the bivariate regressions between green vote share and policy differentiation for these two dimensions.

Figures 2.3 and 2.4 provide pooled evidence of the balancing thesis as well as show how the green parties have evolved as strategic political actors. Figure 2.3 includes the seventy-four party dyads for all five periods. The first graph plots the saliency differences on the environment dimension, while the second shows those differences with regard to the overall green agenda. Both show 95 percent confidence intervals. As in figure 2.2, these graphs plot the difference between the socialist and green policy positions on the x-axis and green vote share on the y-axis. The line is the fitted curve when regressing both the difference variable and the term squared on green vote share, and the data points are the observed values for each party-year dyad. While figure 2.3 shows evidence of the parabolic relationship, the trend curve more strongly supports the policy thesis (H2.1)—that is, too much policy differentiation will reduce vote shares. Thus, levels of policy differentiation beyond Luxembourg's 17.67 in 1994 will lead to reduced vote shares. However, the findings offer less support for H2.2 (the vote-maximization hypothesis that too little variation will result in lower vote shares), since the spread of party dyads is quite wide. With policy differentiation around 10 on the overall green agenda, for example, vote shares vary from 0.02 to 0.1. However, a pattern emerges from the dyads that are below the curve: many of these observations are from manifestos before 1990.

Both of the graphs also show that regardless of whether the Portuguese Green Party's levels of saliency on these issues converge on or diverge from those of the Socialist Party's, the Greens' vote share consistently remained below 0.5 percent during the 1980s. This finding may have to do more with the Portuguese party system and less with the party itself. Portugal had returned to democracy only in 1974 and initially had two center-left parties, the Partido Socialista (Socialist Party, PS) and the Partido Social Democrata (Social Democratic Party, PSD). After its initial manifesto, in which it clearly established itself as a left-wing party, the PSD moved steadily right-

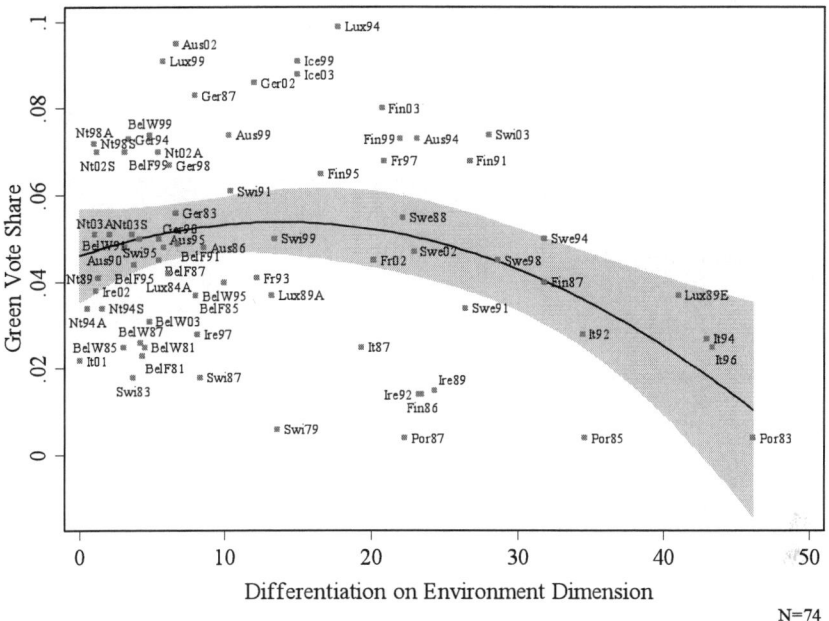

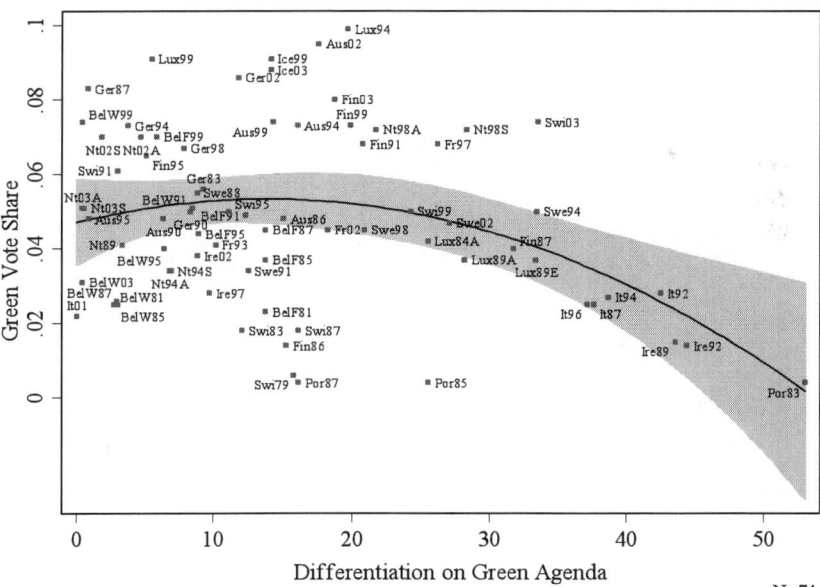

Fig. 2.3. Green-socialist saliency differences, 1979–2003, with 95 percent CI. (Data from Budge et al. 2001; Klingemann et al. 2006.)

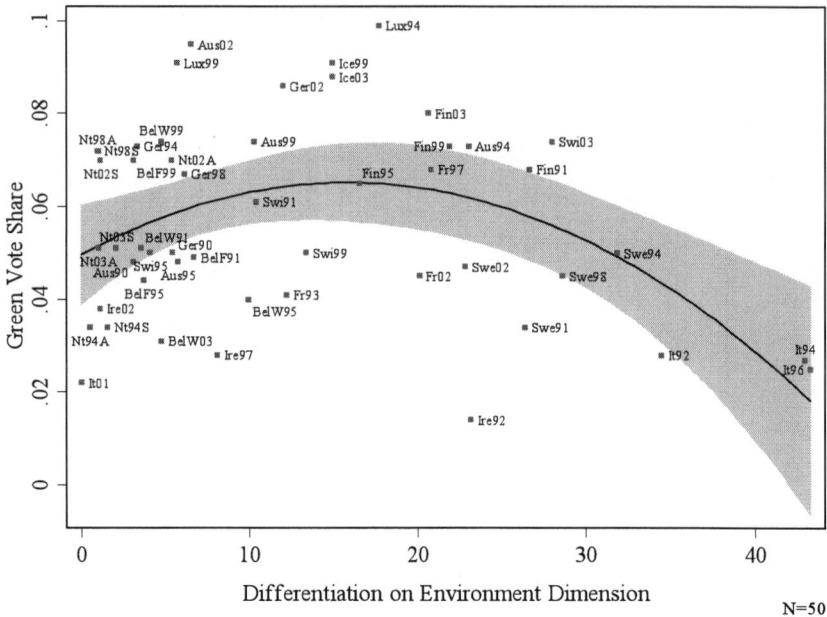

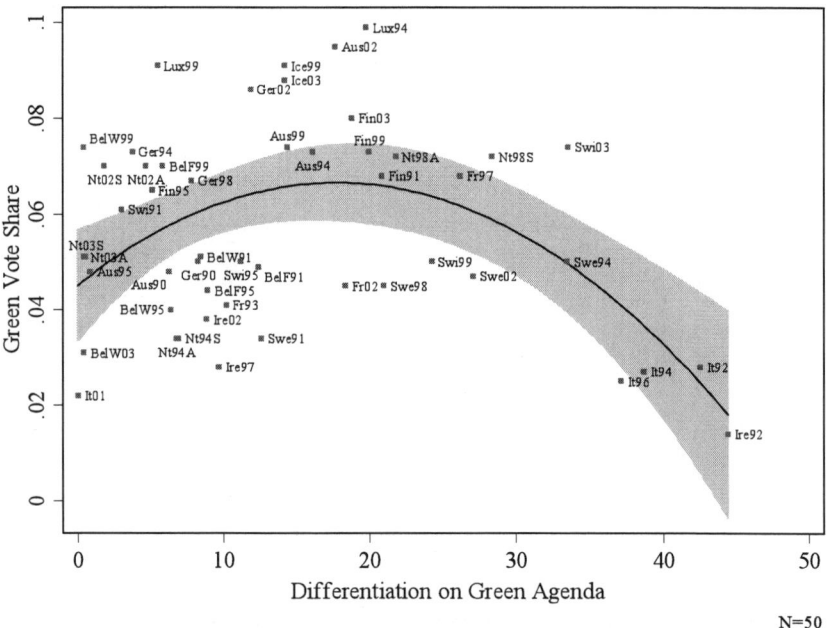

Fig. 2.4. Green-socialist saliency differences, 1990–2003, with 95 percent CI. (Data from Budge et al. 2001; Klingemann et al. 2006.)

ward. However, in the early 1980s, it was still occupying space on the left. Thus, no matter the position of the Greens vis-à-vis the PS, there may have been no room on the left for another party. As a result, the Greens' vote share may have remained low even as it moderated its positions from 1983 to 1987. Once the PSD established itself on the right, we should expect space on the left to open and the Greens' vote share to increase as it continued to moderate. However, this idea cannot be explored empirically because the party joined with the Communist Party to form the Coligação Democrática Unitária (Democratic Unity Coalition) in 1987 and no longer runs its own candidates. Moreover, the CMP data do not include the Greens as a stand-alone party after 1987.

Figure 2.4 shows the same relationship, but only for the third through fifth periods in the analysis. After the twenty-four early party dyads are omitted, there is much clearer evidence of the parabolic balancing thesis (H2.3), especially when looking at the overall green agenda. A comparison of the two figures thus provides strong evidence of party evolution and development. By the early 1990s, most internal green party debates about strategy had subsided, and the focus turned toward how to balance pursing policy agendas and increasing vote and seat shares.

Still, outliers remain, including the French Green Party in 2002. As figure 2.4 shows, the party has nearly the optimal amount of differentiation from the Socialists on the green agenda but still has considerably lower vote shares than the Greens in Austria in the same year, for example. More important, perhaps, the French Greens moderated their position on the overall green agenda considerably between 1997 and 2002 but lost votes. This finding demonstrates the importance of both political context and preelection deals between parties. In 1997, the left came back into control of parliament and government, and the parties that made up the *gauche plurielle* (plural left)—the Socialists, Communists, Greens, and Radicals—collectively won 320 of 577 seats, compared to the 253 won by the right-wing parties, which supported President Jacques Chirac. Although differentiation between the Greens' and Socialists' positions had increased substantially since the 1993 elections (28.25 on the overall green agenda), Green vote share also increased. By 2002, the left lost its majority, as the Greens' vote share demonstrates. Although the Greens moderated their positions, their vote share dropped by more than 2 percentage points. Second, French parties often engage in preelection coalitions (PECs) in which one party stands down and supports the candidate of the other party. The

Greens and Socialists began entering into PECs in 1997. PECs may enable the Greens to take positions more divergent from the Socialists than would otherwise be the case in a non-PR system (for an alternative argument, see Ezrow 2010). The parties do not run joint candidates in all single-member-district constituencies, which may explain why vote shares were so low in 2002 even with policy moderation. Thus, the use of PECs and the political context together offer some insight into the relationship between the French Greens' vote share and policy positions.

Finally, even when examining the data after 1990, we would hope for a stronger relationship. There are still outlier party dyads, such as Sweden in 1998, in the overall green agenda plot. These results thus demonstrate that achieving the optimal policy position is a necessary but not sufficient condition for increasing vote share, as there are outlier green party dyads that are at the optimal point of differentiation but have much lower vote shares that we might otherwise expect. Importantly, no parties fall into the upper-right corner of these graphs. In other words, there are no party dyads with high vote shares and high levels of policy differentiation.[9]

SOCIALIST PARTY REACTION AND THE POLICY GAME

As with the greens, socialist party positions are not static. Socialist parties also update their policy positions on the green agenda issues from one election cycle to the next. This process reflects the socialists' interest in attracting voters who are sympathetic to the greens' positions, as in the devolution example. Moreover, the greens' survival and ultimate electoral success are related to how much the socialists shift their positions. If they move their positions slightly closer to those of the greens, they will attract some green voters. But as long as considerable difference exists between the two parties' positions, green voters will see the merits in voting for the party that is closest to their true preferences. The socialists also need to be cautious about how their policy shifts vis-à-vis the greens affect the socialist ability to attract centrist voters, who are choosing between the mainstream left and the mainstream right. Two examples illustrate socialist party updating while still maintaining position distinction from the greens.

The French Greens strongly supported ending the use of nuclear energy and proposed 2030 as the target date in their 2007 manifesto. In 2002, the French Socialists recognized that nuclear energy remained an important source but argued that it needed to be safe and secure. By 2007, the PS's position had changed so that it now advocated the reduction of nuclear energy use to 20 percent of total energy by 2020 and increasing to 50 percent over the long term the percentage of total energy that comes from renewable resources. Thus, although the Socialists' position had moved closer to that of the Greens, a concrete difference remained between the two parties' positions.

The two parties' positions also converged on the issue of institutional reform, which includes limiting the power of the presidency, instituting term limits, reducing the number of simultaneous elected positions an individual can hold (*cumul des mandats*), and changing the way members of parliament are elected. Both the Greens and Socialists have included this issue in their recent manifestos, though it is not covered by the measures in either the expert or manifesto data. In both their 2002 and 2007 manifestos, the Greens proposed wholesale reform of the national legislative electoral system by instituting mixed-member proportional representation, similar to the system found in Germany. In this system, half of the deputies would be elected through PR on national lists in one round and half would be elected in single-member districts in two rounds. The Socialists, however, supported the introduction of "a dose of PR" in the National Assembly and have proposed that a percentage of deputies be elected through PR on national lists (10 percent in the 2002 manifesto and "about 1 in 5 deputies" in the 2007 manifesto) (Socialist Party 2002, 24; 2007, 22). Thus, the Socialists have not come close to the Greens' preference for total reform of the electoral system but have doubled the proposed number of PR deputies over this period. The Socialists' position has thus approached that of the Greens but remained distinct.

Keenly aware of the socialists' behavior, green parties may respond to the socialists' shift to the left on an issue by moving their position closer to or further away from that of the socialists depending on the political situation in their country. We could also envision the same scenario if the socialists moved their position on a given issue further from the greens to attract voters on their right flank. Over the course of the 1990–2003 period, for example, the CMP data find that both the Sozialdemokratische Partei Österreichs (Austrian Socialist Party) and Suomen Sosialidemokraattinen Puolue (Finnish Social Democratic Party) devoted considerably less of their manifestos to environmental issues. This shift may have been a way of appealing to more centrist voters. Depending on the position of the party to their left, the greens might respond by moving their position closer to the socialists, thus shifting the two parties' overall position on the issue to the right, or might keep their position. Thus, the relationship between green and socialist parties is in constant motion, and proactive party leaders must be aware of the other party's positions and be willing to update positions to maximize potential vote share.

CONCLUSION

Through cross-national analysis, I have demonstrated that the greens need to balance their pure policy desires with their goal of gaining votes and seats. I have found evidence for the balancing thesis (H2.3) using both the expert and manifesto data. I show that while some differentiation is beneficial, if there is too much (H2.2) or too little difference (H2.1) between the parties' positions, the greens will suffer electorally as they lose potential voters who are sympathetic to the greens' policies. Parties lose these voters when a leader moves her party too close to the mainstream left party and the voters do not see the benefit in voting for the small party or when a leader moves or keeps her party too far away from the mainstream left party and the voters consider the party too extreme.

I have shown how the green parties have moderated their policy preferences to attract more voters but have maintained their distinction. In particular, the CMP data illustrate that over the twenty-four-year period, the greens have made their positions less extreme and moved their policy preferences closer to those of the socialists. As the differences became closer to the optimal point, the greens' electoral results improved. This finding highlights not only how the greens have evolved as a party but also how this evolution has enabled them to survive.

Although these data provide a useful test of the balancing thesis, they only address one piece of the puzzle. Chapters 3–5 demonstrate how the parties' balancing of these preferences manifests itself in their electoral and communication strategies. I also show how political context has interacted with the party's policy- and vote-seeking goals to produce a specific set of strategies.

CHAPTER 3

Preelection Coalitions in France: A Lasting Electoral Strategy?

"We are totally dependent on the electoral system, which is unjust and favors bipolarization and thus the big parties. It eliminates the small parties or rising parties, like the Greens. . . . It is therefore impossible for the Greens to elect any deputies on their own."
—NOËL MAMÈRE, DEPUTY FROM BÈGLES AND
2002 GREEN PRESIDENTIAL CANDIDATE

PARTIES OFTEN CREATE preelection alliances or coalitions (PECs) with other parties. Under some of these partnerships, several parties may fuse and run a joint list throughout the country. In Israel, for example, many small parties will fuse before the election and run a joint list against the two dominant parties, Avodah (Labor) and Likud. In Italy, parties form blocs such as the Casa delle Libertà (House of Freedoms) and L'Ulivo (The Olive Tree), in which the parties run individually but agree before the election to work together to form a government. In other countries, a party may support the candidate of a rival party and not run its own candidate. This type of alliance can occur nationwide or on a district-by-district basis. The French Greens have used this latter type of alliance as their general electoral strategy since 1997 as a way of balancing their dual goals of policy differentiation and vote maximization.

This chapter explains this PEC strategy in the 2002 and 2007 election cycles. I explain which legislative districts were likely to be included in the 2002 national alliance as well as which party stood the candidate. For the 2007 election, I discuss why the party chose not to enter into a nationwide PEC as it had during the two previous elections. First, however, I provide a brief background of the French electoral and party system and discuss the constraints and incentives that it establishes for parties.

ELECTORAL RULES

The French use a two-round single-member-district system for elections to the national parliament. A candidate who receives more than 50 percent of the vote in the first round wins. If no candidate receives a majority, any candidate who receives 12.5 percent of the vote qualifies to advance to the second round, with the recipient of the most votes in that round declared the winner. In addition to the high legal (12.5%) and effective (as much as 17%) thresholds,[1] a high level of disproportionality between seat and vote share exists at the parliamentary level. In the 2002 legislative elections, for example, the Greens won 4.5 percent of the total vote: if that number had translated directly to deputies, the Greens would have held roughly 26 of the 577 seats. However, the party won only 3 seats (0.52 percent of the total).

THE FRENCH PARTY SYSTEM AND EXPECTED PARTY BEHAVIOR

Scholars generally agree that through the mid-1990s, France was a four-party system at the popular level (Pierce 1995; Schlesinger and Schlesinger 2000; Gallagher, Laver, and Mair 2006; Dalton 2008). An examination of the effective number of parliamentary parties (ENPP), however, yields even fewer parties. Table 3.1 shows the ENPP from 1988–2007 using Laakso and Taagepera's (1979) measure.[2] Even though an average of nearly fifteen parties ran candidates in the first round of the 2002 elections, the number that won and had representation in the parliament is much lower. The two biggest parties, the Union pour un Mouvement Populaire (Union for a Popular Movement, UMP) and the Parti Socialiste (Socialist Party, PS), won 86.1 percent of the seats (497 of 577). This election represents the culmination of negotiations between the Rassamblement pour la République (Rally for the Republic, RPR) and the Union pour la Démocratie Française (Union for French Democracy, UDF) to consolidate into a single party, the UMP. In 1997, the ENPP was 3.56, with the three largest parties—the PS, UDF, and RPR—holding 85.6 percent of the seats. In 2007, the ENPP was 2.49, which is a slight increase over 2002, when the ENPP was 2.24.

Since the mid-1980s, the extreme right Front National (National Front, FN) and the leftist Greens have also become important players in French politics (Gallagher, Laver, and Mair 2006; Dalton 2008). Under the two-

Preelection Coalitions in France 55

round single-member-district system, the FN won one parliamentary seat in the 1988 and 1997 elections.[3] The Greens won eight seats in 1997, three in 2002, and four in 2007. Unlike the FN, which has run candidates and won seats independently, all of the Greens' seats were won in districts in which there was a preelection alliance with the Socialists.

In France's two-round plurality system, parties have the incentive to fuse either before the election (to increase their chances of qualifying for the second round) or between the two rounds (to increase their chances of winning the election). Over the past three decades, the four main parties (the RPR, UDF, PS, and Parti Communiste Français [PCF]) have traditionally forged alliances that have worked to their mutual advantage. Schlesinger and Schlesinger (1990, 2000) have shown that French parties use four distinctive strategies to win in a system that strongly favors big parties: maximizing support on (1) the first ballot; (2) the second ballot; (3) both ballots; or (4) either ballot. The RPR has tended to prefer strategy 1; the Socialists have used 2; the UDF has employed 3; and the Communists have utilized 4. The RPR and UDF have run joint candidates from the first round in the legislative elections since 1981 and in the second round since 1978. Since 1973, the Socialists and Communists have run a single candidate in some electoral districts in the second round. (For an explanation of why these alliances did not always succeed in the 1980s, see Tsebelis 1990.) These patterns have changed in recent elections with the merging of the RPR and

TABLE 3.1. Effective Number of Parliamentary Parties, 1988–2007

Year of Legislative Election	Effective Number of Parties
1988	2.96
1993	2.93
1997	3.56
2002	2.24
2007	2.49
Average	2.84

Source: Mackie 1989; Le Monde 1993, 1997; National Assembly 2002; and Interior Ministry 2007.

Note: The ENPP reported for 1988 is lower than it actually was. This is because the seat share breakdown reported by Mackie combines the Socialists, Radicals, and other parties of the moderate left. Other sources either did not report seat share breakdown for 1988 or also combined the parties. Therefore, the overall average is probably slightly larger than 3.0.

UDF into the UMP and with the Greens replacing the Communists as the Socialists' preferred coalition partner.[4] The parties do not run joint candidates in all districts, and the two parties engage in elaborate negotiations regarding which districts will be included in the PEC and which party will field the candidate (Schlesinger and Schlesinger 1990, 2000; S. N. Golder 2006a, 2006b). The Greens' strategy follows the expectations of how parties will behave in the French system.[5]

Beginning in 1997, the Greens sought a first-round PEC with the Socialists at the national level. For the legislative elections of that year, the Greens and Socialists entered into a first-round alliance in 107 of the 555 districts in metropolitan France.[6] In 2002, the parties ran joint candidates in 168 districts. In 2007, the parties had no formal national PEC. Table 3.2 describes the 1997 and 2002 PECs in full. Figure 3.1 shows a ballot from a Green candidate in a district in which there was an alliance. The Green, Socialist, and Parti Radical de Gauche (Radical Left Party) logos indicate an alliance, and the *suppléant* (alternate) (see n. 12) is a Socialist.

GREEN-SOCIALIST PREELECTION COALITIONS

In the abstract, we can assume that most Green voters and activists would prefer the election of a Green deputy. Likewise, the ideal outcome for the Socialists is a Socialist deputy. The second-best option for both parties is the election of a deputy of the left, regardless of party affiliation. Both parties often opt for their second choice because of an additional preference: preventing a second-round contest between the right and the extreme right. The threat from the extreme right often supersedes each party's desire to have its own deputy. The second-round contest is typically between the left and the right. In the second round in 2002, for example, only nine three-way contests took place involving the left, right, and FN. The logic holds that reducing the possibilities on the left will help the left candidate and ensure that she qualifies for the second round. It is also important for the parties on the left to win the highest vote share possible in the first round to demonstrate their strength to voters for the second round. This strategy is evident in letters written by the chair of the Socialist Party, François Hollande, asking Socialist voters to support the Green candidate in 2002. One such letter states, "I invite all Socialist voters to vote for Vert candidate Jean-Charles Kohlhaas from the first round, to stand in the way of the right

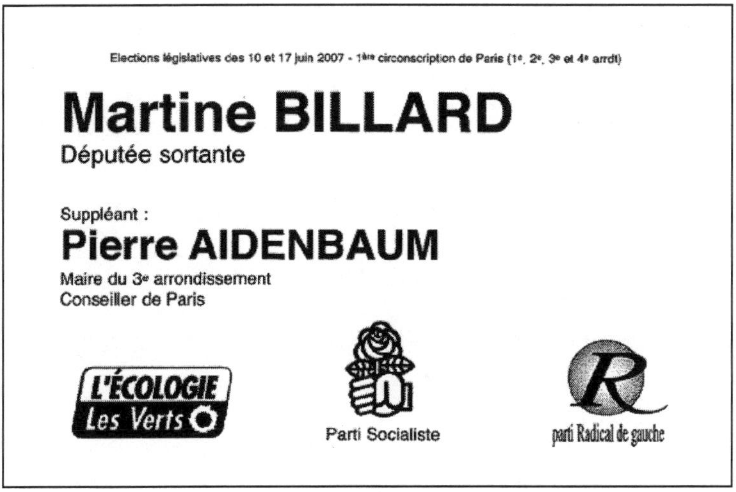

Preelection Coalitions in France 57

> Elections législatives des 10 et 17 juin 2007 - 1ère circonscription de Paris (1e, 2e, 3e et 4e arrdt)
>
> # Martine BILLARD
> Députée sortante
>
> Suppléant :
> # Pierre AIDENBAUM
> Maire du 3e arrondissement
> Conseiller de Paris
>
> **L'ÉCOLOGIE Les Verts**   Parti Socialiste   parti Radical de gauche

Fig. 3.1. Ballot for green candidate in alliance district

and the extreme right" (Kohlhaas 2002).[7] Similar letters were sent to Socialist voters in other alliance districts in which the Socialists supported the Green candidate.

With several parties on the left splitting the vote, the possibility that no left-wing candidate wins 12.5 percent of the vote increases. If an extreme right candidate does pass the threshold, a second-round contest would take place between the mainstream and extreme right, thereby leaving the left without a candidate.[8] For this reason, the much larger and more successful PS has entered into PECs with the Greens. In addition to ensuring that the extreme right candidate does not advance to the runoff, the Greens have chosen to enter into these PECs since it is the only way they can elect deputies in the French system.

Since the mid-1990s, Green Party leaders have generally understood that to win any seats in the National Assembly, the Greens would have to enter into PECs.[9] The party's leaders, members, and voters now generally approve of this national-level strategy, as Martine Billard, a Green deputy from Paris, expressed: "Without these alliances, it would be impossible to have any deputies elected today. This is clear."[10] Even leaders who initially were more reluctant to accept this strategy now see it as their only option for gaining a voice, no matter how small, in parliament. A 1998 survey, for example, found that 89.6 percent of Green Party members felt that the left-wing coalition in government has been a positive way for the Greens to promote their ideas on the environment (Boy 2002, 72).[11]

For both parties, this decision to form a PEC in the legislative elections is also based on party elites' assumption that when faced with a choice of voting Green or voting Socialist (in the absence of an alliance), many Green voters will not coordinate on their own in this type of election—that is, they will not be so-called Duvergerian voters (Duverger 1954), voting for the major party, the Socialists, even if their most preferred party was the Greens. Duvergerian voters know that the party will not win and consequently would not vote for the Greens. Conversely, Green voters will often vote for their most preferred party because they feel best represented by the party's goals and platform—what is often termed a sincere or expressive vote (Schuessler 2000). They will not cast a *vote utile* (useful vote). These voters will "vote with their heart and not with their head," as the French saying goes.

Decisions about which districts will be included in the national PEC are made by a negotiating team comprising officials from both parties. In 2002, these decisions were made in the days after the presidential election and reflected the unpredicted outcome of a second-round contest between the right and the extreme right. The parties also negotiated which districts would have PS candidates supported by the Greens and which would have Green candidates supported by the Socialists.[12]

As the Socialists are the larger party and thus the senior partner in the coalition-making process and the Greens are the junior member, the Greens often got less in the negotiations and had to make more concessions than did the Socialists. One such concession was that the Greens gave the more winnable districts to the Socialists. In 2002, alliance candidates won in 4.9 percent (3 of 61) of the Green districts and in 14.0 percent (15 of 107) in the Socialist districts. Many of the areas where the FN is strongest are traditional Socialist bastions. Thus, by putting their strongest candidate forward, the Socialists and Greens may have been trying to win back supporters in previously leftist areas.

In addition, the parties determine a ratio of Green to Socialist districts. In 2002, the parties agreed that for every Green district, there would be 1.5 Socialist districts. The ratio is more of a blueprint for how the districts are divided than an iron law, and the actual division—61 Green districts and 107 PS districts—reflected a ratio closer to 1:1.75.[13] The parties determined this ratio by considering the aggregate first-round results of the Socialist and Green presidential candidates in 2002 and the parties' results in the 1997 legislative contest. In 1997, the established ratio was 1 Green district for every 3 PS districts. Again, with 29 Green districts and 78 Socialist districts, the actual ratio deviated from what was determined beforehand and was closer to 1 Green district for every 2.7 Socialist districts. The difference in the 1997 and 2002 ratios is attributable to the Greens' increased credibility as a political party after electing eight deputies in 1997 and its experience as a member of Jospin's government from 1997 to 2002. Although the the national party decides which districts will be included in the national accord, the Socialist and Green local groups—and their strength and presence in the district—have some influence over the type of alliance (Green or Socialist).[14]

Table 3.2 presents an overview of the Green-Socialist PECs in 1997 and 2002. The mean first-round vote share for a PS candidate (in a PS-only district) was 28 percent in both years, much higher than the Green candidate vote share (in Green-only districts) of approximately 20 percent in the two elections. The number of Socialist candidates who advanced to the second round was higher in both years than the number of Green candidates. The same relationship holds true when looking at the number of Socialist and Green deputies who were elected. In 2002, 15.5 percent of the PS candidates in the second round won, whereas only 7.7 percent of Green candidates succeeded. In sum, these results demonstrate that the unified left was much more successful where there was a Socialist candidate. Of course, it is not a given that the unified left succeeded because of the type of candidate. Comparing the parties' results in the two elections also reflects the fact that

TABLE 3.2. Green-Socialist PECs in 1997 and 2002

	1997 Alliances	2002 Alliances
Total PS–Green alliance districts	107	168
PS districts	78	107
Green districts	29	61
Mean first-round vote share in PS district	28.0%	28.2%
Mean first-round vote share in Green district	19.1%	21.8%
PS candidates in second round	61	97
Green candidates in second round	20	39
PS deputies (PS–Green alliances)	36	15
Green deputies	8	3

Note: Total districts in metropolitan France = 555.

the *gauche plurielle* (comprised of the Socialists, Communists, Greens, and Radicals) held the parliamentary majority in 1997 and did not in 2002. After the second round of the 2002 presidential contest pitted the right against the extreme right (in large part because of the left's first-round divisions), the left did much worse in the subsequent legislative elections. The parties of the left won 311 of 577 seats in 1997 and only 177 seats in 2002.

THE GREEN-SOCIALIST ALLIANCE FORMATION PROCESS

Various factors influence not only if there was an alliance in a particular district in 2002 but also whether the district was a Green district or a Socialist district. I use the term *alliance* to describe the situation in a specific legislative district. Within the national-level PEC, alliances take place in some districts but not in others. In the nonalliance districts, each party runs its own candidates. Among the alliance districts, a Green district is one in which the Socialists do not run their own candidate and instead support the Green candidate; conversely, in a Socialist district, the Greens do not run their own candidate but instead support the Socialist candidate. The unit of analysis is thus the legislative district in the 2002 parliamentary elections ($N = 555$).

To determine the factors that influence the selection of a district for an alliance, I include whether an alliance existed in 1997, the strength of the Greens in the district, the strength of the mainstream and extreme right, and presence of a left incumbent. (See appendix B for descriptive statistics of all the independent variables.)[15] If the goal of allying is to avoid splitting the leftist vote, I would expect more alliances to occur in districts where the Greens' vote shares in past elections were higher. Thus, the higher the vote share of the Greens in past elections, the more likely an alliance will exist in 2002. The PS and Greens tend to ally to prevent the right and extreme right from succeeding. Therefore, the higher the vote shares of the mainstream right and the extreme right National Front in past elections, the higher the probability that an alliance will form. Moreover, because voters on the left least prefer FN success, high previous FN vote shares increase the likelihood of the creation of a PS district, since the Socialists have a wider appeal than the Greens and thus will produce the strongest candidate. Such a candidate will be more likely to attract voters from across the left and thus ensure qualification for the second round. However, increased strength on the right increases the probability that the district will be Green, since the PS often gives the less winnable districts to the Greens. Conversely, a left incumbent is a strong predictor of no alliance since the parties of the left have little concern about splitting the vote. Therefore, a left incumbent should have the opposite effect than that of a strong right presence, predicting no alliance in 2002.

The models also include several control variables that are predictors of FN or Green support: percentages of the population in a given legislative district who are immigrants, who are unemployed, who are between twenty and thirty-nine years of age, and who have at least two years of postbaccalaureate education (BAC + 2). All of these variables are taken from the 1999 French census, which reports the data at the legislative district level.

First, I include a measure for the percentage of immigrants. Numerous studies have found that the FN's success is related to the percentage of the population who are immigrants, especially those immigrants from Muslim countries (see, for example, Perrineau 1998; Schain 2000; Mayer 2002). There is, however, little evidence that the FN distinguishes between immigrants and naturalized citizens. The best proxy for immigrant status using the 1999 census data is thus nationality.[16] The available census data break out nationality into a handful of non-European groups—Moroccans, Tunisians, Algerians (Maghreb countries), and Turks. I aggregate the percentage of the population from these countries into one "immigrant" group. Concurring with the literature, I find that the correlation between the vote share for Le Pen in the 2002 presidential election and the percentage of immigrants in the district is 0.31. Thus, I would expect that as the percentage of population that is immigrants increases, so will the probability of an alliance.

Second, I include a measure for unemployment. The FN often does well in areas where unemployment is high (Perrineau 1998; Mayer 2002). The party often tries to convince those who are out of work that their situation results from the number of non-European immigrants in France. The correlation between the vote share for Le Pen and the percentage of those unemployed is also 0.31.[17] Therefore, as unemployment increases, so should the likelihood of an alliance. Furthermore, because both of these measures are proxies for FN strength, I expect that the higher the immigrant or unemployed percentage of the population, the more likely it is that a district will have a PS (stronger) candidate. Running a Green candidate could motivate a likely PS voter, who is also concerned about unemployment, to vote for the FN, thus increasing the FN's vote share and reducing the vote share of the Green candidate and her likelihood of qualifying for the second round.

Third, I include variables for age and education. Studies often describe the typical Green voter as young and relatively well educated (Inglehart 1997; Dalton 2008). In the 2002 French National Election Study, for example, 46.9 percent of those who voted for the Greens in the legislative elections were under forty years old, and 42.7 percent had at least two years postbaccalaureate education (compared to 27.1 percent among voters of all parties). Moreover, a strong positive correlation exists between the vote for the Greens' presidential candidate, Nöel Mamère, and the percentage of those with a BAC + 2 and those who are under forty. Thus, the higher the percentage of likely Green voters, the higher the probability that the left would split the vote and thus need an alliance. Therefore, I would expect that the higher a district's percentage of young and well-educated citizens, the more likely it is to have an alliance between the PS and the Greens.

TO ALLY OR NOT TO ALLY: THE SELECTION OF DISTRICTS FOR GREEN-SOCIALIST ALLIANCES

In my analysis of the factors that drive the decision about whether to enter into an alliance in a given district, the dependent variable is dichotomous and is coded 0 if there was no alliance in 2002 and 1 if there was an alliance in 2002. In Models 1–4 (see table 3.3), I show the results when using different measures for Green and extreme right support: the 2002 first-round vote shares of the FN presidential candidate, Le Pen, and the Greens' presidential candidate, Mamère (Model 1); those of Le Pen and the 1999 Green European Parliament list (European99) (Model 2); the first-round results of the 1997 FN legislative candidate (FN97) and Mamère (Model 3); and those of the FN candidate and the European list (Model 4).[18] I find that all of the variables have a positive effect on the probability of an alliance in 2002. In other words, as the vote for Mamère increases in a given district, so, too, does the likelihood that a legislative alliance will exist. However, in the models using FN97 as the FN measure, the Green measures are not significant (Mamère) or are significant only at the 0.1 level (European99). The predicted probability of an alliance in 2002, holding all variables at their means and 97Alliance at 1 (that is, an alliance existed between the parties in the district in 1997), for the two models with Le Pen is 0.45 and is 0.40 for those using FN97. Holding all variables at their means and 97Alliance at 0 (that is, no alliance existed in 1997) decreases the predicted probability to 0.23 for Models 1, 3, and 4 and 0.22 for Model 2.[19]

I have selected Model 1 as the base model for my analysis of alliance formation. With the high correlation between Mamère and the EP Green list ($r = 0.90$), I am confident that either Model 1 or Model 2 would be a good measure of Green support. Although there is little doubt that those who voted for Mamère were expressing their true preferences, some of those voting for the Green list in the 1999 European elections might have been

TABLE 3.3. 2002 Green-Socialist Alliance Formation I

	Model 1	Model 2	Model 3	Model 4
97Alliance	1.03***	1.05***	0.81***	0.83***
	(0.25)	(0.25)	(0.25)	(0.25)
Right	4.78***	4.56***	5.86***	5.68***
	(1.31)	(1.30)	(1.35)	(1.33)
Support for the FN			22.77***	22.63***
FN97			(2.52)	(2.48)
Le Pen	25.47***	25.64***		
	(2.90)	(2.85)		
Support for the Greens	29.65***		11.30	
Mamère	(8.94)		(8.22)	
European99		17.52***		7.09*
		(4.25)		(3.91)
Constant	−8.88***	−8.99***	−7.42***	−7.44***
	(1.15)	(1.08)	(1.02)	(0.94)
Pseudo R^2	0.21	0.20	0.20	0.20
N	555	555	555	555
Log likelihood	−276.89	−273.95	−272.40	−271.73
Pr(02ALLIANCE)[a]	0.45	0.45	0.40	0.40
	(0.35, 0.55)[c]	(0.35, 0.56)	(0.30, 0.51)	(0.30, 0.51)
Pr(02ALLIANCE)[b]	0.23	0.22	0.23	0.23
	(0.18, 0.27)	(0.18, 0.27)	(0.19, 0.27)	(0.19, 0.27)

[a] All variables are held at their means; 97Alliance = 1.
[b] All variables are held at their means; 97Alliance = 0.
[c] 95% confidence intervals.
*$p < 0.1$, **$p < 0.05$, ***$p < 0.01$. Standard errors in parentheses.

doing so to punish the incumbent government, as much of the literature on European elections as second-order elections argues, thus boosting my decision to use Model 1. (See, for example, Reif and Schmitt 1980; van der Eijk, Franklin, and Marsh 1996; Oppenhuis, van der Eijk, and Franklin 1996; van der Brug and van der Eijk 2007. For an alternative view of voting in EP elections, see Ferrara and Weishaupt 2004; Hix and M. Marsh 2007; Hobolt, Spoon, and Tilly 2009.)

The results from estimating this model confirm my hypotheses that a previous alliance in the district and the vote shares of the right bloc, Le Pen, and Mamère increased the probability of an alliance between the Socialists and the Greens in 2002.[20] Holding all variables at their means and 97Alliance at 1, I find that as the vote shares of Mamère, Le Pen, and the right bloc increase, so does the probability of an alliance. However, moving from the minimum to the maximum vote share, the probability of an alliance has the largest increase for Le Pen. Figure 3.2 demonstrates this trend over the different values of Le Pen's vote share. The biggest change in the probability of an alliance is when Le Pen's vote share increases from 0.15 to 0.25, as the predicted probability of an alliance increases from 0.33 to 0.86.[21]

Taking each of the three variables in turn and setting them at one standard deviation below the mean[22] while holding the other variables constant at their means and 97Alliance at 1, I find that the probability for an alliance decreases from 0.45 to 0.19 for Le Pen, 0.34 for the right bloc, and 0.35 for Mamère. This finding demonstrates that the vote shares of the right and of Mamère have roughly the same effect on a 2002 alliance. Holding Le Pen at its value two standard deviations below the mean, the effect is even more dramatic. The predicted probability of an alliance drops to 0.06 for Le Pen and decreases to only 0.25 for both the right and Mamère.

When adding age, education, immigrant population, and unemployment variables to the basic model, only the percentage of the population with at least a BAC + 2 and the rate of unemployment are significant (see table 3.4). Models 5 and 6 demonstrate these results. Education is positively correlated with the vote for Mamère and has a positive effect on the probability of an alliance. Thus, as the percentage of those with at least a BAC + 2 increases, so does the likelihood of an alliance in the district. Conversely, as unemployment increases, the probability of an alliance decreases. One possible explanation for this result could be that those who are unemployed are voting both for the Socialists and for the FN. There is a 0.27 cor-

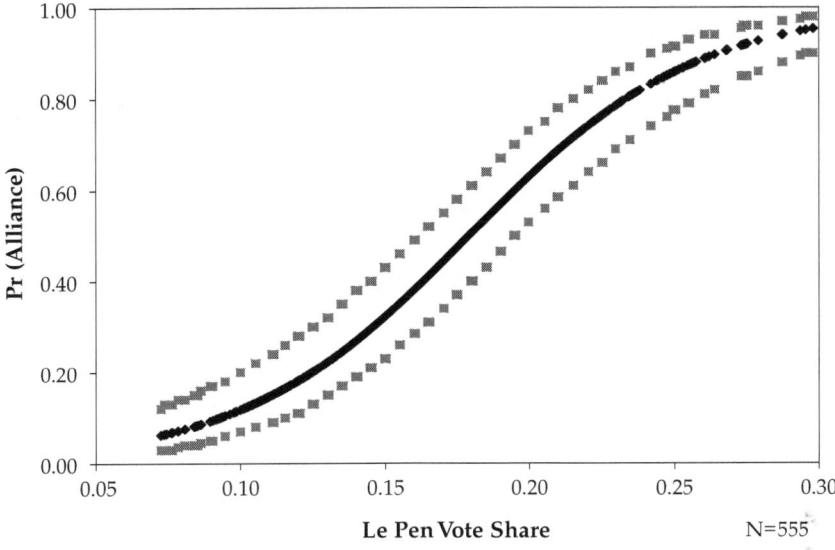

Fig. 3.2. Predicted probability of alliance in 2002 varying Le Pen Vote share, with 95 percent CI

relation between the vote for the Socialists' presidential candidate, Lionel Jospin, and unemployment and a 0.31 correlation with the vote for Le Pen. Thus, those who are unemployed are voting either for the PS because they like its policies or for the FN because they fear immigrants taking jobs. Voting for the PS is an indicator of Socialist strength, thus reducing the need for an alliance.

The percentage of immigrants does not have an impact on the probability of an alliance as expected.[23] Only when Le Pen is removed does the percentage of immigrants become significant (Model 7). However, this result is at the cost of the percentage correctly predicted by the model, which drops to 0.07. This finding demonstrates that both the vote share for Le Pen and the percentage of immigrants are good measures for where an alliance is likely. However, because only one variable at a time is significant, they are highly collinear.

Age is also not significant. Although there is a relatively strong bivariate relationship between age and the vote for Mamère, this correlation does not carry over to the probability that there will be an alliance. Many of the thirty-seven districts in which the percentage of the population aged be-

TABLE 3.4. 2002 Green-Socialist Alliance Formation II

	Model 5	Model 6	Model 7	Model 8	Model 9
97Alliance	1.05***	0.98***	0.98***	1.04***	1.03***
	(0.25)	(0.25)	(0.23)	(0.25)	(0.26)
Right	3.78***	3.61**	−0.09	1.06	−0.86
	(1.42)	(1.55)	(1.30)	(1.75)	(2.04)
Le Pen	26.55***	24.54***		23.24***	24.20***
	(2.98)	(3.02)		(2.96)	(3.20)
Mamère	19.16*	22.08**	−17.54**	24.36***	8.71
	(11.13)	(9.85)	(7.68)	(9.24)	(12.17)
Min. BAC+2	4.36**				3.88*
	(2.09)				(2.14)
20–39 years	−0.25				0.44
	(4.03)				(4.44)
Immigrants		9.22	23.29***		4.38
		(6.10)	(5.29)		(6.65)
Unemployment		−6.99**	−7.67**		−6.63*
		(3.32)	(3.20)		(3.43)
Left incumbent				−0.91***	−0.81***
				(0.29)	(0.29)
Constant	−8.76***	−7.20***	0.35	−6.39***	−5.05***
	(1.41)	(1.39)	(0.94)	(1.37)	(1.77)
Pseudo R^2	0.19	0.19	0.07	0.20	0.21
N	555	555	555	555	555
Log likelihood	−274.27	−274.23	−316.08	−271.84	−267.86
Pr(02ALLIANCE)[a]	0.45	0.44	0.47		
	(0.34, 0.55)	(0.33, 0.54)[g]	(0.38, 0.57)		
Pr(02ALLIANCE)[b]	0.22	0.23	0.25		
	(0.18, 0.27)	(0.18, 0.27)	(0.21, 0.29)		
Pr(02ALLIANCE)[c]				0.35	0.35
				(0.25, 0.47)	(0.25, 0.48)
Pr(02ALLIANCE)[d]				0.32	0.31
				(0.24, 0.41)	(0.23, 0.39)
Pr(02ALLIANCE)[e]				0.16	0.16
				(0.12, 0.22)	(0.12, 0.22)
Pr(02ALLIANCE)[f]				0.57	0.55
				(0.44, 0.69)	(0.41, 0.68)

[a]All variables are held at their means; 97Alliance = 1.
[b]All variables are held at their means; 97Alliance = 0.
[c]All variables are held at their means; 97Alliance = 1; left incumbent = 1.
[d]All variables are held at their means; 97Alliance = 0; left incumbent = 0.
[e]All variables are held at their means; 97Alliance = 0; left incumbent = 1.
[f]All variables are held at their means; 97Alliance = 1; left incumbent = 0.
[g]95% confidence intervals.
*$p < 0.1$, **$p < 0.05$, ***$p < 0.01$. Standard errors in parentheses.

tween twenty and thirty-nine is 35 percent or higher (mean is 28 percent) are urban, and several house universities or are near universities. Thus, education may be taking away some of the explanatory power of age. In addition, alliances occurred in only nine of these districts. Importantly, support for the FN is weaker among young, educated voters in the aggregate.[24]

When examining individual-level data instead of aggregate data, I find that roughly 35 percent of those who either voted for an FN candidate in the first round of the legislative elections in 1997 or for Le Pen in 2002 were under forty years of age (Centre d'Etude de la Vie Politique Française 2003). Therefore, age also may not be significant in predicting the strength of the Greens and thus the probability of an alliance in a district because many younger voters also voted for the extreme right in 2002. If age is a measure of FN strength, then I would expect a high probability of a PS alliance in districts with a younger population, according to the individual-level data. But, since age is not significant in any of the models, I cannot necessarily distinguish what effect, if any, age has on vote for the Greens versus vote for the FN.

In Model 8, I have included a dummy variable for a left incumbent. A left incumbent has a negative effect on the probability of an alliance. With the addition of this variable, the coefficient for the variable measuring the right bloc's strength is no longer significant, a result that follows my expectations. If there is a left incumbent, then the right does not have a strong foothold in the district and the left is strong enough that there is little concern that the parties of the left will split the vote among themselves. Hence, there is little need for an alliance.

In sum, given the likelihood of Green voters to vote sincerely and the desire of both the Greens and the Socialists to minimize the success of the right and extreme right, the parties enter into preelection coalitions. This analysis has demonstrated that alliance districts are selected based on the strength of Le Pen, Mamère, and the right bloc. As the value of each of these variables increases, so does the probability of alliance formation. When considering the control variables, the higher the percentage of the population in a given district that has at least a BAC + 2, the more likely that an alliance between the Socialists and the Greens will occur. Conversely, if a district had a left incumbent or a high rate of unemployment, then the likelihood of an alliance decreases. (See Model 9 for a fully specified model with all of the control variables included.)

WHICH TYPE OF ALLIANCE? SELECTING A GREEN OR SOCIALIST CANDIDATE

With an understanding of the key determinants of whether there is a Green-Socialist alliance in a given district, I now turn to the question of what influences whether the alliance will feature a Green or a Socialist candidate. Extending the binomial logit analysis to a situation in which there are more than two choices requires the use of multinomial logit (MNL).[25] The dependent variable here is trichotomous (no alliance, Green alliance, PS alliance).

Table 3.5 shows the results for the basic model, in which the base category is no alliance. Each coefficient indicates the effect on the likelihood of observing a particular choice relative to the alternative.[26] In column 1, for example, the coefficient indicates the relationship between the independent variables and the probability of a Green candidate. The predicted probabilities of alliances using the basic model (holding all variables at their means and 97Alliance at 1) demonstrate that where the right is stronger, the

TABLE 3.5. Multinomial Logit Analysis of Type of Alliance in 2002

	Green/None	Socialist/None	
97Alliance	0.92***	1.09***	
	(0.34)	(0.28)	
Right	8.42***	2.63*	
	(1.85)	(1.55)	
Le Pen	22.21***	28.16***	
	(3.81)	(3.40)	
Mamère	55.45***	7.63	
	(11.69)	(11.64)	
Constant	−12.04***	−8.02***	
	(1.63)	(1.31)	
Pseudo R^2	0.18		
N	555		
Log likelihood	−370.32		
Pr(Green)[a]	0.15	Pr (PS)[a]	0.27
Pr(Green)[b]	0.08	Pr (PS)[b]	0.12

[a]All variables held at their means; 97Alliance = 1.
[b]All variables held at their means; 97Alliance = 0.
*$p < 0.1$, **$p < 0.05$, ***$p < 0.01$. Standard errors in parentheses.

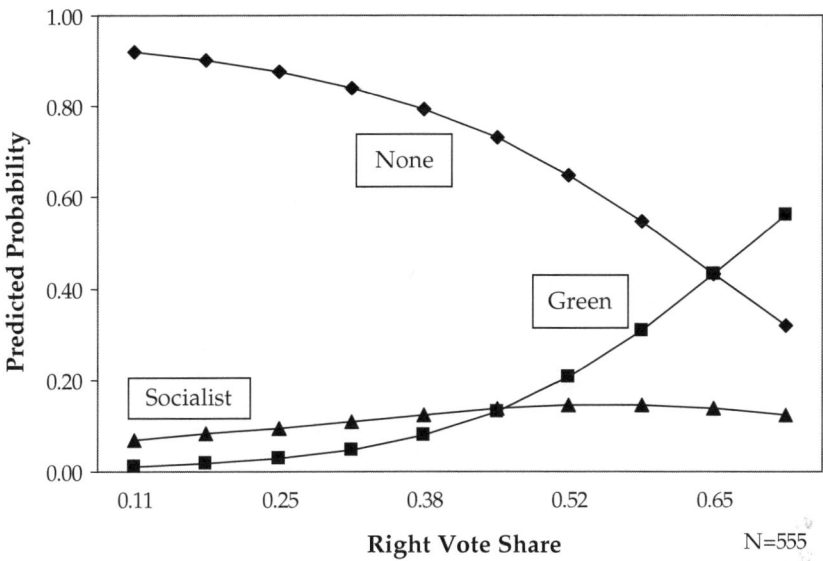

Fig. 3.3. Predicted probability of type of alliance varying mainstream right vote share

probability that it will be a Green district increases. But as the FN's vote share increases, so does the likelihood of a Socialist candidate (figures 3.3 and 3.4). This finding confirms the hypothesis that the Greens receive the districts in which the left is least likely to win; in the districts where there is more concern that the extreme right will advance, there will be a Socialist candidate. This strategy is chosen to ensure that the FN is kept out.

The MNL results from the basic model demonstrate that a 1997 alliance in the district increases the probability of a Green alliance by 7.1 percent but increases the likelihood of a Socialist alliance by 14.3 percent. However, the type of alliance in 1997 also plays a role in predicting the type of alliance in the district in 2002. Adding a dummy variable for a 1997 Green alliance to the basic model shows that the probability of a Green alliance in 2002 is 7.0 percent if there was a PS alliance in 1997 and nearly five times that if there was a Green alliance existed. The magnitude of the impact of the type of alliance in 1997 on the alliance type in 2002 is much lower for the Socialists. If a Green alliance existed in 1997, the probability of a PS alliance in 2002 is 20.3 percent, increasing only to 28.9 percent if a Socialist alliance existed. This finding highlights the fact that after controlling for

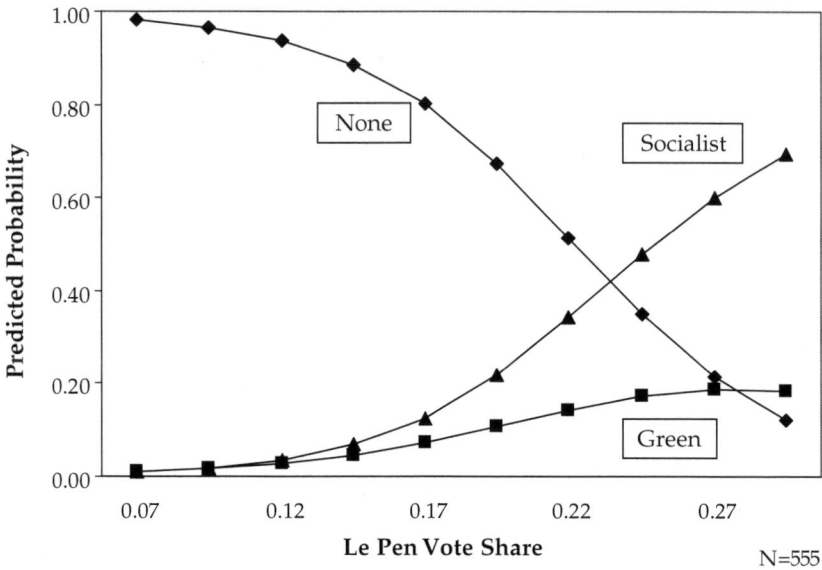

Fig. 3.4. Predicted probability of type of alliance varying Le Pen vote share

all other variables, the existence not only of a previous alliance but specifically of a Green alliance is a key predictor of a Green alliance in 2002. However, for a Socialist alliance, other factors play a much larger role. For example, without an alliance in 1997, holding Le Pen at 0.25 (instead of its mean of 0.17), the probabilities that it will be a Green or Socialist district are 20.2 percent and 47.3 percent, respectively.

Moreover, repeating the same test to determine which of the three key variables—Le Pen, Mamère, and the right bloc—has the biggest effect on the probability of a Socialist alliance, I find that as in the logit model, Le Pen has the largest impact on the alliance decision. Holding Le Pen one standard deviation below its mean reduces the likelihood of a Socialist alliance by almost 20 percent, from 0.27 to 0.10. Performing the same analysis on the right and Mamère variables does not decrease the probability of an alliance at all. These values are 0.24 and 0.27, respectively. Conversely, when considering the probability of a Green alliance, reducing the variables by one standard deviation decreases the chances of an alliance, but the probabilities are roughly the same for all three variables—about 0.08. Thus, all three of the variables have the same influence on the probability of a Green alliance.

In three separate models, I add level of education, unemployment, and left incumbent in a given district to the basic model. Both education and unemployment do not add much explanation to the overall model.[27] However, education is significant in predicting a Green alliance, whereas unemployment is significant for the likelihood of a Socialist alliance.

As in the logistic results, education has a positive effect, and unemployment has a negative effect. For education, a fairly strong correlation (0.51) exists between the vote for Mamère and the percentage of the population that has at least two years of postbaccalaureate education. Therefore, an increase in the percentage of the population with a higher level of education in a given district is a measure of the strength of the Greens and thus serves as an indicator of where a Green alliance is most likely.

Unemployment, however, has a negative effect on a Socialist alliance. I would argue that this result holds because in the majority of alliance districts, the vote for the Socialists is high enough that there is little concern of splitting the vote if there is no alliance. High unemployment has a stronger impact on the PS vote share than on that for the FN and thus adversely affects the likelihood of a Socialist alliance. Indeed, in 171 of 313 districts that had left incumbents in 2002, the unemployment rate was above the national mean of 0.13.

Similar to the binomial analysis, the existence of a left incumbent in a given district is significant only in predicting the probability of a Green alliance. It is negative and significant at the 0.01 level. A left incumbent signifies that there is little concern that the Greens will split the left if they run a candidate by themselves. In all but a handful of the 313 districts, the left incumbent was not a Socialist, thereby providing further evidence that the Greens tend to receive the unwinnable districts in their alliance negotiations with the Socialists.

These findings confirm my expectations. The higher the FN's vote share, the more likely there will be a PS alliance. Conversely, the higher the right bloc's vote share, the higher the probability of a Green alliance. The type of alliance that existed in 1997 is a key predictor of a Green alliance but is less important in predicting a PS alliance. Finally, education is only significant for the likelihood of a Green alliance, whereas unemployment is significant only for a PS alliance.

These analyses show that the Greens have become adept at navigating the constraints of both the French party and electoral systems. With the goal of gaining a voice in the parliament, the party has demonstrated a willingness to sacrifice its ideological purity in favor of winning. To this end, it has chosen to enter PECs, running its own candidates in some districts and supporting Socialist candidates in others. In terms of electoral strategy, by entering into PECs, the party has given more weight to maximizing its likelihood of winning seats than to differentiating its ideological preferences. But the Greens have chosen to enter into these alliances with the mainstream left, which shares similar policy positions with the Greens. This choice has resulted in an increase in the party's seat share in parliament, demonstrating that it has balanced its competing goals.

In addition to maximizing seats, the Green Party elites seek to prevent the extreme right from advancing to the second round and winning seats. This goal is attainable in some districts only if the stronger of the two parties runs a candidate. In most situations, the stronger candidate is the Socialist. My findings have shown that the PS has the upper hand in the negotiations and that the Greens remain the junior partner. The Greens accept this position because they know that given the constraints of the electoral system, this is the only way they will be able to gain seats in the National Assembly. Furthermore, by winning a few seats in the parliament in the current election, they increase their future credibility as a viable political party.

This analysis has also demonstrated that exogenous forces play the largest role in determining whether an alliance will exist and what form it will take. Although the vote shares of Mamère and the Green list for the European elections influence the probability of alliance formation, the vote shares of the right bloc and the FN candidate in the past legislative election and those of Le Pen in the presidential election are the strongest predictors of an alliance and the type of alliance it will be. The Greens and PS want to ensure that the left parties do not split their vote, thus preventing a left-wing candidate from qualifying for the second round. In deciding the strategy for the legislative election, the parties have arguably been influenced equally by the voting behavior of other cohorts of voters—those who vote for the right and extreme right—and by their own core supporters, whose voting tendencies led them initially to consider alliances.[28]

ALTERNATIVE EXPLANATIONS

Although these results have shown that the Greens are both policy- and seat-driven, one could argue that policy—specifically, the desire to implement leftist policies—really provides the underlying motivation for the party's behavior. The mere fact that the parties of the moderate left enter into alliances demonstrates that the goal is not necessarily winning the seat for themselves in a given district but rather putting someone in that seat who would vote for and advance leftist policies. Wittman (1973) argues that parties often collude against the voters to get policy implemented. He talks about this practice as it relates to the parties' platforms, but this notion of collusion can also be applied to preelection alliances. Although not necessarily conspiring against the voters, the parties are sending the message that it is acceptable for a Socialist voter to support a Green candidate in an alliance district, for example, because this deputy will subsequently work to implement policies that will be generally favorable to the Socialist electorate. In addition, by cooperating with the Socialists and ensuring a victory for the left, the Greens may be rewarded with a side payment. One such payment was the Ministry of the Environment, which the Socialists gave to the Greens after the left won in 1997. As the Greens were not a needed coalition partner to form a government, this was truly a thank you to the Greens for working with the Socialists to minimize the seats won by the right and extreme right.

Moreover, the goal may not be winning but may be a combination of installing a leftist deputy (regardless of party affiliation) and preventing the advancement of the FN. Winning may then be only a means to this end. And who wins, as long as it is a candidate of the moderate left, does not matter, as is evidenced by the Green Party's 2007 message that its voters should support "the best placed candidate on the left" (Les Verts 2007b). Thus, advancing a leftist agenda is most important. Although this may be a short-term scenario, in the long term, the Greens participate in elections with the ultimate goal of winning their own seats, even if they have to compromise in the immediate electoral contests and enter into PECs. In the end, winning seats is ultimately how the party achieves electoral success and increases its credibility among voters. Both of these strategies ensure the party's survival. Furthermore, even this alternate reading of the results demonstrates another facet of the party's strategic behavior: the balancing of both short- and long-term goals.

GOING IT ALONE IN THE 2007 FRENCH LEGISLATIVE ELECTIONS

Following the left's successful preelection coalition strategy of 1997 and 2002, most observers expected a similar strategy in 2007. However, the

Green Party decided not to enter into another nationwide PEC with the Socialists in light of the party's defeat in the presidential elections, debates about which districts to include, and programmatic disagreements. Even without a nationwide PEC, the Socialists did not run candidates against the three Green incumbents, Martine Billard, Yves Cochet, and Nöel Mamère, all of whom were reelected. In three other districts where there were either local or department-level agreements, no PS candidate stood against a Green. In one of these districts, in the Loire-Atlantique department (44-1), the Green candidate, François de Rugy, won. Thus, without a formal national alliance, the Greens kept their three incumbents and gained an additional deputy in the National Assembly. Is this decision representative of a shift in strategy, the result of the political context, or some combination of the two?

According to interviews with those involved on the Greens' negotiating team, the party's stated goal was to increase its number of deputies in the parliament.[29] On 29 June 2006, the party proposed that the PS would not run candidates and would support the Green candidate in twenty-four districts. The PS responded on 1 July 2006 by offering that it would not run candidates in fourteen districts. Both proposals included the three incumbents' districts. After months of additional negotiations, the Greens refused the Socialists' final proposal in the weeks following the presidential election in May 2007.[30]

Even without the formal national-level PEC, the Socialists still strongly supported the three Green incumbents, thus ensuring their reelection. The *suppléants* of all three incumbents were well-known Socialists, such as mayors of two *arrondissements* in Paris. Cochet, the incumbent from district 75-11 in Paris, received the endorsements of several prominent Socialists, including Bertrand Delanoë, the Socialist mayor of Paris; Jacques Delors, the former Socialist president of the European Commission; and Ségolène Royal, the 2007 Socialist presidential candidate. Billard, the incumbent from district 75-1, also in Paris, had the endorsement of several local Socialist elected officials, including Delanoë and Royal. These individuals' names, pictures, and endorsements were prominently featured in both Billard and Cochet's election propaganda, including leaflets and posters distributed throughout the districts. An example of such an endorsement was Delanoë's statement of support for Cochet: "I trust Yves Cochet and Pierre Castagnou, mayor of the Fourteenth Arrondissement [Cochet's *suppléant*], to carry the colors of the left in the Eleventh District of Paris. I know they will defend your interests in the National Assembly with energy and conviction" (Cochet 2007). Similarly, Royal's endorsement read, "I support my friend, Martine Billard, a hardworking and active deputy. When you have a very good deputy, you keep her! She truly deserves your trust" (Billard 2007a). A leaflet distributed to voters in Billard's district by the local Socialist Party provides further evidence of the PS's efforts to ensure the reelection of a leftist deputy, regardless of party. It called on voters to support Billard because "what brings us together is more important than what divides us" (Billard 2007a). For their part, the Greens also recognized the importance of the left (regardless of party) winning seats. On the campaign poster above the photograph of Cochet and Castagnou was the slogan "The left in motion" (Cochet 2007). In a letter to her constituents before the first round of the legislative elections, Billard explained, "We need deputies on the left, in large number, to guarantee our democracy" to oppose the plans of the UMP government, and to propose alternatives (2007b). Thus, the Socialists' strong support of the incumbent Greens and a mutual understanding that the most important result was a leftist deputy meant that the Greens' decision not to enter into a formal national PEC would not hinder its deputies' reelection.

There are several explanations for the differences between 2002 and 2007. The political context had changed considerably over the five years. Voters wanted to prevent an outcome resembling that in the 2002 presidential election, in which the second-round contest pitted the UMP's Jacques Chirac against the FN's Le Pen. Five years later, however, the FN no longer posed such a serious threat, so this motivation likely did not affect the interparty negotiations.[31] Moreover, by 2007, the Socialist Party was internally divided, as was evidenced by the results from its first-ever presidential primary, held in June 2006. In addition to Royal, Dominique Strauss-Kahn, and Laurent Fabius sought the Socialist nomination. Royal won the nomination with 60.6 percent of the vote, while Strauss-Kahn took 20.8 percent and Fabius won 18.5 percent (Keaten 2006; Sciolino, 2006, 2007). As a comparison, Nicholas Sarkozy won the UMP's nomination with 98.1 percent of the vote. In addition, some of Royal's policy positions, including her stance on reviewing the thirty-five-hour workweek, diverged from those of the party in the subsequent legislative elections, according to the Greens' 2007 elections coordinator. Finally, the Greens were in a weaker position after the presidential elections but still felt they could win more districts than the PS was offering. Dominique Voynet, the

Greens' 2007 presidential candidate, won only 1.57 percent of the vote, the lowest vote share ever for a Green presidential candidate and less than half the 5.34 percent won by the 2002 Green candidate, Mamère.[32]

The parties also remained divided by some programmatic issues, most importantly nuclear energy, genetically modified food, and electoral reform, three central issues on the Greens' agenda.[33] The Socialists' plan to reduce the use of nuclear energy still remained far from the Greens' position of ending the use of nuclear energy completely. The Greens favored a mixed electoral system, like that of Germany, whereas the PS supported adding "a dose of proportional representation" into elections to the National Assembly (Parti Socialiste 2007, 22). The Greens advocated a ban on genetically modified food, while the Socialists' position was more cautious and focused on food safety (Parti Socialiste 2007; Les Verts 2007a). In sum, the Greens' behavior in 2007 may have diverged somewhat from that of a vote- or seat-maximizing party. But a closer examination of intra- and interparty divisions and negotiations and the political context demonstrates that the party was still working toward a goal of increasing representation while balancing its desire for policy differentiation.

By 2007, new parties had developed and entered the political discussion. In the weeks following the 2007 presidential election, François Bayrou, leader of the centrist UDF, formed a new party, the Movement Démocrate (Democratic Movement, MoDem), effectively ending the UDF's more than thirty-year existence. Most of the UDF's elected officials, activists, and supporters followed Bayrou to the MoDem, as did activists, members, and even elected officials from other parties on the left and center-left. The MoDem won four seats in the National Assembly, while the UDF won no seats after winning twenty-nine in 2002.

Several leading members of the Greens left the party and joined the MoDem, most notably Jean-Luc Bennahmias, who had been the Greens' national secretary from 1997 to 2002 and was elected as a Green member of the European Parliament in 2004. At the first public appearance of the MoDem, Bennahmias commented that by joining the party, he was in "a better place to work on *écologie*" (Zappi 2007b).[34] Four Paris city councillors were also among the defectors, including Olivier Pagès, who ran as a MoDem candidate for the legislative elections. Bayrou appears next to Pagès on his campaign leaflet, which states that "the big challenges that await us, in particular the urgency of environmental issues, have gone beyond traditional political cleavages" (Pagès 2007). Pagès thus implies that environmental issues are no longer only a concern of the left and that the traditional parties, in which he includes the Greens, are not addressing the issues in a productive way.

At the same time, Daniel Cohn-Bendit, copresident of the Greens–European Free Alliance group in the European Parliament and one of the most well-known European Green politicians, announced a manifesto that would "restructure ecological politics." Given the left's growing internal divisions, this effort sought to consider a political alternative that would be a coalition of social democrats, ecologists, and centrists. Many of the more pragmatic Greens signed the manifesto. In reaction to the Greens' disappointing results in both the presidential and legislative elections, Cochet proposed that the party dissolve itself, thereby enabling it to be "reborn" and giving party leaders and activists the opportunity to reorganize internally and reformulate how the party could reach both its electoral and ideological goals. In the end, a large majority of eligible voters rejected Cochet's proposal (Virot 2007; Zappi 2007a). A week later, Cohn-Bendit launched a new organization, Horizons Ecologie (Ecological Horizons), which he viewed as an innovative way of attracting and mobilizing voters beyond ideological and partisan divisions (Renard 2007).[35] After this tumultuous period, there has been little further discussion of this new organization.

The combination of the decision to not enter into a national PEC and the defection of several Greens to the MoDem might seem to signal that the Greens had moved significantly away from their goal of vote and seat maximization. However, a multipronged party press release between the two rounds of the legislative elections demonstrates both the importance of policy and the recognition that the policies of any party on the left were preferable to those of the right and the extreme right. The document first called on voters to support the candidate on the left who had the best chance of winning "to enable firm opposition to the politics led by Nicolas Sarkozy." However, the party also urged voters not to support seven leftwing candidates in the second round because of positions that are "antienvironmentalist or discriminatory." Finally, in the event of second-round contests between the UMP and MoDem, the party did not advise its voters on how to vote. Rather, it laid out two important goals: beating candidates who support the presidential majority and advocating for diversity and pluralism in the National Assembly. To this end, leaders trusted voters to make "the most sensible choice that is in agreement with these principles" (Les Verts 2007b). Thus, although the party was focused on parliamentary representation, it was not willing simply to throw away its policy preferences. One of the Greens' television broadcasts further emphasized this goal. Cécile Duflot, the party's national secretary, explained that beyond voting for Green candidates, what is most important is building a *"projet écologiste"*—an ecological agenda, which includes environmental, social justice, and grassroots democracy issues. Finally, the suggestion that the current party may not be the best way to achieve the goals of *écologie* offers further evidence of the party's electoral ambitions.

CONCLUSION

The Green Party is continually seeking to balance its preferences of vote and seat maximization and policy differentiation. Given the context of a particular election, the focus may swing more toward one goal, and it may swing back during another election cycle. Regardless of which way the pendulum swings, the Greens have demonstrated their overall ability to survive under plurality rules by continually balancing their electoral and policy goals through PECs with the Socialists. Furthermore, the party's presence in parliament increases its credibility in the eyes of the French electorate, thus increasing its potential survivability.

As with many small parties, especially those in plurality systems, the Green Party finds itself in somewhat of a catch-22. To gain representation in the short term, the Greens need to compromise and enter into PECs, but this strategy could have both beneficial and harmful effects for the party's longevity. It may signal to voters that the party is credible, both because the Socialists are willing to enter into alliances and because the Greens are gaining experience in parliament. Or it could lead to the party's demise as the pragmatist and electoralist wing of the party, which has driven this strategy, becomes one of many factions within the Socialist Party (or another party). Most important, the rules of the French electoral system and the history of the party system have demonstrated that the Greens are not likely to win seats in parliament if they do not work with, but rather compete against, the Socialist Party.

CHAPTER 4

Focusing Locally and Targeting Nationally in the United Kingdom: Working toward Representation in Westminster

"Objective and Aims: [T]o develop and implement ecological policies consistent with the Philosophical Basis of the Party as expressed in the Manifesto for Sustainable Society;[1] to that end to win seats at all levels of government."
—GREEN PARTY OF ENGLAND AND WALES, CONSTITUTION, SPRING 2006

AT THE 1989 BRITISH GREEN PARTY CONFERENCE, a motion was introduced that advocated collaboration with Labour and the Social and Liberal Democrats (SLD) so that only one candidate would run in each constituency. The motion did not receive the two-thirds majority necessary to pass (Frankland 1990, 23). Three years later, the local Green Party in the Welsh constituency of Ceredigion and Pembroke North actively supported the Plaid Cymru (Party of Wales) candidate, Cynog Dafis, and did not run its own candidate. The parties ended their agreement in 1995, largely over policy disagreements, and Dafis finished the rest of the term as a Party of Wales member of Parliament (MP). In the 1997 general election, the Ceredigion Greens again chose to support Dafis as a joint Plaid/Green candidate; however, after a lengthy debate, the Green National Executive declined to enter into an alliance because of ideological differences between the two groups. It also did not field a candidate against Dafis (O'Neill 1997; Burchell 2000, 2002; Fowler and Jones 2006).

These three experiences with Party of Wales represent the British Greens' only attempts at balancing electoral and policy goals through the formation of preelection alliances or coalitions (PECs) with other parties in the same way as the French Green and Socialist Parties. However, unlike the breadth and depth of the Green-Socialist alliances in France, which have resulted in the election of Green MPs, the British Greens' efforts at forging even a singular constituency-level alliance have not been a successful long-term strategy.[2] Much of the reason for the Greens' failure to work formally with other parties comes from their philosophy of engaging in an alternative type of politics, which is very bottom-up and grassroots-focused, as Peter Cranie, the Green Party executive (GPEx) elections coordinator in 2006, posits: "Part of the Green ethos, philosophy, and vision is a different type of politics."[3]

Without this tactic in their strategic toolbox, the British Greens have thus had to find more creative electoral strategies for surviving in the United Kingdom's restrictive plurality, or first-past-the-post (FPTP) system. The party's twofold strategy of focusing locally and targeting nationally has enabled it to persevere and become both credible and viable at the local, national, and European levels. Through this strategy, the Greens are engaged in two types of balancing. First, they balance their desire to gain representation and credibility within the constraints of the FPTP system. Second, they balance their desire to "do politics differently" inside the party with the external goal of winning a parliamentary seat.

Table 4.1 illustrates the British Greens' steady progression in the general elections from 1992 to 2005. The party has increased both the number of constituencies in which it stands candidates and its vote shares in these

TABLE 4.1. Green Party General Election Results, 1992–2005

	1992	1997	2001 (EWS)	2005 (EWS)	2001 (EW)	2005 (EW)
Number of constituencies contested (of total number of constituencies)	253/ 651	95/ 659	146/ 659	202/ 646	140/ 566	180/ 566
Average vote share in constituencies contested (%)	1.3	1.4	2.8	3.4	2.8	3.3
Highest vote share (%)	3.8	5.5	9.3	21.9	9.3	21.9
National vote share (%)	0.5	0.3	0.6	1.1	0.6	1.1
Constituencies in which deposit was saved (%)	0 (0)	0 (0)	6.9 (10)	11.9 (24)	5.7 (8)	11.1 (20)

Source: Data for 1992 and 1997 are from Mackie 1993; O'Neill 1997; Carter and Rootes 2006; Carter 2008; United Kingdom Election Results. Data for 2001 and 2005 are from British Parliamentary Constituency Database, 1992–2005 (Norris 2005b).

Note: For 1992 and 1997, all of the data were not disaggregated by country and include Scotland. For 2001 and 2005, the data were available by country and are reported for both England, Wales, and Scotland (EWS) and for England and Wales (EW) only. The Scottish Greens are an independent party, and so the relevant numbers for the green party under study are those for England and Wales. I provide the other values for a more complete over time comparison.

constituencies. The percentage of districts in which the party has received more than 5 percent of the vote and subsequently had its deposits refunded has also increased during this period.[4] In 2005, ten of the saved deposits were in London. Many of the others were in urban constituencies, several with large student populations, including Bath, Brighton Pavilion, Bristol South, Leeds West, Norwich South, and Sheffield Central (Norris 2005b; Carter 2008, 225). Finally, and perhaps most promising for its future success, the party's highest vote share increased fourfold from 1997 to 2005, as table 4.1 shows. In addition to the Greens' 21.9 percent in Brighton Pavilion, the party's results were higher in the constituencies of Lewisham Deptford (11.1 percent) and Hackney North and Stoke Newington (9.9 percent) than its highest single score in 2001 (Norris 2005b).

The chapter begins with a closer look at how the British Greens work with other parties during both election and nonelection periods. I explore the party's position on both pre- and postelection alliances. Next, I examine the party's two-pronged electoral strategy of focusing locally and targeting nationally. I illustrate the complexities of these strategies through in-depth analysis of the campaign tactics of the Brighton and Hove, Oxfordshire, and Norwich Green Parties, which have had varying levels of success in local and national elections. I then explore whether a pattern can be identified among the constituencies in which the party chose to run candidates in the 2005 national elections.

My analysis relies primarily on two types of data. The first set of data are from thirty-three interviews I conducted with party leaders, activists, and elected officials between June and August 2006. I use the interview material to demonstrate the Greens' strategic behavior and its underlying logic. The second set of data are taken from the *British Parliamentary Constituency Database* (Norris 2005b), which includes constituency-level election results as well as census data from 1992 to 2005. I use these data as contextual information and to test the hypothesis that there is a systematic pattern for where the party stands candidates.

DECENTRALIZED DECISION MAKING IN PRE- AND POSTELECTION ALLIANCES

The British Greens have taken a more decentralized or local approach to working with other parties than have their French counterparts, as stated in their constitution (2006, 6):

> When entering into agreements with other political parties, politicians, and groups, elected members and other representatives must take into consideration the long-term best interests of the Party. Such decisions should be made after consultation with the relevant local or regional party/parties.[5]

The national party thus lacks the ability to enter into preelection coalitions (more commonly referred to as "electoral deals" by the Green Party) with other parties in a parliamentary election and then subsequently consult the local parties in deciding which constituencies to include, as is often the case in France. Rather, the national party can make recommendations to the local group based on demographic and past election data. Cranie elucidated this sentiment in discussing the party's response to the left-wing Respect, Equality, Socialism, Peace, Environmentalism, Community, and Trade Unionism (RESPECT) Party, which approached the Greens in 2005 to form an umbrella anti–Iraq War party and then to enter into a national PEC.

> I don't think we could impose something top-down in our party. I could not say, "We're going to do a deal with the Labour party, RESPECT, the Lib[eral] Dem[ocrat]s, or Conservatives." . . . As decentralists, regional and local parties would say, "No, we disagree."[6]

Although this decision rests solely on the shoulders of the local parties, after the Welsh Greens' rocky experience with the Party of Wales in the early 1990s, both local and regional parties have generally eschewed any sort of preelection alliances.

For lower-level elections, the local and regional parties can also choose whether to work with another party in support of a single candidate, where one party stands down and supports the candidate of the other. These deals are often informal arrangements. In other words, the Greens may target some wards in a given city while another party targets other wards based on their respective strengths or on a specific campaign strategy. These do not represent any kind of official coordination between the parties, however. In one Oxford ward, for example, the antiwar RESPECT party did not run a candidate against the Green candidate in the 2005 local elections. The Green candidate had been a very active member of the antiwar coalition, and RESPECT did not want to take votes away from an antiwar Green candidate who had the possibility of winning. In the end, the Green candidate defeated the Labour candidate and won the seat.[7]

Darren Johnson, Green member of the Greater London Assembly, explained that in the London borough of Lewisham, "different parties were working on different seats according to their campaign strategies, their strengths, and where they had the most support." Echoing Cranie's sentiments, member of the European Parliament (MEP) Jean Lambert posits that much of the reason for this focus on more informal arrangements is based on the party's view that "if you want to be a different political party, you have to earn" it.[8]

A second type of electoral alliance or coalition is the postelection governing coalition, which is ubiquitous in parliamentary systems. Most European countries outside the United Kingdom typically have some form of coalition government, whether minority, minimum winning, or oversized (Laver and Schofield 1998; Müller and Strøm 2000).[9] Except for the brief Lib-Lab pact of the late 1970s, the United Kingdom has had single-party national governments throughout the entire postwar period.[10] At the local level, however, multiple parties often jointly govern in city and county governments.

Two models of local government exist in England and Wales, excluding London. In the first model, there is a district or city council (for example, the councils in Norwich and Oxford) and a county council (as in Norfolk and Oxfordshire). The city council is typically responsible for housing, waste collection, and local planning, while the county council is in charge of education, health care, other social services, and waste disposal. In the second model, the city and county councils are merged into a unitary authority, which consolidates the functions of the two councils. Unitary authorities were set up as part of the Local Government Act of 1992. Cities and counties can apply for unitary status.[11] London has both the Greater London Authority and a council in each borough.

Councillors typically serve four-year terms. Councils use several different election calendars, including elections for the entire council every four years; elections of one-third of the council each year, with no election in the fourth year; and elections of half of the council every two years.

The British Green Party has taken no official stance on governing deals or alliances at the local level, other than to allow local parties to decide what is best on their local council. Thus, the local Green parties have entered into both formal coalitions and more informal arrangements with Labour, the Liberal Democrats, and the Conservatives on various councils. In 2003 in Leeds, for example, the Labour Party lost control of the council for the first time in twenty-three years. The Greens subsequently joined a ruling coalition with the Conservatives and Liberal Democrats that lasted until 2007, when the Greens pulled out over concerns about the council's backing of a new garbage incinerator (BBC News Online 2007). The Oxfordshire Green Party made a similar decision following the Labour Party's loss of its majority in the 2000 elections. The eight Green councillors decided to join with the Liberal Democrats in a governing coalition on the Oxford City Council. The local Greens viewed this arrangement as a shared governing agreement or a "business relationship" and not as a coalition, since there was no voting agreement between the parties. The arrangement ended following the 2002 elections, when the districts were redrawn and Green representation was reduced to three seats.[12]

Following these experiences, many elected officials and party leaders have concluded that it is best for the Greens to work with other parties on local and regional councils on an issue-by-issue basis. This strategy has two benefits. First, the party remains autonomous. It avoids the blame for either bad policies or mismanagement of funds and the appropriation of its policy ideas and achievements by the larger party. The Greens thus can take credit for what the coalition has done well. Second, the strategy enables the party to be selective about working with other parties. It can choose the issues on which it is willing to compromise based on the other parties' positions.[13]

In sum, the British Green Party's approach to both formal coalitions and informal working arrangements with other parties differs significantly from that of the French Greens. I argue that the British party follows this strategy not because it is less electorally focused than its French counterpart but rather for more context-based reasons.

First, the party systems in the two countries provide some explanation for the variation in strategy. In the United Kingdom, the left has traditionally had only one electable party. In France, in contrast, there has been at least an electable communist and a socialist party active on the left for most of the last century. Today, the French left is even more diversified with the advent of the Parti Radicale de Gauche and Greens.[14] In addition, voter socialization to the United Kingdom's two- (and perhaps three-) party system poses a double hurdle for the Green Party. As a small party, it not only has the very difficult if not impossible task of attracting voters on its own, but leftist voters are already conditioned to vote for the Labour Party in national elections.[15] The Greens are not even on the radar screen of many British voters. Furthermore, Britain and France have very different party system cultures. Whereas first- and second-round PECs have been the norm for the major parties during the French Fifth Republic (see Tsebelis 1990; Schlesinger and Schlesinger 2000), PECs are much less common in Britain.

Second, differing party organizational traditions may help explain the difference. Similar to most parties in France, the French Greens are much more centralized than are the British Greens. As MEP Lambert succinctly states, "The French Green Party thinks much more in terms of a national collective than we do." To this day, the "electoralist-decentralist" division embodied by the Green 2000 and Basis for Renewal initiatives of the 1990s still plays a fairly prominent role in debates in the British Green Party.[16] No similar debate over a centralized versus more decentralized decision-making structure ever played a large part in French Green intraparty discussions. Moreover, debates in the French Green Party over the PEC strategy have mostly ended, with the vast majority in the party agreeing that this approach represents the only way to elect Greens to the parliament.

Since I conducted these interviews, the British Greens have taken a further step in the electoralist direction, arguably making the party more centralized. From its founding, the party rejected having a single leader, which would have gone against its grassroots traditions (Rüdig 2008). Beginning with the 1991 Green 2000 initiative, the party had two principal speakers, one male and one female. Debate and discussion within the party over this strategy continued for years. Some members felt that the absence of a single leader was the embodiment of grassroots politics and approaching politics "differently," while others argued that this structure was holding the party back from its true potential. Many Greens contended that a party leader would increase the party's credibility, would provide the media with a single representative, and would reduce confusion over "strange job titles and unfamiliar structures" (Carter 2008, 233; Rüdig 2008). In a November 2007 party referendum, 73 percent voted to move to a single-leader model (Green Party of England and Wales 2007). In September 2008, Caroline Lucas, MEP and candidate in the Brighton Pavilion constituency for the next general elections, was elected party leader by a margin of 90 percent, and Adrian Ramsay, leader of the Green group on the Norwich City Council, ran unopposed for the post of deputy leader (Green Party of England and Wales 2008).

FOCUSING LOCALLY AND TARGETING TO WIN

Without the PEC strategy as a real option, the British Greens have used other proactive electoral strategies to gain credibility as a viable party and to reach their goal of representation in the national parliament. With a sophisticated understanding of how the electoral system works, the Greens have focused their efforts on building up support at the local and supranational levels (city, county, unitary authority, and European) and are working systematically toward translating this support into winning seats in Westminster through targeting specific constituencies, much as other "third" parties in Britain have done. The Greens' steadily improving vote shares in general elections are the result of these two activities.

The Green Party's current strategy has in some respects paralleled that of the Liberal Democrats (Russell and Fieldhouse 2005), another party that has more limited financial, activist, and member resources than Labour and the Conservatives. Recognizing these limitations, the Liberal Democrats have focused their efforts on selected constituencies at the national level and selected wards at the local level. Patterning their behavior after that of the Liberal Democrats, the Greens have demonstrated the tensions within the party to balance a different kind of politics with the goal of electoral representation. In so doing, the Greens have shown that they can be as strategic and electorally savvy as other parties yet have raised the question of how different their politics really are.

The Liberal Democrats have held the status of the third party in the British system for most of the past century. They have lagged behind Labour and the Conservatives in size, resources, and vote and seat share. Since 1992, the party has compensated by targeting select constituencies in general elections and focusing on grassroots politics at the local level. By 1997, the Liberal Democrats had organized the Key Seats Initiative to target their limited resources and increase their seat share without necessarily increasing their vote share. In other words, the party sought to attract a plurality of votes and no more in a given constituency, thereby spreading its support across constituencies and maximizing its seat share. From polling data, the party also developed a program of targeting likely voters called Target Voters in Target Seats. Campaign leaflets were then hand delivered to voters in the targeted constituencies. Through the Key Seats and Target Voters programs, the party more than doubled its seat share from twenty in 1992 to forty-six in 1997. Denver, Hands, and Henig (1998) found that the party's vote share increased in targeted seats. The Liberal Democrats won twenty-four of thirty-four targeted seats in 1997 and thirty-five of fifty-eight targeted seats in 2001 (Denver 2001; Russell and Fieldhouse 2005, 210–11; Cutts and Shryane 2006, 437). In 2005, the party adopted a more varied targeting strategy, seeking to unseat prominent Conservative MPs. This strategy ultimately failed (Johnston and Pattie 2006, 205).[17]

Beginning in the mid-1990s, Green Party leaders also realized that to win as a small party in a plurality system required that resources be focused on the most winnable seats. The internal debates over whether the party was to engage in electoral politics or an issue-based campaign or social movement politics had somewhat subsided, and the electoralist wing was driving party strategy, as Lambert explained:

> I think we've got more people in the party now who see it as an effective political force. So I do think there's been a shift, which a number of us have been trying to work on for a considerable period of time. I think that because we're elected, you get more people in [the party] who are interested in being part of a party that's elected.[18]

Recognizing that initially setting their sights on Westminster was unrealistic, the Greens concentrated on building up their base of support in local elections. The 1993 Basis for Renewal plan shifted the party's focus to the local level, where representation was more achievable. The party targeted wards that already had strong bases of activists and support, using a strategy that "did not ignore national elections, but saw them as more of an opportunity to challenge the major parties on policies, [and] raise the party's profile" (Burchell 2002, 69).

To meet this goal of building up its credibility as an electable party, the Green Party has focused on electing local councillors through the plurality system and electing members to representative bodies that utilize more proportional electoral systems, such as the Greater London Assembly (GLA).[19]

The GLA was established in 2000 after fourteen years without a London-wide representative body. Its predecessor, the Greater London Council, had been abolished by Margaret Thatcher in 1986, and the new body was created by a 1998 referendum and a 1999 parliamentary act. The Greater London Authority consists of both a directly elected assembly and a mayor. The first assembly and mayoral elections were held in 2000. The GLA has twenty-five members, fourteen elected from constituencies and eleven elected from party lists. Elections are held every four years using a mixed-member proportional system, whereby voters have two votes, one for a constituency candidate and one for the party, similar to the system used to elect members to the German Bundestag. The Greens have had GLA representation since 2000, with three members from 2000 to 2004 and two members since 2004. All of the party's representatives have been elected as at-large members from party rather than constituency seats. Although only the Labour and Conservative Parties have won constituency seats in the three GLA elections, the Greens have contested all twenty-five seats as well as the mayoral position since 2000. The London Greens' electoral strategy has, however, focused on the party or list seats. According to Darren Johnson, member of the GLA and mayoral candidate in 2000 and 2004, the party's 2004 campaign strategy did not involve a "decision to target," an approach that is

> very different than a general election or a local council election, where we do very much concentrate on targeting seats. But we didn't target particular constituencies for the GLA elections because the prize that we wanted was winning the list seats. And it was important to get a London-wide vote, even though more activity went into some areas where we were stronger.[20]

London party leaders have also recognized the challenge of winning a constituency seat and believe that focusing resources where the party can actually win seats is a more fruitful strategy. Furthermore, even if the party could win a constituency seat, it might lose a list seat, given the intricacies of the conversion of votes to seats. Thus, the Greens would not necessarily be in a better position with a constituency seat; the party could, in fact, be worse off, since focusing on a constituency seat is a bigger risk.[21]

Targeting in local elections remains at the discretion of the individual local parties. The national party advises the local parties using both demographic data on likely Green voters and electoral data to identify which wards to target. But the ultimate decision remains in the hands of local party organizations, much like the decision to work either formally or informally with other parties. Furthermore, whereas some local parties will stand candidates only in selected wards, others will try to stand candidates in all wards to increase the party's visibility. The Oxfordshire Greens, for example, have a policy of standing candidates in all wards, even if some are paper candidates and do not receive any resources from the local party. Oxford city councillor Elise Benjamin explains that the party takes this approach "to give everybody the opportunity to vote Green and to show that we're serious as a political party."[22]

When wards are targeted, a comprehensive year-round door-knocking campaign is planned, both inside and outside of the formal election period. According to party leaders and elected officials, the Greens' comparative advantage over their major-party competitors is both their willingness to work throughout the year using face-to-face campaigning and their councillors' focus on casework at the local level. As Richard Mallender, GPEx chair, elaborated,

> The best way to get more people to vote Green is, in my opinion, to get out on the doorsteps and talk to people. You can put things in the media, you can be on the radio—they all help—but in my experience, nothing beats face-to-face contact. You have to get out there and talk to people and listen to what they have to say . . . make sure there's good communication.[23]

A Norwich city councillor explained the importance of the focus on casework:

> What has surprised me is that even if you're not successful, the fact that you've done something is what really matters. People are awfully grateful if you've tried [to help them] . . . If you're doing something for someone, word gets around. And the Greens seem to have a reputation all over [the city] of listening and getting things done.[24]

To convey information to voters, many local parties produce newsletters or newspapers that they distribute by hand to constituents in the wards in which they have representation or that they are targeting for a future election. According to one Brighton and Hove city councillor,

> The *Greenleaf* [newspaper] goes to the whole of the [Brighton] Pavilion constituency that we target and it also goes to the wards that are outside where we are hoping to get Green councillors. . . . It's a big job getting that out. We deliver them all on foot, except for a small amount in the north part of the

Pavilion constituency which we pay for the delivery. . . . We don't have many members out in that area, but we do feel that as they are part of Pavilion, that they should get the newspaper.[25]

Local parties may lack financial resources, but they do have dedicated volunteers and councillors who are willing to put in the time to convey their message to voters. Moreover, these grassroots activities enable the party to distinguish itself from its competitors and to realize its strategy. Chris Rose, the national election agent, further justified these tactics:

Candidate X really showed that you could blow the opposition away by knocking on doors outside of the election period. [A voter's reaction may be that] "it doesn't matter that you're the Green Party, but that you're X and that you came around to talk to me, which is shocking but wonderful. And I'm going to vote for you because no else has bothered [to come around] . . . And maybe you helped me sort out a problem, and so I tell my neighbor that you helped me with that."[26]

The local parties also recognize their limitations and where their resources are best spent, as demonstrated by the Brighton and Hove party's decision to not hand-deliver newspapers outside of the city center, where residences are further apart and harder to reach with a limited pool of volunteers.

The second piece of the Greens' electoral strategy, called Target to Win, focuses directly on electing an MP to Westminster. Much as is the case with the Liberal Democrats' Key Seats Initiative, the national Green Party selects constituencies to target. The national party plays a distinctive role in this process, which, unlike other party decisions, is very centralized. Local parties apply to the national party for selection as a targeted constituency. The Party Executive then selects both primary and secondary targets. Primary target constituencies receive funding, staff, and volunteers from the national party. For example, of the 202 constituencies where the Greens stood candidates in the 2005 general election, 3 primary targets were selected: Brighton Pavilion, Lewisham Deptford (part of a London borough), and Norwich South.[27] Table 4.2 illustrates how the Greens' vote shares increased in the targeted and selected geographically proximal nontargeted constituencies. In 2005, the Green candidate in Brighton Pavilion, Keith Taylor, received the highest vote share ever by a Green candidate, 21.9 percent, and came in third, behind Labour's 35.4 percent and the Conservatives' 23.9 percent, and well ahead of the Liberal Democrats' 16.5 percent. Most in the party expect that Brighton Pavilion will be the first Green seat in Parliament. Current party leader Caroline Lucas has been selected by the Brighton and Hove Green Party as the candidate in this constituency for the 2010 general elections. Because she is the most well-known individual in the national party, it was a clear strategic choice for the local party to select her as its candidate for the seat, which is likely to be its first in Westminster.

On the whole, although PECs are not among the British Greens' electoral tools, they have used other tactics to succeed in a restrictive plurality system. With a local focus and targeting at both the local and national levels, the party has slowly elevated its credibility and viability, leading to increases in local representation and ultimately to national representation.

LOCAL PARTY STRATEGIES

I now turn to a more in-depth discussion of the electoral strategy of the Norwich, Oxfordshire, and Brighton and Hove local parties.[28] As table 4.2 shows, several parliamentary constituencies fall into the area covered by each of these local parties. The strategies illustrate the complexities of suc-

TABLE 4.2. Green Vote Share in 2005 in Select Constituencies, 1997–2005 (in %)

Constituency	2005 Target	1997[a]	2001	2005
Brighton Pavilion	yes	5.5	9.4	21.9
Brighton Kemptown	no	1.5	3.3	7.0
Hove	no	5.4	3.3	5.7
Lewisham Deptford	yes	3.0	6.5	11.1
Lewisham East	no	2.2	N.C.[b]	4.0
Lewisham West	no	1.5	N.C.	4.6
Norwich South	yes	3.1	3.4	7.4
Norwich North	no	2.0	1.7	2.7
Oxford East	no	2.2	2.8	4.3
Oxford West and Abingdon	no	3.6	3.8	4.0

Source: Norris 2005b; Green Party of England and Wales.

[a]The Greens' vote share was not disaggregated from the "other" category in the election results. Thus, the results also include other small parties' vote shares. However, based on subsequent election results, the Greens' vote share is the majority of this total.

[b]N.C. = No Green candidate.

ceeding at the local and national levels for a small party in a plurality system as well as shed light on several facets of the Green Party's electoral strategy. Constituencies in Norwich and Brighton and Hove have been among those targeted by the national party, and both local parties have increased their vote and seat shares over the past several elections.[29] Brighton Pavilion's candidate in the 2001 and 2005 national elections was Keith Taylor, one of the national leaders of the Green Party, whereas the candidate in Norwich South, Adrian Ramsay, was the leader of the local party and a rising figure in the national party. Over a six-year period, Ramsay led the party from relative obscurity to holding one-third of the seats on the local council. Conversely, although the Oxfordshire Greens' seat shares at both the city and county levels have also increased, Oxfordshire's two constituencies have not been among those targeted by the national party. Given the history of radical politics in the city of Oxford and the Greens' long-standing local presence, the fact that Oxford has not been targeted at first seems puzzling and merits some explanation. I discuss the party's strategy in Norwich to show the importance of traditional grassroots campaigning for Green Party success at the local level and how this can translate to success at the national level. I then explain why the constituencies in Norwich and Brighton have been targeted while those in Oxford have not.

Norwich: Anatomy of a Political Strategy

The Green Party in Norwich, a city of about 135,000, in Norfolk County, East Anglia, has engaged in both targeting and grassroots politics. The city council is made up of thirty-nine councillors, three from each of thirteen wards. Every two years, one-third of each ward's councillors is up for election to four-year terms. As of May 2008, the council was run by a minority Labour administration, which held fifteen seats. The Liberal Democrats previously ran the city, also as a minority. The Green Party held thirteen of the council seats, making it the largest group on a city council in the country, both in absolute numbers and proportionally. Following the 2009 local elections, Greens held seven of the eighty-four seats on the Norfolk County Council, an increase of two from the previous election.

Norwich is divided into two parliamentary constituencies, Norwich North and Norwich South. Norwich South lies wholly within the city of Norwich and includes nine of its wards. In the 2001 census, its population was roughly 91,000, of which 13.6 percent were students. The Greens' city and county councillors represent four of the wards in Norwich South, which was one of the Greens' primary target constituencies in the 2005 election. The party's vote share increased by more than 50 percent from 2001 to 2005, although it only won 7.4 percent in 2005. Table 4.3 illustrates the Norwich Green Party's rapid growth at the local level from 2002 to 2008. Since 1987, the constituency has been represented by a Labour MP, and until 2005, it was considered one of the safest Labour seats in Norfolk. Following a shift in votes to the Liberal Democrats, it is now a more tenuous Labour seat, with the party's victory margin dropping from 20.7 percent in 2001 to 8.7 percent in 2005. Norwich North is made up of the four wards on the north side of the city plus several suburbs, which combined had a population of just over 97,000 in the 2001 census. Only 4.2 percent of the Norwich North residents were full-time students. It is a somewhat marginal seat, as it has been held by both Labour and Conservatives for long periods since its creation, along with Norwich South, in 1950. In 2005, Labour won by 11.7 percent, thus making it a safer Labour seat than Norwich South.

The Norwich Greens' strategy followed the conventional wisdom that all effort should go into one ward until it has been won. The Greens initially chose Henderson, a ward in Norwich South that had a good base of members and likely Green voters and that was not fiercely being contested by the other parties. In 2002, just two election cycles later, the Greens elected two councillors in this ward. The Greens built on this initial success by incrementally expanding their targeted wards and efforts within them. Adrian Ramsay, head of the Norwich Greens, city councillor, and deputy leader of the national party, explained,

TABLE 4.3. Green Seat Share on Norwich City Council

Election Year	Seats	Total Seats on Council	Seat Share (%)
2002	2	48	4.2
2003	3	48	6.3
2004[a]	5	39	12.8
2006	9	39	23.1
2008	13	39	33.3

Source: Norwich Green Party.
[a]Boundary change. Council went from 16 wards (48 councillors) to 13 wards (39 councillors). All seats were up for election in 2004.

I'm always keen that we're realistic over what's achievable during a particular period. And although there is urgency to the policies we want to implement, if we try to do too much, if we try to target too many wards, we could risk not winning any of them.[30]

The Norwich Greens, like the rest of the British Green Party, have actively engaged in traditional constituency campaigning, or face-to-face politics. Scholars of electoral campaigns generally agree that campaigns are becoming more professionalized, centralized, and modernized. With this movement, both traditional methods of campaigning and the influence and necessity of local party organizations are being superseded by more technologically advanced methods of contacting voters by the central party organization (Panebianco 1988; Farrell 1996; Farrell and Webb 2000; Norris 2002; Denver et al. 2003). At the same time, a second group of scholars argues that local party organizations are still important and play a role in electoral campaigns. This "revisionist school" (A. Clark 2004, 35) has demonstrated that both local campaigning and party members provide important political linkages between not only voters and government but also voters and the national party (Whitely and Seyd 1994; Denver and Hands 1997; Widfeldt 1999; Scarrow 2000; Cutts and Shryane 2006). These scholars argue that grassroots politics is not in decline and is still needed alongside today's modern campaign techniques.

As evidence of the revisionist school of campaigning, Green Party volunteers and councillors go door to door and drop off newsletters on a regular basis, even in nonelection periods. The newsletter, the *Norwich Green*, focuses on what the Greens are working on and have achieved on the council and their policy positions on both local and national issues. The publication also seeks to show the multifaceted nature of the Greens' policies and to demonstrate that they are neither a single-issue party, with a sole focus on narrowly-defined environmental issues, nor a local party, without positions on national issues. According to Ramsay,

> The other thing we're trying to do on our leaflets is to have more detailed pieces on national issues so that people can see that we have positions on these issues, that they do make sense, that we have thought them through, that they are distinctive, and that we do need Greens in Westminster [to get these issues on the agenda].[31]

Newsletters have highlighted the Greens' work in keeping a large grocery store chain from opening a store in an already well-served area, promoting affordable housing, defending the founding principles of the National Health Service, and diversifying national energy policy. The paper has also covered the local Greens' actions on more traditional green issues and campaigns, such as increasing recycling, fighting a proposed incinerator, and opposing the cutting down of trees along a local road. According to activists and city councillors, the party's local success has resulted from traditional campaign tactics in targeted wards, with careful consideration of the party's limited resources.

> I think our success is partly targeting and partly the door knocking. And it's the year-round door knocking, focusing on one area, and once you've got that area established, gradually working out [from there]. And it's not taking on too much at one time—going at it fairly steadily and not trying to blanket the whole of Norwich with limited resources. We are a small party, and we don't have much money. We have to be careful where we spend our resources—human and financial—and I think that's what we've done.[32]

Even though the Norwich Greens have used face-to-face campaigning to win local seats, translating this local representation into national representation is the party's biggest hurdle. Tactical- or wasted-vote arguments (Niemi, Whitten, and Franklin 1992; Cox 1997; Alvarez and Nagler 2000) often fuel this challenge. Put simply, voters in a plurality system are typically Duvergerian strategic (Duverger 1951) and often will not vote for their most preferred party for fear that their least preferred party will get elected. Depending on the particular political context of the constituency, this least-preferred party can be the Conservatives, Labour, or the Liberal Democrats. Given this tactical thinking, many Green supporters in Norwich will vote Green locally, where they know the Greens can succeed, but will vote Liberal Democrat in the general elections to ensure that Labour is defeated. According to one councillor, in the 2005 general election in Norwich South,

> When I was door knocking last year, when we had the general election at the same time as the county council election, there were an awful lot of people who said, "Yes, I'll vote for you in the county elections, but not in the general elections. . . . You can't possibly get elected."[33]

Norwich party leaders argue that tactical-voting arguments can only be overcome by increasing representation locally and showing that the party can be a serious contributor to local government, whether in a governing or an opposition role on the city council. The party then must use this local success to demonstrate that it can be a serious political player nationally and that it has the ability to win not only election but also reelection, as local councillors reflected:

> The key thing is turning local votes into parliamentary votes. . . . We need to convince people to vote for us in the parliamentary election. We can do it, we just need to put the effort into really building that local vote.

> We need to highlight that we have a whole range of coherent policies that are relevant in national politics. . . . In the last local elections, we defended several seats, and we kept them all and gained others. And that's telling us that the electorate likes what we're doing. Now we need to multiply that and really concentrate in Norwich South and continue to grow. . . . We need to build on the ground from what the councillors are doing here.

> It's us continuing to grow in local elections, which gives us the credibility that people need to see to vote for us in the general election.[34]

Like many local Green parties, the Norwich Greens are trying to balance the goals of local and national representation and policy distinction. For a small party, however, defining success is complicated. Activists and leaders in the Green Party across the United Kingdom have different opinions about whether it is success when other parties adopt its policies and promote its ideas. In Norwich, many Greens refer to the idea of "greenwashing"—that is, when other parties endorse Green ideas but then do not follow through with policies after winning election.

> I don't see other parties taking on Green issues as success. . . . If you look at their philosophies, there's no other party that even remotely has something like the *Manifesto for a Sustainable Society*. Most of the other parties are just built on the idea of continuous growth and that there is no alternative to the current system. It's success in way—it's putting the issue on the agenda. But I'm more worried if they try to take on these issues because it's just for the short term. . . .

I think it's a mixture of both being beneficial and frustrating at the same time. When the Labour MP did a walking tour a week before the general election and saw the masses of Green posters up, he immediately started talking about the Labour Party's environmental policy. And we were flattered in a way. . . . But the other parties aren't translating this stuff on the ground. . . . I think most of the electorate will see through it . . . [Conservative leader David] Cameron on his bike with the Lexus behind him is the reality.[35]

I would say that to have any credibility with the general public, we've got to be recognized for what we're doing. I see what David Cameron is doing now as greenwash.[36]

By targeting its resources and focusing on traditional face-to-face campaigning, Norwich Green activists and elected officials have made substantial progress toward overcoming the hurdle of tactical voting in a plurality system and have gained representation at both the city and county levels. In addition, the Greens' vote share in the European Parliament (EP) elections in the Eastern region, of which Norwich is a part, increased from 6 percent in 2004 to 9 percent in 2009. In Norwich, the Greens finished first, winning 25 percent of the vote in the 2009 EP elections. Overall, the local party organization recognizes the importance of gaining credibility in the eyes of the voters in both the short and long term and how to achieve this goal.

Oxfordshire, Brighton and Hove, and Norwich: Does Local Success Lead to National Success?

The goal of the Greens' focus on local grassroots politics is to build up the party's credibility with voters, as outlined in the 1993 Basis for Renewal initiative. In this regard, success at the local level would seem to be a necessary condition for selection as a targeted general election constituency. However, it is by no means a sufficient condition, as the Oxfordshire Greens have demonstrated. Some of the British Greens' earliest successes came on the Oxford City Council and the Oxfordshire County Council, yet the party has not replicated these successes in parliamentary elections (see table 4.2). If the Green Party's overall objective is to achieve representation in Westminster, then why has one of its most successful local parties not been able to do better in national elections and have one of its constituencies targeted by the national party?

The Green Party has a long history in Oxford, a university city that is also home to a car manufacturing plant and several hospitals and has about 165,000 residents. Over the past thirty years, the city council has bounced back and forth among Labour and Conservative control as well as minority or coalition governments. As of 2008, Labour was in a minority administration. The first Green was elected to the city council in 1993. Until 2000, the council was elected in thirds every year, with no election in the fourth year. In the wake of election reforms in 2000, half of the Oxford City Council is up for election every two years. In 2002, however, the entire council was up for election because of ward boundary changes. After winning their first seat in 1993, the Greens built up to eight seats in 2000 (15.7 percent of the seats) but then fell back to three following redistricting in 2000. Since 2000, the Greens' seat share on the council has returned to seven or eight seats (see table 4.4). At the same time, the party also increased its representation on the Oxfordshire County Council from one councillor in 1993 to five (of seventy-four) by 2005 before losing three in the 2009 county elections.

The city of Oxford is split between two parliamentary constituencies, Oxford East and Oxford West and Abingdon. Oxford East, created in 1983, has been a Labour stronghold, home to the car factory, a large council estate, and a high percentage of student voters (19 percent in 2001). It has been represented by Andrew Smith since 1987. However, Smith won by only 2.3 percent of the vote in 2005, a sharp drop from his 26 percent margin of victory in 2001. Thus, it is becoming a more marginal Labour seat.

TABLE 4.4. Green Seat Share on Oxford City Council

Election Year	Seats	Total Seats on Council	Seat Share (%)
1994	1	51	2.0
1995	1	51	2.0
1996	3	51	5.9
1998	4	51	7.8
1999	7	51	13.7
2000	8	51	15.7
2002[a]	3	48	6.3
2004	7	48	14.6
2006	8	48	16.7
2008	7	48	14.6

Source: Oxfordshire Green Party.
[a]Boundary change. Entire council was up for election in 2002.

Oxford West and Abingdon, also created in 1983, was represented by Liberal Democrat Evan Harris from 1997 to 2005. It includes several villages and towns to the north and west of Oxford and also has a high student population (19.7 percent in 2001). Through 2005, it was a strong Liberal Democrat seat. Harris won by a margin of at least 10 percent in the 1997, 2001, and 2005 elections. On the city council, most of the Greens' seats have been in the Oxford East constituency, though they have had one councillor representing a ward in Oxford West and Abingdon. As table 4.2 shows, the Greens' vote share did not top 4.5 percent in either constituency in the the 1997, 2001, and 2005 general elections.

Over the years, the Oxfordshire Green Party has concentrated its electoral efforts at the local level. Although electing an MP is widely considered by Green Party leaders and elected officials as the most important means to achieve credibility in national politics, this belief has not translated into a dedicated on-the-ground effort for the Oxfordshire Greens. Oxford city councillors and leaders argue that the party has not recruited candidates committed to running in successive elections and that this absence of repeat candidates has hindered the party's potential for electoral success. Explained one Oxford city councillor, "I think running constantly is really important, and something that we don't do well is to have the same candidate time after time. And so, of course, people don't build up a relationship with one candidate."[37] The Oxfordshire Green Party elections agent concurs: "Having someone who's prepared to campaign in the longer term . . . I think it's worth a few percent at least if you can stay in the same area and keep campaigning. People slowly get to know you."[38]

Many Oxfordshire Greens posit that the party has succeeded in the Brighton Pavilion constituency because of Taylor, a high-profile candidate who ran in successive elections. In addition to serving as one of the national party's principal speakers from 2004 to 2006 and serving as a city councillor, Taylor was the party's candidate in the constituency in 2001 and 2005. In July 2007, the Brighton and Hove Green Party selected party leader and MEP Caroline Lucas as its candidate in the next parliamentary elections. In 2010, she became the first Green representative elected to Parliament.

The timing of the candidate selection decision is also important. The Brighton and Hove party selected its candidate long before parliamentary elections were even scheduled, thus enabling the party to campaign unofficially for three years. The Oxfordshire party learned from its earlier mistakes and chose its candidates in early 2007 as well. However, the Oxfordshire candidates are local activists without the broader name recognition that Taylor and Lucas enjoy, both among party supporters and among potential Green voters.

Brighton and Hove has been represented by three parliamentary seats since 1950: Brighton Pavilion, Brighton Kemptown, and Hove. From 1997 to 2005, the Brighton Pavilion constituency was represented by a Labour–Co-operative candidate.[39] Though it remained a safe Labour seat, the Labour–Co-op MP, David Lepper, saw his vote share decrease from 54.6 percent in 1997 to 35.4 percent in 2005. This decline parallels the steady increase of the Liberal Democrats' and Greens' vote shares in the constituency. Hove has been a Labour seat since 1997, but the party's winning margin steadily decreased to 1 percent in 2005. Brighton and Kemptown was also a Labour seat from 1997 to 2005, but the party's winning margins have not declined as steeply. The Labour MP, Des Turner, won by 6.9 percent in 2005.

Like its Oxfordshire counterpart, the Brighton and Hove Green Party has steadily increased its representation on the city council through grassroots campaigning. As of 2007, it held 22 percent of the seats (see table 4.5). All of the Green city councillors represent wards in the center of Brighton, which is in the Brighton Pavilion constituency. In 1997, the governments of Brighton and Hove merged into a unitary authority, which now represents roughly 254,000 people. For most of the last decade, the Labour Party has controlled the council either as a majority or minority party. The council is currently run by a minority Conservative administration.

One of the key differences between the Oxfordshire and Brighton and Hove parties is the type of candidates that they stand as well as a short-ver-

TABLE 4.5. Green Seat Share on Brighton and Hove City Council

Election Year	Seats	Total Seats on Council	Seat Share (%)
1996[a]	1	78	1.3
1999	3	78	3.8
2003	6	54	11.1
2007	12	54	22.2

Source: Brighton and Hove Unitary Council.
[a]In 1997, the East Sussex districts of Brighton and Hove became a unitary authority and now have a single local council.

sus long-term parliamentary campaign strategy. Whereas the Brighton and Hove Greens have selected nationally known figures who have been willing to run repeatedly, the Oxfordshire Greens have struggled to find candidates who have broad appeal and are willing to run in successive elections.[40] This difference has given the Brighton and Hove constituency of Brighton Pavilion the prized position of a targeted constituency and left the Oxford constituencies with little national resources. In the words of one Brighton and Hove city councillor,

> We are very high-profile locally, and we do have a way of getting our message across through our local [party] paper and through the press. . . . And of course, Keith [Taylor] is now one of the principal speakers. . . . He's very well known locally. He's been active in Brighton a long time.[41]

The Norwich Greens exemplify the strategy of working locally while simultaneously building on this work to achieve the ultimate goal of electing an MP. Norwich South was one of three targeted constituencies in 2005, and the party views electing a Green in this constituency as a realistic objective in the foreseeable future. One of the key factors that differentiates Norwich from Oxfordshire is the local party's focus on this goal. In Ramsay, it has found a charismatic and outspoken young candidate. As the leader of the Green group on the city council and deputy leader of the national party, he is an up-and-coming figure in the party with growing name recognition among both Greens and likely Green supporters in the constituency. Furthermore, he led the Norwich Greens' highly successful 2008 local campaign. The Norwich Greens run a candidate in the Norwich North constituency, but the bulk of local resources are targeted to the Norwich South constituency.

These case studies have demonstrated the complexities of the Greens' two-pronged strategy of focusing (and targeting) locally and targeting nationally. While both are crucial to building the party's credibility, they involve different tactics. A local party's choices may affect success not only at the local level but also at the national level. A party may choose to focus on building up local representation (Oxfordshire), select a nationally known figure to run for Westminster and use local representation as a means of building credibility and support for the national-level election (Brighton and Hove), or try to increase its presence locally and its vote share in the general elections (Norwich). As Ramsay said,

> We've clearly shown that we can win at local elections. [However,] an enormous number of the people who voted for us in the local elections in 2005 didn't vote for us in the general election because they thought that we couldn't win. I think that by the time we get to the next general election, . . . we can win. We're very close to being the second-largest party on the council now. There's another local election again before the general election, and this will really boost our credibility gap and will show that we haven't just got councillors in a couple of wards, but we're second across Norwich South. . . . In summary, it's us continuing to grow in local elections which gives us the credibility for people to vote for us in the general election.[42]

In the end, the local parties seek to balance their preferences for getting their issues on the agenda and increasing their representation both locally and nationally. Local parties have chosen a variety of foci for their efforts, and this choice affects not only their success in national elections but also whether their constituencies are targeted; this decision, in turn, affects subsequent success.

A NATIONAL PATTERN OF STANDING PARLIAMENTARY CANDIDATES?

The British Greens are behaving strategically given the confines of their internal party organizational structure and of the electoral system. But can a pattern be identified in the party's decisions about where to stand candidates? Traditional quantitative analyses of national party strategy typically focus on the party's activities in national-level politics. However, unlike the French Greens' coordinated national PEC strategy, the very decentralized British Greens have little control over where local parties choose to stand candidates in national elections. The national party does not formally decide where to stand candidates and then funnel resources to the constituencies, as Cranie explained.

> It's very decentralist. If a local party is willing to put up a candidate, that's great. We'll support it and that's fantastic. And often we will say to the regions to stand one-sixth of the total candidates because previously the BBC guidelines have been very clear that unless you're standing in one-sixth of the available seats, they will give you less coverage. So we've always looked

at this as a goal. . . . There is currently no top-down system which says, "This is where we're standing." . . . It's been considered and discussed at GPEx meetings . . . whether we want to become more sophisticated than that. . . . Ideally, we would love to stand everywhere, but we're not at that level yet.[43]

Because of this decentralization, it would not be fruitful to use a measure such as the past strength of the extreme right British National Party (BNP), as I did with the National Front to predict Socialist-Green PECs in France. Indeed, the results of a bivariate logistic regression between BNP vote share in a given constituency in 2001 and a Green candidate in 2005 are negative and not significant. While the nonsignificant relationship may be attributable to the lack of a coordinated strategy about where to stand candidates, it also results in part from the fact that the BNP's vote share was only greater than 0.05 percent in 6 of the 33 constituencies in which it stood candidates in 2001. Therefore, this potential effect is washed out by the high number of constituencies where the threat from the BNP was of little concern. In 2005, the BNP ran candidates in 115 constituencies and won 0.05 percent or more of the votes in 34 constituencies. Thus, it will be useful to reexamine this relationship after the 2010 general elections.[44]

Trying to predict where there were Green candidates in 2005 based on traditional factors such as vote shares in previous elections and constituency demographics is equally challenging. In the 2005 general election, the Greens ran candidates in 180 constituencies in England and Wales, up from 140 constituencies in 2001. The results of a bivariate logistic regression between Green vote share in a given constituency in 2001 and a Green candidate in 2005 is positive and significant at $p < 0.01$, demonstrating that the local parties considered past experiences in choosing where to stand candidates. When 2001 Green vote share is at 1.0 percent, the probability of a Green candidate in 2005 is 0.06. Increasing vote share to 9.0 percent increases the likelihood of a Green candidate to 0.19. However, the fact that 76 constituencies had Green candidates in 2005 and not in 2001 suggests that the party's past experiences in a given constituency tell only part of the story.

To demonstrate further that the traditional variables only provide partial insight into where the Greens run candidates, I conducted a multivariate logistic regression analysis. The dichotomous dependent variable is whether there was a Green candidate in a given constituency in 2005. The unit of analysis is the parliamentary constituency. The independent variables are Green, Labour, Liberal Democrat, and Conservative vote shares in 2001 and the size of the majority of the 2001 winning candidate (measured as the difference between the winner and second-place finisher). Following from previous research that has demonstrated a strong positive correlation between voting for a European green party and age, level of education, being a full-time student, and living in cities (see, for example, Inglehart 1995, 1997; Dalton 2008; see also Birch 2009 for an analysis of the districts in the United Kingdom where Green candidates have the most support), I also include several demographic control variables from the 2001 census that represent these characteristics of the population: the percentage of the constituency's population that takes public transportation to work (there is no measure of urban area in the data set), rents property, is full-time students, has higher professional occupations, and is nonwhite. (See appendix C for the descriptive statistics of the variables included in the analysis.)

Table 4.6 illustrates the results for all constituencies and for only those constituencies that had Green candidates in 2001. Among the electoral variables, only the Greens' vote share in the 2001 elections is significant and positively predicts the probability of a Green candidate in that constituency in 2005 in both models. The 2001 vote shares of Labour, the Liberal Democrats, and the Conservatives in a given constituency have no significant effect on the likelihood of a Green candidate. Among the demographic variables, only the percentages of the district that are renters, professionals, and nonwhite are significant. For all of these variables, as the percentages of these populations increase, so does the likelihood of a Green candidate. Turning to predicted probabilities, I set all of the variables at their means and varied the Greens' 2001 vote share. In the model that includes all of the constituencies, the probability of a Green candidate in 2005 ranges from 0.20 (when the 2001 Green vote share is 1.0 percent) to 0.36 (when vote share is at its maximum of 9.0 percent). In the second model, which includes only the constituencies with Green candidates, the values range from 0.07 to 0.25 (see table 4.7).

In the model using all constituencies, the size of the majority for the winning candidate is negative and significant at the 0.1 level. In other words, as the difference between the winner and second-place finisher increases, the probability of a Green candidate decreases. This result is somewhat counterintuitive. As a policy-focused party, the Greens might be expected only to run in safe seats where they know that their vote share will

TABLE 4.6. Probability of a Green Candidate in 2005

	All Constituencies	Only Constituencies with Green Candidates in 2001
01 Green vote share	1.02***	1.73***
	(0.12)	(0.56)
01 Labour vote share	–0.03	–0.03
	(0.02)	(0.07)
01 Lib Dem vote share	–0.03	–0.02
	(0.02)	(0.07)
01 Conservative vote share	–0.02	–0.03
	(0.02)	(0.06)
Majority	–0.02*	–0.03
	(0.01)	(0.03)
Renters	0.07***	0.10*
	(0.02)	(0.06)
Public transport	–0.01	–0.07
	(0.02)	(0.04)
Students	–0.01	–0.12
	(0.04)	(0.08)
Professionals	0.19**	0.35*
	(0.08)	(0.21)
Nonwhite	0.03**	0.06
	(0.02)	(0.04)
Constant	–1.52	–3.30
	(1.97)	(5.90)
Pseudo R^2	0.32	0.27
N	530	130
Log likelihood	–222.99	–55.58

Source: British Parliamentary Constituency Database (Norris 2005b).
*$p < 0.1$, ** $p < 0.05$, ***$p < 0.01$. Standard errors in parentheses.

TABLE 4.7. Predicted Probability of Green Candidate in 2005

Green Vote Share (%)	All Constituencies	Only Constituencies with Green Candidates in 2001
1.0	$p = 0.20$	$p = 0.07$
3.0	$p = 0.23$	$p = 0.10$
5.0	$p = 0.27$	$p = 0.13$
7.0	$p = 0.31$	$p = 0.18$
9.0	$p = 0.36$	$p = 0.25$

not interfere with the outcome—that is, where the party can convey its policy agenda to potential voters without much concern that the votes it receives will harm the chances of its second-most-preferred party.

Furthermore, if the British Greens followed the same pattern as their French counterparts in regard to PECs, we might expect the party to stand candidates in only the more safely left seats. But such is not the case. When adding variables to the model for safe Labour, Liberal Democrat, and Conservative seats (that is, one that was won by a margin of 20 percent or greater), none of the variables are significant. One reason for this may be that the Greens may not yet differentiate among and see faults with all three major parties. Or, depending on the local political context, Labour, the Liberal Democrats, or the Conservatives may be Green voters' second-most-preferred party.[45] These discrepancies contribute to the difficulty of identifying a national pattern of where the party is most likely to stand candidates.

However, these results suggest an alternative motivation. If the party is policy-driven, then it follows that it should run in marginal districts where it can become the kingmaker and force other parties to adopt its positions as a way of winning over potential Green voters (Meguid 2008). As Meguid (2008, 122) notes, the Green Party's presence contributed to seven Conservative-held and two Labour-held constituencies changing from safe to marginal seats in 1987. Had the parties tried to win over Green Party voters, they might have lost fewer votes. These results lend additional support to the argument that the Greens are behaving strategically. But we do need to be somewhat cautious about accepting this explanation. The Greens do not necessarily trust other parties' environmental promises and thus would not want to sacrifice potential Green votes to a party that might not follow through on its proposed agenda. Moreover, many party leaders do not see this tactic as success.

While these explanations may offer some insights into where the Greens stand candidates, the local parties still put a great amount of effort into determining not only in which constituencies to stand candidates but also where to focus resources. A local or regional party may choose to stand paper candidates in some constituencies to gain visibility but will focus only on constituencies where the party has local representation, where the demographics are favorable, or where it has been involved in a particular local issue.[46] Thus, local parties are acting strategically and working to increase their credibility, as the case study of the two Norwich constituencies demonstrates.

CONCLUSION

The British Greens seek to balance their vote- and policy-seeking goals. While the British party has had less electoral success than its French counterpart, it has demonstrated an ability to navigate the restrictive plurality system while remaining committed to "doing politics differently." It is following in the footsteps of the Liberal Democrats, the largest third party in the United Kingdom, by focusing locally, relying heavily on grassroots campaign tactics, and targeting nationally. In general elections, the Greens have increasingly sought to have a single cohesive message for voters. In 2005, for example, the national party coordinated the text and images in all election leaflets and other campaign paraphernalia, thereby enabling voters easily to recognize a candidate as being part of the Green Party and representing its agenda. Over time, the party has slowly built up its credibility with voters as it has gained more seats on local councils and has controlled or been the chief opposition on several local authorities. The Greens now use their best-known personalities in the most high-profile elections. As a result, voters increasingly see the party as a credible political actor and a viable party at least at the local and European levels.

However, the Greens still have a steep hill to climb in the British political system. First, local representation presents a double-edged sword for a small party. While it does give the party legislative and governing experience, it also means that the party can be blamed when outcomes are not positive. Although all parties face such blame, negative experiences and media coverage can be more detrimental to small, less established parties. Second, many voters who consider themselves Green Party supporters will support the party only in second-order elections, such as those to local councils and the European Parliament, and will not vote for Green candidates in general elections. In the 2009 European Parliament elections, for example, the Greens received 8.6 percent of the vote, a 2.4 percent increase from the 2004 elections, but did not increase their number of MEPs. These results, however, far exceed the party's 3.3 percent of the vote in the constituencies it contested in the 2005 general elections. The June 2010 general election will provide further evidence of how the party's success in second-order election contests may boost its national-level support.

Few observers would contest the view that the British Greens have had less electoral success then the French Greens, but the constraints in the United Kingdom are arguably higher. Britain has little tradition of PECs and a strong tradition of having only one viable party on the left. The political space is simply not as open to different approaches to left-wing politics as is the case in France, making entry into Westminster even harder for the British Greens. But the party is standing its ground; running candidates in local, national, and European elections; and refusing to let the larger parties appropriate its issues. Through this behavior, the party is balancing its vote and policy preferences.

CHAPTER 5

Communicating Credibility: Elected Officials and Media Strategies

THE WAY THAT PARTIES communicate their message to voters is another key piece of the credibility puzzle, especially when a small party is seeking to balance its goals of maximizing its vote share potential and of avoiding straying too far from its core policy preferences. The party's communication strategy is as central to its survival as are its electoral and policy strategies. Who speaks on behalf of the party, what they are speaking about, and how its ideas are conveyed to the public go a long way toward demonstrating how a party wants to be perceived by voters. Such approaches are important for all parties but are perhaps even more crucial for small parties that are trying to break through and work their way into the hearts and minds of voters. A carefully crafted communication strategy can contribute a great deal to a party's survival.

Communication strategies fit into the parties' role in the electorate (Key 1958). Parties use these tactics to educate and organize voters in general as well as specifically to convey their policy messages and their viability to voters. Small parties with electoral and governing goals, like the greens, must focus especially on the latter. How can they convince voters that supporting one of their candidates is not a wasted vote? While a "wasted vote" can take on many meanings, I use the idea to refer to voting for a party that has no chance of getting elected either in the short or long term—a true throwaway vote—akin to voting for the Green Party candidate in a U.S. presidential election.

One way parties can achieve this goal is through their coverage in the print media. If a voter who is sympathetic to the agenda and positions of the small party reads only articles on internal debates and divisions, she will most likely not be encouraged to cast her vote for the party. Conversely, if the same voter reads articles concentrated on the party's policy positions and its local, national, or supranational activities, she may be more encouraged to support this party, since it is being portrayed as serious and credible. New parties with little or no representation have to focus much more on how their coverage conveys viability than do older, larger parties. Newspaper articles about internal party debates and divisions may not bode well for attracting voters to any party but can be especially harmful for a newer party trying to gain political footing. These types of articles shift the public's focus away from the party's policy positions and visions for change and toward intraparty fighting. Thus, in essence, these parties have triple the task: first, recognition by the voters; second, conveying their credibility; and third, convincing voters to support them.

Parties have agency in how they are covered and are not simply pawns of the media. A party's coverage can be simply reactive, at the whim of the writers and editors; however, parties also can take a more proactive approach by ensuring that they control not only how much coverage they receive but also the substance and tone of the coverage. They can do this by having prominent party members write guest articles and news analyses, letters to the editor, and opinion pieces or by creating newsworthy events, staging protests, engaging in illegal activities, or taking positions on controversial issues.

DO THE MEDIA MATTER?

Research has demonstrated that the media have some influence on voters' opinions and behavior. Through their agenda-setting ability (Iyengar and Kinder 1987; Iyengar 1997), the media can shape how voters think about issues, candidates, and political parties. Studies have demonstrated that exposure to various media sources (newspapers, television news) has some influence on voters (Curtice and Semetko 1994; Dalton, Beck, and Huckfeldt 1998; Newton and Brynin 2001; Gerber, Karlan, and Bergen 2006). This influence can be positive or negative—from reinforcing a voter's existing beliefs or changing her opinions to generating cynicism and a lack of confidence in institutions and subsequently reducing the likelihood of voting (Norris et al. 1999; Moy and Pfau 2000; Norris 2000). Other research has found that only when the news media and another cue-giver, such as a preferred party, reinforce each other will the voter's opinion be affected (Carey and Burton 2004). Thus, if newspapers can influence voters' opinions and subsequent voting decisions through both what they choose to cover and how they choose to cover it, then it follows that a party would devote resources and time to its media strategy as a part of its larger communication strategy.

Recent surveys show that European citizens still obtain some of their information about current events from newspapers. In 1999, 45 percent of citizens in the EU-15 read a newspaper every day, while 71 percent of respondents watched television news on a daily basis. For French citizens, the results were 26 percent and 58 percent, respectively, and in the United Kingdom, the corresponding numbers were 49 percent and 71 percent (European Commission 1999; Norris 2000, 80). Similarly, the 2004 European Election Study found that 51.5 percent of residents of the EU-15 read newspapers and 72 percent watched television news programs at least five days a week. Among French respondents, the figures were 36.4 percent for newspapers and 67.5 percent for television, while among Britons, those values were 51.9 percent and 80.4 percent, respectively (European Election Study 2004). In the 2009 European Election Study, voters were asked how many days a week they follow the news (including newspapers, television, and radio). In the EU-27, 68.7 percent of respondents reported following the news seven days a week; in France, that number was 70.7 percent, and in the United Kingdom it was 72.2 percent (European Election Study 2009). Moreover, many people use newspapers, especially the national dailies, for in-depth background information and analysis on the key issues of the day, supplementing those sources with radio and television. (For further discussion of the French media, see Kuhn 1995, 231–32.)

Here, I am not entering into the debate about the influence of the media; rather, I use these findings to motivate my study of party communication strategy. If the media had no effect on voters' opinions and decisions, there would be little reason to focus on the party's newspaper coverage. Since the media do have some influence, looking at how the party uses them is a useful exercise for understanding one piece of its larger strategy of achieving credibility among voters.

PROFESSIONAL PARTIES AND THE MEDIA

Recent literature has described parties in developed democracies as becoming professional organizations, idealized by Panebianco's (1988) electoral-professional party. The parties are staffed by professionals who are specialists in their fields, such as polling, advertising, or public relations (Farrell 1996; Swanson and Mancini 1996; Farrell and Webb 2000; Norris 2002). Part of this professionalization includes hiring media specialists and advisers to develop media strategies, both during electoral campaigns and at other times. These individuals craft the message that the party conveys, assure that this message is communicated coherently and cohesively by politicians and party elites, and develop a strategy for publicizing this message through various outlets, including newspapers, television news programs, Web sites, and blogs.

In addition, parties in parliamentary systems are becoming more leader-driven (Bowler and Farrell 1992) and even "presidentialized" (Norris et al. 1999; Poguntke and Webb 2005). Party leaders, for example, are being put on pedestals as never before, as if they are seeking the voters' direct support for prime minister rather than support for the party.[1] This presidentialization is evident in how the parties—both those that are viable prime ministerial contenders and those that are not—present their candidates to the public, campaign, and use the media.

Small parties also want to take advantage of the media as well as put their leaders out front. In fact, it is even more essential that small parties become professionalized to convey their message to the public. According to Villalba (2008, 51), the French Greens "have, over time, acquired . . . electoral *savoir faire,* technical skills, negotiation abilities. . . . In short, they have gone through a professionalization process." Similarly, Peter Cranie, the United Kingdom Green Party Executive's (GPEx) elections coordinator, explained,

> The planning weekend that's taking place this weekend is the first of its kind. It's planning for local elections in 2007 and it's happening now in June 2006 and it's the start of the process. . . . It's identifying the likely political agenda. It's identifying weaknesses and strengths and what message we need to communicate. We've got a professional communications agency involved in what we're doing. We've got experienced marketers. And we've got an adviser that formerly worked at Downing Street at the highest level also providing advice. And we are stepping up the game in terms of planning. . . . Preparations are key, so that when something does hit the news agenda, we can react to it because we're already prepared for that. This is the first time that we've taken that kind of approach.[2]

As further evidence of this professionalization, the French Greens have increased their staff and communications budgets since the mid-1990s, while the British Greens have done so since the early 2000s.³ The French party nearly tripled what it spent on staff between the mid-1990s and 2007.⁴ Between 2002 and 2007, years in which both legislative and presidential elections took place in France, the Greens almost doubled the amount they spent on staff (nearly $3 million). On propaganda and communication expenses (an all-encompassing category that includes conferences, rallies, press, publications, television, and publicity), the party spent a total of $2.8 million in 2007, nearly $1.6 million more than it spent in 2002. The official reports did not further break down these expenses. (Commission Nationale des Comptes de Campagne et de Financements Politiques 1996, 1997, 2002, 2004, 2005, 2006, 2007a, 2007b, 2008).

Similarly, the British Greens' staff expenditure increased over the 2001–7 period. The $210,000 it spent in 2007 was $50,000 more than it spent in 2001. The party also significantly increased its expenditures on external communications over this period, with the most money spent in 2004, for the European elections (Green Party of England and Wales 2002–8). In fact, the British Greens spent more in the year of the European elections on external communications than they did the following year for the general elections. The reports filed with the U.K. Electoral Commission allow the parties to provide further explanation of their expenses. Through these, we see the clearest evidence of the Greens becoming more professionalized, particularly in their focus on the media.

> The Press Office is currently undergoing a revamp, with new equipment being installed and more importantly of all, a full time Press Officer. (2005)
>
> External Communications now employ a full time press officer which has improved efficiency and output. (2006)
>
> External Communications had another productive year, building capacity further. A second press officer was appointed in the second half of the year to cover the work of the London election campaign. (2007)

Moreover, after years of debate and discussion, the British Greens' November 2007 vote to move to a single leader and deputy leader further demonstrates that the party recognizes the importance of conveying its credibility through the media (Green Party of England Wales 2007; see also Carter 2008, 233; Rüdig 2008).

To study the communications strategy of the French and British Green parties, I examine the media coverage of both parties' members of the European Parliament (MEPs) as well as the coverage of the French Greens' members of Parliament (MPs). I thus provide both cross-country and intra-country comparisons. Both parties strive to put their best face forward to get their messages across to voters as a way of increasing the party's credibility, but they are not equally successful.

I begin with an overview of the political experiences of the eleven elected officials under consideration. Next, I discuss how elections to the European Parliament (EP) affect small parties before turning to the data and methods for studying the parties' communication strategies. I then analyze the coverage of the three groups of elected officials. Finally, I explain the differences across groups and the implications of my findings.

GREEN NATIONAL AND EUROPEAN POLITICIANS

The eleven politicians who comprise this analysis possess a range of political experience and positions in their parties and represent different geographical areas. Table 5.1 provides an overview of these individuals and their positions during the study.

British MEPs

Of the two British MEPs elected in 1999 and reelected in 2004 and again in 2009, Caroline Lucas is the more well-known politician, though Jean Lambert has also had a substantial amount of experience. Lucas has served in prominent party positions, including national press officer (1987–89), cochair of the National Party Council (1989–90), female principal speaker (2003–5 and 2007–8), and party leader (September 2008–). In 1993, she became the second Green elected to a county council seat in England and Wales. She held this position on the Oxfordshire County Council until 1997. In the 1999 EP elections, Lucas headed the Green list in the South East region and won one of the region's 10 seats. She was reelected in both 2004 and 2009. In July 2007, Lucas was selected to be the party's candidate for

Communicating Credibility

the next general elections in the Brighton Pavilion constituency, and in 2010, she became the first Green elected to the British Parliament.

Lambert represents the London region. Prior to being elected MEP, she also held several prominent party positions, including the posts of female principal speaker (1992–93 and 1998–99) and chair of the Party Executive (1994).

French MEPs and MPs

In 2004, Greens were elected as MEPs representing six of the seven regions in Metropolitan France: Marie-Hélène Aubert (Ouest), Marie-Anne Isler Béguin (Est), Jean-Luc Bennahmias (Sud-Est), Hélène Flautre (Nord-Ouest), Alain Lipietz (Ile de France), and Gérard Onesta (Sud-Ouest). The six MEPs

TABLE 5.1. **Summary by Individual Politician, 2004–7**

Name	Position	Articles (as % of total for group and raw number)	Largest Category for MP/MEP (as % of articles for individual)
Martine Billard	French MP	13.6 (128)	general policy (38.3)
Yves Cochet	French MP	28.5 (268)	presidential election (25.7)
Nöel Mamère	French MP	58.0 (546)	domestic events (25.6)
Marie-Hélène Aubert	French MEP	13.7 (53)	internal party politics (32.1)
Marie-Anne Isler-Béguin	French MEP	4.7 (18)	European policy (33.3)
Jean-Luc Bennahmias	French MEP	25.9 (100)	presidential election (33.0)
Hélène Flautre	French MEP	5.4 (21)	world events (38.1)
Alain Lipietz	French MEP	31.3 (121)	domestic events (21.5)
Gérard Onesta	French MEP	18.9 (73)	domestic events (41.1)
Jean Lambert	British MEP	22.0 (40)	general policy (42.5)
Caroline Lucas	British MEP	78.0 (142)	general policy (38.7)

have a range of party and elective experience. Aubert was a member of the party's Executive Committee (1993–95), national spokeswoman (2002–4), regional councillor (1992–98), MP (1998–2002), and MEP (2004–9). Bennahmias was the national secretary (1997–2001), regional councillor (1992–6), chair of the Green Group in the Provence–Alps–Côte d'Azur Regional Council (2004–), and Green MEP (2004–7).[5] In 2007, Bennahmias left the Green Party and joined François Bayrou's new party, the Mouvement Démocrate (MoDem). Bennahmias now represents the MoDem in the EP. Isler-Béguin was a member of the National Council and Executive Committee (1986–89), national spokeswoman (1994–99), and MEP (1991–94, 1999–2009). Flautre was a city councillor (1989–1992, 2001–) and was elected to the EP in 1999 and reelected in 2004 and 2009. Lipietz was a city councillor (1995–97), was a regional councillor (1992–94), was national spokesman (1997–98), and was elected MEP in 1999 and again in 2004. Finally, Onesta was a member of the National Council (1987–99), national spokesman (1994–95), and MEP (1991–94, 1999–).

In France, newspaper coverage of the MEPs can be compared with coverage of the MPs. During this period, France had three Green MPs, Martine Billard, Yves Cochet, and Nöel Mamère. (A fourth Green MP, François de Rugy, was elected in June 2007 but was not included in this analysis because he was not in parliament for the entire period.) All three of the included MPs were elected through a 2002 preelection coalition (PEC) with the Socialists in which the Socialists did not run a candidate; all were also reelected in 2007. Billard and Cochet represent Parisian districts (75-1 and 75-11, respectively), and Mamère represents a district near Bordeaux, in southwest France (33-3).

Billard was the spokesperson for the Paris Greens (1996–97), the national spokesperson (1999–2000), and a member of the Executive College (2000–2002).[6] She also served as a Paris city councillor (1995–2001).

Cochet helped to found the Greens in 1984 and served as the party's spokesperson from its inception until 1986 and again from 1992 to 1997. Since 1984, Cochet has also served on the National Interregional Council. He was elected to the city council in Rennes and to the EP in 1989. In 1997, he was elected to the parliament from Val d'Oise, also through a PEC with the PS. Cochet became minister of the environment in Lionel Jospin's government in 2001, holding the position until the June 2002 elections.

Mamère began his career in green politics in the rival party, Génération Ecologie (GE), before joining the Greens in 1998. As a member of GE and later the Greens, Mamère has been the mayor of Bègles since 1989 and was the vice president of the Communauté Urbain de Bordeaux from 1989 to 2001. He was the spokesperson for GE and a regional councillor from 1992 to 1994. From 1994 to 1997, he served as a GE MEP. In 1997, he was elected MP as part of a preelection pact that included GE. In 2002, Mamère was the Greens' candidate for president.

ELECTIONS TO THE EP

Parties use these second-order elected officials to boost their credibility on the first-order stage—that is, at the national level. A vast literature describes European elections as second-order elections (see, for example, Reif and Schmitt 1980; van der Eijk and Franklin 1996; M. Marsh 1998; Carrubba and Timpone 2005; van der Brug and van der Eijk 2007), in which voter turnout tends to be lower than in first-order national elections, government parties are punished by voters, and small parties receive a higher percentage of votes. Voters also tend to cast their votes in European elections based on domestic issues rather than on European issues. However, recent studies have begun to challenge this assumption (Ferrara and Weishaupt 2004; Hix and M. Marsh 2007; M. Marsh 2007; Hobolt, Spoon, and Tilley 2009). For many of these reasons, both the French and British Green Parties have gained representation in the EP.

However, with second-order elections, parties may not put their top candidates on the electoral lists but rather use the lists to groom future candidates for national office or as a place where ex-national politicians can still play a role (see Judge and Earnshaw 2003, 93–95). Small parties that have no or very little national representation are less likely to follow this practice. The EP is one of the institutional settings, along with local and regional councils, where small parties can gain credibility. Thus, placing potential or existing party leaders on the European list is more common among these parties.

Another reason that explains small parties' ability to elect individuals to the EP is the electoral system. Beginning with the first direct election to the EP in 1979, member states could choose their own method for electing representatives. Most states decided on proportional representation (PR), following their national electoral rules, while a handful kept their respective majoritarian national systems.

For the first four EP elections, the United Kingdom used a first-past-the-post (FPTP) system, similar to the one used for elections to the House of Commons. Although the Greens' overall vote share was respectable for these four elections, reaching an all-time high of 14.9 percent in 1989, the party never won any seats because the votes were dispersed across the country rather than concentrated in a handful of constituencies. The Liberal Democrats won two seats in the 1994 EP elections with 17 percent of the vote, thereby demonstrating the impact of vote concentration in an FPTP system.

In 1999, the British Parliament passed the U.K. European Parliament Elections Act, which changed the electoral system to closed-list PR with regional electoral districts. Following this reform, the United Kingdom was divided into twelve regions, or electoral districts, for elections to the EP. Nine of the regions are in England, while the others are Scotland, Wales, and Northern Ireland. Each region has between three and ten MEPs. As of 2009, the total British EP delegation was seventy-two. The Greens and other small parties, such as the United Kingdom Independence Party, first won seats in the EP in the elections following the change in electoral rules.[7]

The British Greens did not win any seats until the 1999 European elections. In 1994, the party received only 3 percent of the vote, and five years later, the party's vote share did not approach its 1989 high. However, the rule change to PR meant that the Greens' 6.25 percent resulted in two seats—one of ten seats in the South East region (Lucas) and one of nine seats in the London region (Lambert).

Beginning with the first EP elections in 1979, France has used a closed-list PR system with a 5 percent threshold. Since 1989, the Greens have had representation (with the exception of 1994–99). Until 2003, there was one nationwide district for EP elections, but reform then created eight regions or electoral districts for the 2004 election. Seven of these regions are in Metropolitan France, and one represents the overseas territories and departments. Each region has between three and fourteen MEPs. As of 2009, France's delegation to the EP was seventy-two.

The French Greens have seen some of their greatest successes in elections to the EP. As with their British counterparts, the French Greens won their highest vote share in 1989. However, their 10.6 percent of the vote resulted in the election of nine MEPs; Green MEPs have subsequently been elected in 1999 (nine), 2004 (six), and 2009 (fourteen).

In 1994, the Greens' vote share decreased to 3.0 percent, and a competing green party, GE, won 2 percent of the vote. In addition, François Mitterrand encouraged the newly formed Mouvement des Radicaux de Gauche (Movement of Radicals of the Left, MRG), under the leadership of Bernard Tapie, to invite independent ecologists to join the party's list as a means of undermining the Parti Socialiste (Socialist Party, PS) leadership of Michel Rocard, a longtime Mitterrand foe. The MRG won 12 percent of the vote and thirteen seats, the PS received 14.5 percent of the vote share and fifteen seats, and the Greens' won no seats (Ysmal 1995, 336–37)

In the 2009 EP elections, both the British and French Green Parties performed well. The British Greens maintained their representation with two MEPs, but their vote share increased 2.4 percent to 8.6 percent overall. The French Greens, running on the Europe Ecologie list, increased their seat share from six to fourteen MEPs, finishing third overall with 16.28 percent of the vote, just 0.2 percent below the Socialists. Because the European level is the focus for most small parties, it is also where we would expect them to concentrate their communication strategies.

DATA AND METHODS

To study the communications strategy of the French and British Greens, I analyze the coverage of their MEPs and MPs (France only) in two national newspapers in each country over a nearly four-year period—15 June 2004–31 December 2007 (42.5 months).[8] During this period, several important events took place. First, the 2004 European elections were held on 13 June in France and 10 June in the United Kingdom. Second, the period encompasses the British general elections in May 2005 and the French legislative and presidential elections in April–June 2007. Finally, the vote on the European Constitution referendum was held on 29 May 2005 in France. No such vote was held in the United Kingdom because the Constitution as it stood was abandoned after being rejected in France and in the Netherlands (on 1 June). The months I examined were also filled with an assortment of policy discussions, internal party debates, and various domestic events. Thus, while this period is not meant to be representative of any period of the same length (and there may be more elections and voting during this time than is typical), it does provide a great deal of material to analyze and compare.

For each party, I analyzed its coverage in two national newspapers. In

France, I used *Le Monde* and *Libération* (*Libé*), both of which provide in-depth coverage of national events and political parties. *Le Monde* is considered a more centrist/objective paper, while *Libération* has a more left-leaning focus. In the United Kingdom, I chose the *Guardian* and the *Independent*. The *Guardian* has a fairly left-leaning perspective; in recent years, the *Independent* has devoted more coverage to environmental issues and by extension the Green Party. Thus, the four newspapers provided a large number of articles to analyze. The newspapers were read and coded in their original languages, and I tracked the coverage of the three French MPs, six French MEPs, and two British MEPs.

There are other ways to measure the parties' communication strategy. For example, one could look at the coverage of the party itself and examine any article that mentions the party, regardless of reference to an individual politician. I did not pursue this approach because I was interested in how the party uses its representatives. Given the national FPTP systems in both France and the United Kingdom, individuals play a very large role not only in the electoral system but also in the political system more generally, making it essential to understand their role in representing the party to the public. While large parties may use the EP as a training ground for future MPs (Judge and Earnshaw 2003, 93–95), for small parties, especially those in FPTP systems, the EP is one of the few spaces where future MPs can gain legislative experience. Thus, we can learn a great deal about the parties' strategies through the coverage of their MEPs.

OVERVIEW OF DATA

Table 5.2 provides an overview of the number of articles analyzed for each group of elected officials—French MPs, French MEPs, and British MEPs—during the 2004–7 period. In addition, the number of articles for the entire 1999–2007 period is included for the British MEPs. The first column shows the number of distinct articles in which an MP/MEP is quoted or mentioned or that an MP/MEP authored. Many of these articles cite or are authored by more than one individual, so an article may be counted more than once. A second category of nonduplicated articles counts each article only once, regardless of how many MPs/MEPs are cited or are the author. The subsequent columns show the breakdown of the nonduplicated articles by newspaper.

The articles were coded in three primary areas: subject, role of the individual, and tone.[9] Each article was first coded by its overall subject. We developed eleven categories that fit the vast majority of the articles. We also had one residual category for the articles either that did not fit into one of the more strictly defined groupings or for which there were not enough articles in one broad area to create an additional category. The twelve categories are Domestic Events, Domestic Policy Statements, European Union (EU) Constitution, European Elections, European Policy, Internal Party Politics, Interview with MP or MEP, Legislative/General Elections, Miscellaneous, Municipal Elections, Presidential Elections, and World Events.

Some articles could fit into two categories; however, for parsimony and clarity, we concentrated on the primary focus of the article. For example, some of the articles on the EU Constitution referendum in France emphasized the divisions within in the party, whereas other articles were concerned with the content of the referendum or the campaign itself. In the first case, these articles were coded as internal party politics; in the second case, they were coded as EU Constitution. Second, the Legislative/General Elections category refers to the 2007 legislative election in France and the 2001 and 2005 general elections in the United Kingdom. There were no municipal elections in France during this period. In the United Kingdom, local elections are held each year in different parts of the country, so there are always a few articles that discuss such elections in any given year. Third, the presidential election category is only for France. Table 5.3 shows the breakdown by subject category for each group for the 2004–7 period.

The second area for which the articles were coded was the politician's role. This was a clear-cut trichotomous scheme—whether the individual was mentioned or quoted or wrote the article. If the MP or MEP was both mentioned and quoted, the articles was coded as "quoted," since the quo-

TABLE 5.2. Summary Statistics by Newspaper

	All Articles	Nonduplicated Articles	Le Monde	Libé	Guardian	Independent
2004–7						
French MPs (3)	942	799	349	450	—	—
French MEPs (6)	386	316	149	167	—	—
British MEPs (2)	182	171	—	—	106	65
1999–2007						
British MEPs (2)	305	280	—	—	173	107

Note: — = not applicable.

TABLE 5.3. Subject Categories (as % of articles for group and raw number)

	French MPs	French MEPs	British MEPs
Domestic Events	19.5	20.9	4.1
	(156)	(66)	(7)
Domestic Policy	**22.3**	4.3	**41.5**
	(178)	(14)	**(71)**
European Constitution	6.5	13.3	1.8
	(52)	(42)	(3)
European Elections	0.3	6.0	4.1
	(2)	(19)	(7)
European Policy	0.13	11.1	24.6
	(1)	(35)	(42)
Internal Party Politics	12.6	14.2	5.8
	(101)	(45)	(10)
Interview with MP or MEP	3.3	1.3	1.2
	(26)	(4)	(2)
Legislative/General Elections	7.5	2.2	2.9
	(60)	(7)	(5)
Miscellaneous	9.5	2.5	8.2
	(76)	(8)	(14)
Municipal Elections	0.3	1.3	2.3
	(2)	(4)	(4)
Presidential Elections	16.6	16.1	N.A.
	(133)	(51)	
World Events	1.5	6.6	3.5
	(12)	(21)	(6)
Total articles	799	316	171

Note: Bold entries represent the largest category for each of the three groups of politicians.

tation was usually in the context of mentioning the person. Most authored articles were guest opinion pieces, articles, or letters.[10] Table 5.4 highlights the role each group of elected officials played in the articles. For this analysis, I use the total number of individual articles, since some articles may quote one MP/MEP and mention another, for example.

The third area coded was the tone of the article. The article was read and coded for how the article discussed the Green Party rather than the individual politician. We developed six categories for the tone of the article: Positive, Positive/Neutral, Neutral, Negative/Neutral, Negative, and Not Applicable (NA). The Neutral category was reserved for articles that mentioned the Green Party only in regard to the MP or MEP's party affiliation. The NA category was used when the MP or MEP was the author of the article or when the Green Party was not mentioned at all. As the focus of the analysis is how the party's image is conveyed through coverage of these individuals, we assumed that pieces written by the MP or MEP were meant as a way to lend the party credibility and would have inflated the Positive category but would not have reflected the newspaper's overall coverage of the party. Table 5.5 shows the tone of the articles by group and newspaper, again using the nonduplicated number of articles.

TABLE 5.4. Role of Elected Officials in Article (as % of articles for group and raw number)

	French MPs	French MEPs	British MEPs
Mentioned	56.8	57.0	31.3
	(535)	(220)	(57)
Quoted	41.5	37.3	30.8
	(391)	(144)	(56)
Author	1.7	5.7	37.9
	(16)	(22)	(69)
Total articles	942	386	182

TABLE 5.5. Tone of Articles by Newspaper (as % of articles in newspaper and raw number)

	Positive	Pos/Neutral	**Neutral**	Neg/Neutral	Negative	**NA**	Total
French MPs							
Le Monde	7.7	16.0	**61.3**	2.0	0.6	**12.3**	349
	(27)	(56)	**(214)**	(7)	(2)	**(43)**	
Libération	8.7	17.1	**50.0**	4.2	1.3	**18.7**	450
	(39)	(77)	**(225)**	(19)	(6)	**(84)**	
Total	66	133	**439**	26	8	**127**	799
French MEPs							
Le Monde	14.1	18.8	**42.3**	9.4	4.7	**10.7**	149
	(21)	(28)	**(63)**	(14)	(7)	**(16)**	
Libération	13.8	26.3	**41.3**	6.0	2.4	**10.2**	167
	(23)	(44)	**(69)**	(10)	(4)	**(17)**	
Total	44	72	**132**	24	11	**33**	316
British MEPs							
Guardian	8.5	3.8	**29.2**	2.8	3.8	**51.9**	106
	(9)	(4)	**(31)**	(3)	(4)	**(55)**	
Independent	1.5	1.5	**38.5**	6.2	6.2	**46.2**	65
	(1)	(1)	**(25)**	(4)	(4)	**(30)**	
Total	10	5	**56**	7	8	**85**	171

ANALYSIS

Figure 5.1 provides an overview of the number of nonduplicated articles for each group of politicians. Each data point represents the number of articles during the previous 6-month period (except for the first period, which covers 5.5 months, and the last period, which includes 7 months) and highlights some of the key dates during this period of analysis. The figure shows that many more articles were devoted to the French MPs than to the other two groups as well as the high points for the numbers of articles. For the French MPs and MEPs, the number of articles peaked just after the June 2004 European elections, although articles about these elections do not figure significantly into the total count for either of the groups. The vast majority of the French MPs' articles in the first six-month period concern two events: when Mamère performed a marriage ceremony for two gay men in Bègles and when a group of Greens, including several elected officials, were arrested for uprooting genetically modified crops.

Table 5.2 shows that the three French MPs have more than twice as many articles as their EP counterparts (799 versus 316). However, the French MEPs have nearly twice as many articles as their British counterparts (316 versus 171). The Greens did not have equal coverage in both of the French and British newspapers. In France, *Libération* had more articles than *Le Monde* for the MPs and MEPs, and the *Guardian* had more articles on the British MEPs than did the *Independent*. A higher percentage of *Le Monde*'s articles concentrated on domestic policy than was the case for *Libération,* but *Libé* devoted more space to coverage of the presidential elections. For the French MEPs, a higher percentage of *Le Monde*'s articles focused on domestic events, whereas *Libération* focused more on internal party politics. Finally, the *Independent* devoted more of its coverage to domestic policy than did the *Guardian*. However, since many of the *Independent* articles were written by the MEPs, the difference in coverage of certain issues is more of a decision of the party than of the paper.

Table 5.6 illustrates key differences in the coverage of the three groups of politicians. Hardly any of the British MEP articles concentrated on domestic events, perhaps because the two MEPs are the Green Party's best avenues for gaining credibility as a viable party and the MEPs and the party have made a conscious decision to avoid having these individuals appear in the media for participating in illegal activities, as is a common tactic for the French Greens. The Green Party of England and Wales may also be less in-

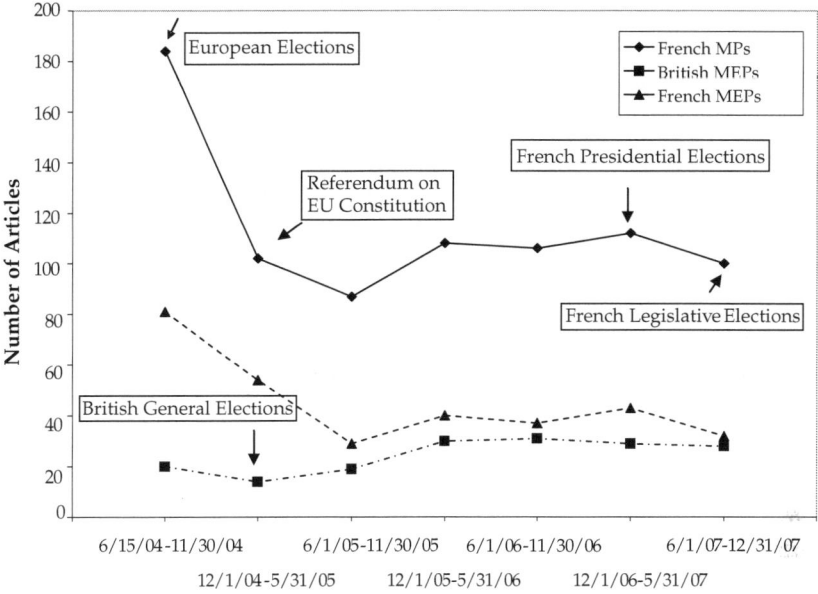

Fig. 5.1. Number of articles by group over time

volved in domestic events because unlike many other European Green parties, it did not originate in a social movement (see Carter 2008, 229–30; Rüdig 2008). Lambert and Lucas may, therefore, be inclined not to take part in or create contentious politics (see Tarrow 1998) but rather to concentrate on more conventional and policy-focused activities for elected officials—debates, meetings, and speaking on the floor of the EP. Although both parties want some control over the context of their newspaper coverage, they accomplish this goal in different ways. Whereas the French Greens to some extent generate coverage based on domestic events, the British Greens write the vast majority of their articles, focusing on policy positions and policy-related activities. Of Lucas's eighty-nine policy-centered articles, for example, she wrote forty-three (48.3 percent); similarly, Lambert authored seventeen of her twenty-five policy-focused articles (68 percent).

A second key difference between British and French coverage is the concentration in the French articles on internal party politics, a topic that garnered virtually no coverage in the British media. Again, these differences could result from the British MEPs' practice of writing articles and thus not wanting to highlight intraparty divisions and thereby lessen the public's view of the party. Only ten articles (5.8 percent) cover internal party issues in the United Kingdom, less than half the amount for the French MPs (12.6 percent) or the French MEPs (14.2 percent). This phenomenon could also be explained by the fact that the British Greens, unlike their French counterparts, face no competition from other environmental parties. In the 2007 legislative elections, the center-right GE and Mouvement Ecologiste Indépendant (Independent Ecologist Movement, MEI) continued to run candidates. In the 2009 EP elections, these parties ran a joint list, the Alliance Ecologiste Indépendant, and won 3.6 percent of the votes. As a way of generating at least the perception of competition between the Greens, GE, and MEI, the French media may choose to focus on internal party debates.

This intraparty focus is evident in a set of French articles from 2004. Both MPs and MEPs were quoted and mentioned in several articles that highlighted the party's divisions in the run-up to the annual conference, held in Reims in December. The disagreements centered on ideological differences and the party's relationship with the Socialists and other parties of the plural left, including the Radicals; the party's position on the upcoming referendum on the EU Constitution; and the selection of the new party leader. Many of these articles concentrated on the differences between two factions within the party, one headed by Mamère, the other led by Do-

TABLE 5.6. Summary of Key Differences across Groups (% of total articles)

	French MPs (3)	French MEPs (2)	British MEPs (2)
Domestic events	19.5	20.9	4.1
	(156)	(66)	(7)
Internal party politics	12.6	14.2	5.8
	(101)	(45)	(10)
Policy (domestic or European)	22.4	15.5	66.1
	(179)	(49)	(113)
Authored	1.9	5.1	39.8
	(15)	(16)	(68)
Letters to the editor (as % of authored)	6.7	6.3	85.3
	(1)	(1)	(58)
Total articles	799	316	171

minique Voynet. Article titles from this period included "Mamère Breaks His Alliance with Dominique Voynet; Six Months from their Congress, the Greens Are Still in Search of a 'Stable Majority'" (van Eeckhout 2004); "The Factions in the Greens Prepare for the Succession of Gilles Lemaire [retiring party leader]" (Cordier 2004); and "Five Motions in Competition" (Auffray 2004). The clearest example of these divisions is probably Cochet's call for a dissolution of the Greens in January 2005, after many of the debates were left unresolved at the party's conference. He wanted to disband the current party and create a new more effective party ("Verts" 2005).

Third, the British MEP articles contain a much greater emphasis on policy, both domestic and European. Two-thirds (66.1 percent) of British MEP articles focus on policy, compared to 22.4 percent and 15.5 percent for the French MPs and MEPs, respectively. The British Greens are committed to conveying their credibility to voters as a viable party and are using their MEPs to accomplish this goal. Having media coverage focus on policy, as opposed to internal party divisions (or extrainstitutional, or even illegal, actions), works toward this goal. Since the possibility of coalitions with other parties is not on the table for the British Greens, the party uses its MEPs very instrumentally, and the MEPs, in turn, use their media exposure instrumentally as well.

This concentration on policy is also tied to a fourth key difference between the French and British coverage—that of authorship. More than 30 percent of the articles in the British newspapers were written by the British MEPs, much higher than the figure of 7 percent for the French politicians. The prevalence of MEP-authored articles in the United Kingdom also contributes to the number of articles in the NA tone category. In fact, 80 percent of the NA articles for the British MEPs were self-written, versus 11.8 percent and 51.5 percent of NA articles for the French MPs and MEPs, respectively. Moreover, 52.2 percent of the British policy-centered articles were written by the MEPs. Thus, the party, through its MEPs, has some control over the media's agenda and how the public perceives the party.

In this way, when the average reader recalls what she has recently read about the British Greens, policy positions will come to mind rather than internal party fighting or contentious or illicit activities. Another way of looking at this phenomenon is that without the Greens' proactive strategy of writing letters to the editor and contributing opinion pieces, the MEPs' print coverage would be greatly decreased, since the newspapers themselves are not covering the MEPs and their activities. This phenomenon, of course, is most likely a result of the second-order nature of not only the EP elections but also of the EP and its members (Reif and Schmitt 1980; van der Eijk and Franklin 1996; van der Brug and van der Eijk 2007).

Among MEP/MP-authored documents, letters to the editor are much more common in the British newspapers than in the French publications. The articles authored by the French MPs and MEPs included only one letter: a letter to the editor at *Libération* by a majority of the French national and European Green delegation encouraging the government to honor an earlier commitment to allow Italian refugees into France ("Réfugiés Italiens" 2004). Conversely, fifty-eight of the sixty-eight (85.3 percent) British MEP-authored articles were letters to the editor.

In contrast to the differences on issues and authorship, there is more consistency in the tone of the articles across the three groups, reflecting attitudes toward the party. As table 5.5 demonstrates, for the three groups across all four papers, the majority of articles were coded as Neutral. There are more positive or positive-leaning articles than there are negative or negative-leaning articles for the French MPs and MEPs. This finding also holds true for the British *Guardian* but not for the *Independent* (which had the smallest number of articles). Although many of the French articles focus on internal party divisions, the tone reflects a more objective reporting of the story. It is possible to argue that the focus on the divisions makes the articles appear more negative, but an important difference exists between the subject of the article and how it is written. Thus, even an article about a party's successes, for example, could be presented with a negative tone.

Table 5.3 shows the breakdown of articles by individual for each group. For the three French MPs, the largest categories are domestic policy (22.3 percent), domestic events (19.5 percent), and the presidential election (16.6 percent). For the French MEPs, the three largest subject groups are domestic events (20.9 percent), the presidential election (16.1 percent), and internal party politics (14.2 percent). The three largest groups for the British MEPs' articles are domestic policy (41.5 percent), European policy (24.6 percent), and miscellaneous (8.2 percent). These results offer great insight into how the party is using these elected officials. In France, both the MEPs and MPs as a group focus on domestic politics and policy rather than on European-level issues and events, perhaps because the party has national-level representation and thus does not need to rely on the second-order sphere of the EP to raise credibility. Conversely, more than 66 percent of the articles on the British MEPs cover policy issues. The party is clearly using these MEPs to convey its credibility as a viable political party. Moreover, 59 of the 113 policy-centered articles (52.2 percent) are written by the MEPs, and 39.8 percent of all British MEP articles are self-written, compared to only 5.4 percent of articles for the French MEPs and 1.9 percent for the French MPs. The British party thus uses this strategy to control its press coverage.

Variation occurs among individual politicians as well as among groups. As table 5.1 shows, Mamère, Lipietz, and Lucas have the most articles in their respective groups. Mamère and Lucas have significantly more articles than do the other individuals in their groups. Mamère is the subject of 546 of the 942 articles. In June 2004, Mamère became the first French mayor to perform a gay wedding, challenging the country's ban on same-sex marriage.[11] He was subsequently sanctioned for this action, and his duties as mayor were suspended for one month. Mamère also received extensive coverage for his role in a protest against genetically modified food. A group of protesters picked genetically modified crops without permission. The group members were arrested, tried in court, and subsequently fined and sentenced. A quarter of Mamère's articles (140 of 546) concern domestic events rather than his service as MP, and half these articles refer to the gay wedding and the food protest. In comparison, 1.6 percent of Billard's articles and 7.5 percent of Cochet's articles focus on domestic events. Lucas's large number of articles (142 of 182) can be attributed to her status as one of the most visible Green politicians as well as her time at the top of the party's leadership. Finally, many of Lipietz's articles (121 of 386) also concern two domestic events: the food protest, in which he participated, and a case he and his sister brought against the French national railway on behalf of their father and uncle, who were transported to the Drancy deportation camp during World War II. Following the court's ruling that the railway was liable and required to pay damages to the Lipietz family, several hundred other descendants of deportees brought a second wave of lawsuits against the railroad, and these cases are now being considered by the European Court of Justice. Figure 5.2 shows these three individuals' article counts over time.

Furthermore, as table 5.1 shows, the articles concerning each elected official have widely varying emphases that demonstrate the different roles they play within the party. A total of 38.3 percent of the Billard articles focus on policy—particularly on her activities in the National Assembly—compared to 19.0 percent for Cochet and 16.1 percent for Mamère. These

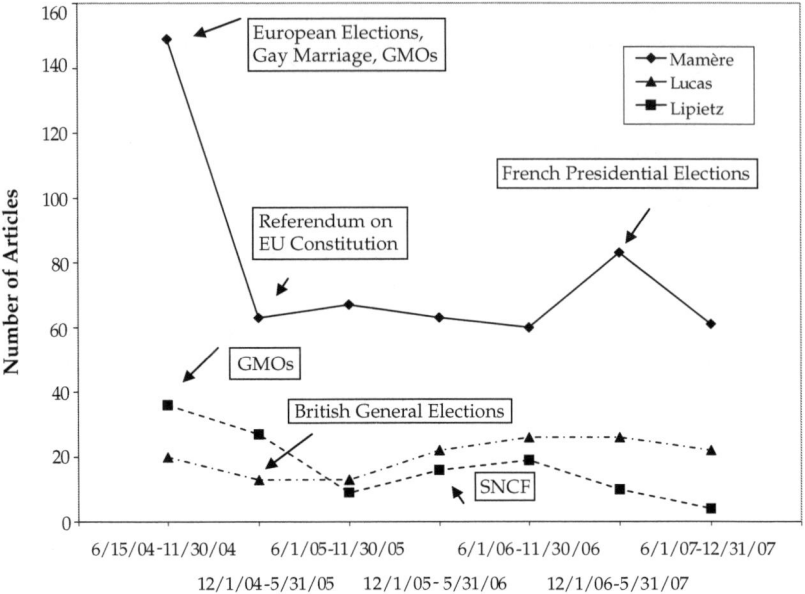

Fig. 5.2. Number of articles by leading individual over time

articles discuss parliamentary debates and legislation, especially those concerned with health care, employment, environment, and civil rights. These present Billard (and through her, the Greens) in a very professional and policy-minded manner. In addition, many of these articles discuss issues other than the environment, thereby portraying the party, through Billard, as more than a single-issue party. A quarter of Billard's articles concern the legislative elections, a significantly higher proportion than for either of the other two MPs (though the absolute numbers, just over thirty, are similar). These articles discuss her district, candidacy, the reelection campaigns of the three Green MPs, and the election results.

Cochet's articles, conversely, are concerned predominantly with the presidential election. Just over one-quarter (25.7 percent) of his articles fall into this category, much higher than the 8.6 percent for Billard or the 16.3 percent for Mamère. Cochet ran against Dominique Voynet to be the party's presidential candidate in 2007, explaining this focus.[12] The articles discuss the intraparty election, the debates, and the two rounds of voting: the first produced a virtual tie, while in the second, Voynet won fifty-seven more votes than Cochet and thus the nomination. Roughly 19 percent of Cochet's articles cover domestic policy and internal party politics (the second- and third-largest groups). In terms of policy, Cochet primarily focused on environmental, energy, transportation, and sustainability issues. The articles concerning internal party politics concentrated on divisions in the party over the vote for the presidential candidate, the EU Constitution referendum, and negotiations with the Socialists for the legislative elections. In sum, these articles provide more of a window into the party's inner workings. Given Cochet's long history within the party, this emphasis is intuitive. On the one hand, it shows a somewhat divided party; on the other hand, it demonstrates the transparent process by which the presidential candidate is chosen, for example. Cochet's policy focus on environmental and energy issues highlights the party's loyalty to its roots.[13] Cochet's emphasis on these core green issues, compared to Billard's more catholic approach to green politics, can be explained either by personal preference or by his role as one of the party's founders. Billard came to the Greens later (in 1993) after starting her political career as a far-left activist.

Mamère's articles are concerned primarily with domestic events. Domestic policy and the presidential elections are the second and third categories, each accounting for about 16 percent of the articles. But given the large number of articles involving Mamère, these two categories represent 177 articles, or almost 40 percent more than Billard's total. Many of the domestic policy articles focused on the broader implications of the gay marriage and the genetically modified crop protest. Mamère, who had been the party's 2002 presidential candidate, again sought the nomination in 2007; shortly after announcing his candidacy, however, he withdrew to support Voynet. In addition, as a prominent member of the party, Mamère was often mentioned or quoted in articles about the 2007 presidential elections.

A total of 316 articles appeared on the French MEPs: 18 on Isler-Béguin, 21 on Flautre, 53 on Aubert, 73 on Onesta, 100 on Bennahmias, and 121 on Lipietz. Policy, either domestic or European, does not figure heavily in these individuals' articles, with the exception of Isler-Béguin, where European policy comprises 33.3 percent and 13.7 percent of the articles, respectively. Even for Aubert, the vice chair of the Greens–European Free Alliance (EFA) group in the EP, articles on European policy constitute only 7.5 percent of her total.[14] The results of the European elections also produced few articles. However, articles on the European Constitution referendum made up one of the top three categories for four of the MEPs. These articles discussed the substantive debate within the party, divisions among the left in general over the Constitution, and individual MEPs' support for the referendum. Internal party politics was one of the top three categories for four of the MEPs as well. These articles emphasized intraparty divisions over the nomination of a presidential candidate, leadership, party structure, and positions on key policy issues.

MEPs Bennahmias and Lipietz had the most coverage in the French newspapers. One-third of Bennahmias's articles concentrated on the presidential election. Many of the articles concerned his support for another ecological (non–Green Party) candidate, Nicolas Hulot, whom Bennahmias supported as the sole ecological candidate.[15] A total of 18 percent of Bennahmias's articles concerned internal party politics—divisions as well as his decision to leave the Greens in May 2007 and support Bayrou and the MoDem for the presidency.[16] Thus, we can attribute much of his coverage to these two key events. The third-largest category for Bennahmias is the European Constitution (13.0 percent). Given Bennahmias's long history with the Greens, coverage of a prominent individual portraying divisions within the party does not help either the party's image or its credibility in the eyes of the voters.

Lipietz's articles were somewhat evenly split among domestic events (21.5 percent), the European Constitution (17.4 percent), and internal party politics (15.7 percent). The domestic events articles primarily focused on the deportation issue and the genetically modified food protest. The articles on the EU Constitution and internal party politics also covered similar topics as those on Bennahmias. Moreover, many of these articles either mentioned or quoted multiple MEPs.

Thus, we see both differences and similarities when comparing the French MP and MEP articles. Policy constituted the largest category of articles for Billard (38.3 percent of articles) and Isler-Béguin (33.3 percent of articles). Both politicians had the smallest percentage of articles for their respective groups—13.6 percent for Billard and 4.7 percent for Isler-Béguin. The results were quite different for the two most visible French Greens, however. Cochet had more than twice as many articles as Billard, and Mamère had four times as many articles as Billard, but 19 percent of Cochet's articles and 16.1 percent of Mamère's articles focused on domestic policy. Policy was not anywhere close to a predominant category for any of the other MEPs. Furthermore, for four of the MEPs, non-European categories (internal party politics, presidential election, and world or domestic events) dominated. Thus, these findings offer very strong evidence that the French Greens do not use their MEPs as a way of conveying their governing or policy-driven credentials to voters.

In contrast to both the French MP and MEP articles, the largest categories of articles for both British MEPs was those addressing policy issues. Articles on both domestic and European policy dominated the coverage of the two MEPs in both newspapers. Of Lambert's forty articles, 42.5 percent focused on domestic policy, and 20 percent covered European policy. The only other category that even came close was Miscellaneous, with 5 articles (12.5 percent of the total). The distribution of Lucas's 142 articles was similar, with 38.7 percent on domestic policy and 23.9 percent concerning European issues. Again, the next-largest category was Miscellaneous, with 11 articles (7.7 percent of the total). For Lucas, both types of policy articles focus on the environment, energy, food safety, animal welfare, transportation, and sustainability issues. Lambert's articles address employment, immigration (migrants and migration), civil rights, the environment, and energy.

Other than the subject differences between the British and French parliamentarians, the other major distinction between the two groups is the use of the print media by the representatives themselves. From 1999 to 2007, roughly one-third of both Lambert's and Lucas's articles were self-written. However, of a total 305 articles, 75 were written by Lucas (24.6 percent), with only 1 coauthored with Lambert. Furthermore, 63 of these articles (84 percent) concentrated on either domestic or European policy (see table 5.7). In sum, while the articles were substantively similar for the MEPs, the important difference lies in the number of articles in which Lucas's name appears. According to scholars and practitioners alike, Lucas is by far the most prominent Green politician. Neil Carter, a leading British authority on the Green Party, states that "Lucas is certainly the party's most high-profile politician and arguably its most effective public performer" (2008, 237).

Another important difference between the two MEPs is the number of nonletters (that is, opinion pieces or guest articles) written. All but 1 of Lambert's 28 authored pieces were letters; whereas only 23 of Lucas's 75 pieces were not letters but were opinion pieces and articles that appeared in other sections of the paper, 69.6 percent of which focused on policy. This finding offers evidence of Lucas's high-profile position from both the party's and the newspapers' perspectives.

Finally, I examine whether holding a leadership position affects an elected official's role in the newspapers. Lucas was co–principal speaker of the British Greens for part of the period under analysis, enabling me to explore whether her coverage changed based on her leadership status. One might expect the emphasis to change with her return to this prominent position in 2007 and subsequent election to the position of single leader in 2008. Figure 5.3 shows that the number of articles in both the *Guardian* and the *Independent* that were focused on internal party politics was higher during her two periods of leadership. Policy-centered articles reached their high point in 2006, when Lucas was not speaker but had established herself as a leader in environmental politics not only in the United Kingdom, but also in the EP. The number of articles she authored also peaked in this interim period.

The articles focusing on the British Greens' internal party politics differ substantially from similar articles in the French press. Among the 171 total articles, many concerned the party's decision to adopt a single-leader model and changes to the party's overall policy agenda. In general, the ar-

TABLE 5.7. British MEPs Compared, 1999–2007

	Lambert	Lucas
Total articles	75	230
Policy	52.0	48.7
	(39)	(112)
European elections	14.7	10.0
	(11)	(23)
Internal party politics	9.3	7.4
	(7)	(17)
Domestic events	2.7	8.3
	(2)	(19)
Authored	37.3	32.6
	(28)	(75)
Letters to the editor (as % of authored)	96.4	69.3
	(27)	(52)

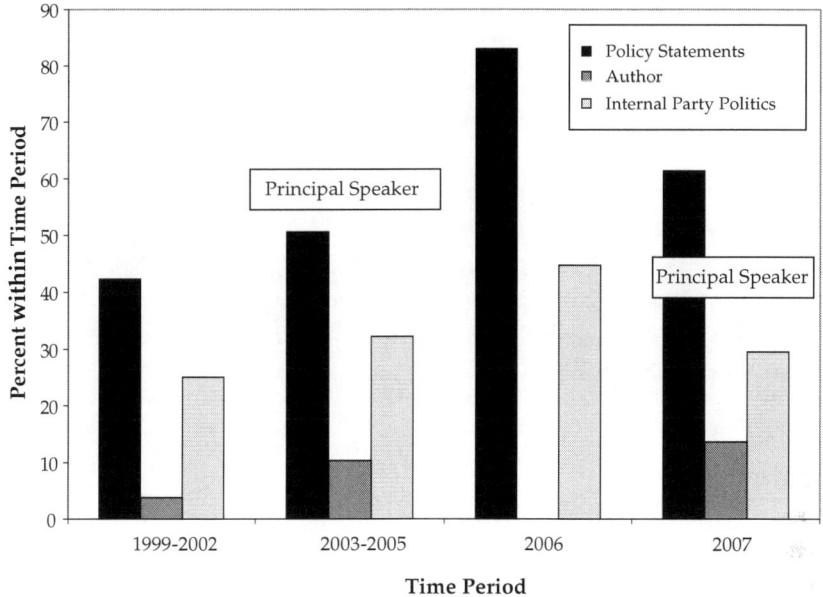

Fig. 5.3. Lucas articles by period. (There were no articles on internal party politics in 2006.)

ticles did not concentrate on intense internal divisions and debates, as did the French articles in this category. This phenomenon may reflect the fact that there are fewer divisions within the party and that the votes to change the leadership structure and policy agenda were fairly unified. Although the overall focus of the articles differed from the focus in the articles about the French Greens, not all British party members agreed with the leadership structure change, as evidenced by an article headlined "Leader Question Dominates Green Conference" that describes the different camps—those who favor a single leader and those who want to retain the cospeaker model (Tempest 2003).

As one of the most prominent party members, Lucas's leadership experience benefits her political resume. Whereas the shift from more policy-dominated coverage to a focus on internal party politics could be problematic for the party if the articles concentrated on divisions and debates, such was not the case for Lucas.

However, one could imagine a different scenario. Because the party leader is the media's source for information about internal party decisions and debates, an increase in this kind of coverage may not bode well for the public's overall perception of the party or of the leader. The result is another possible catch-22 for small parties with a limited pool of potential elites.

Preelection coalitions in France posed a similar conundrum. The only way for the party to gain representation in parliament, given the dominance of the two main parties and the electoral rules, is through PECs. But reliance on these coalitions may prevent the party from gaining representation on its own and succeeding without the help of the Socialists, especially in a plurality system.

DISCUSSION

Two somewhat different patterns of party communication strategies emerge. Whereas the overall coverage of the French Greens can be summarized as mentions and quotations in event-focused articles (many of which party members have created), the British Greens' coverage is self-authored and policy-oriented. Both parties are proactive in seeking media coverage, but they do so in different ways. Important differences also exist between the French MPs' and MEPs' articles. The French MPs garner more policy coverage, but it represents only one-fifth of their articles. The largest category for the MEPs remains domestic events, which underlines the second-order nature of these elected officials.

The differences between French and British coverage may result from the British Greens' precarious position in their country's party system. Lacking national-level representation, the party needs to establish itself as a credible political player and is using the EP to do so. Casual observation also shows that the party concentrates on policy-centered coverage at the local and county levels and through other higher-profile elected officials—mainly its two representatives on the London Assembly, Darren Johnson and Jenny Jones. The French Greens, with their national-level representation, are less dependent on their MEPs as the only way to gain credibility with voters. In sum, whereas the French Greens can use the existence of their MPs to establish credibility, the British Greens need to rely on press coverage to achieve this goal.

The French Greens won seats in the National Assembly only through

PECs. While the British Greens attempted this strategy with Plaid Cymru in 1992 in one constituency in Wales, the alliance fell apart after this election. Alliances with the Socialists have relieved the French Greens of some of the burden of establishing credibility on their own. Therefore, we cannot make a direct comparison between the underlying mechanism that drives the parties' patterns of coverage and media strategies. Although this analysis does not do so, it would be possible to go back to the pre-1997 period in France and analyze coverage of the party's representatives. The French Greens had representation in the EP from 1989 to 1994 but not from 1994 to 1999. This would yield a more direct comparison to the function of the two current British Green MEPs.

The two countries also have different newspaper cultures. While the British press has a tradition of letters to the editor and guest opinion pieces, such articles seem to be less common in the French media. As a result, the number of authored pieces may be much higher for the British Greens than for the French Greens. Wahl-Jorgensen (2007, 46) argues that the development of the letters section of newspapers in England and the United States is a historical construction. Newspaper editorial boards also function as gatekeepers and agenda-setters in choosing which letters to include on their pages (Wahl-Jorgensen 2002). Thus, the British newspapers analyzed may have a longer tradition of letters to the editor as well as editors who are more open to letters from Green politicians.

Contributors to opinion pages are often regular columnists, political insiders, public intellectuals, or celebrities. Ian Mayes, readers editor of the left-leaning *Guardian,* described his paper's Comment and Analysis section as "committed to publishing 'opinions that conflict with government, the majority of the public opinion, and the view of the *Guardian* as a whole'" (quoted in Wahl-Jorgensen 2004, 62). Such a viewpoint may help to explain the number of Lucas's articles featured on these pages, since she is the voice of the Green opposition in the United Kingdom. Furthermore, this approach clarifies why so many of the French Greens' authored articles are guest opinion pieces. But the difference in the number of articles written by the two parties' politicians may come back to national tradition or a difference in the relationship between these small parties and the newspaper editors (or how they perceive the parties). Testing these hypotheses would require the collection of data on letters to the editor and opinion pieces by politicians of all parties, a fruitful topic for future research.

CONCLUSION

While it is difficult to pinpoint a causal explanation for the parties' distinct media strategies and coverage, this analysis suggests three conclusions. First, voters in France and the United Kingdom would have differing perceptions of the parties from reading these four newspapers. Second, the parties use their elected officials in different ways. And third, the parties use the media differently, a strategy driven in part by the parties' positions in their respective party systems and in part by diverse media cultures. Moreover, these different patterns of media use and coverage have important implications for the parties' ability to maximize potential vote share. These media strategies reflect how they are seeking to balance policy differentiation and vote maximization and establish their credibility as parties.

These findings also demonstrate that coverage in the media is yet another balancing act in which the parties must engage. Newspaper coverage can be beneficial, but coverage that focuses on negative debates and divisions may hurt the party more than the coverage helps to boost party credibility. Thus, the parties need to balance their desire for presence in the media with a careful crafting of the message they want to convey to the public. This balancing is intimately connected to parties' efforts to build credibility for future elections.

CHAPTER 6

The Balancing Act Synthesized: Policy, Electoral, and Communication Strategies

Sous le pavé, la plage. (Under the pavement, the beach.)

IN MAY 1968, student activists ripped up cobblestones and hurled them at the Paris police, yelling, "Under the pavement, the beach." These activists and others in France and across Europe wanted to usher in a new era in which the hierarchical top-down relationship between politicians, institutions, and the citizens was upended and reconfigured. Through this slogan, the students conveyed their desire to lift the constraints of post–World War II Europe, which was embodied by a university system that was "bourgeois, authoritarian, and static" (Hitchcock 2003, 248), and replace it with something new, liberating, and different. The green and women's movements grew out of the student revolts, as did the new politics parties of the left. The parties wanted to change how politics was done—who the actors were, how they were organized, and what issues were on the agenda.

These small new politics parties, or niche parties, have undeniably changed European politics over the past four decades. The parties' organizations, electoral goals, ideologies, and priorities have affected "politics as usual." The changes are evident in countries with differing political, party, and electoral systems. Indeed, even the most unlikely of systems—in countries that use restrictive plurality rules—have seen the political landscape changed by these parties. These small new politics parties have persevered, balancing their competing interests of vote maximization and policy differentiation through their policy, electoral, and communication strategies.

I have developed an alternative model of party competition that stresses the importance of both vote maximization and policy differentiation for small-party survival. To survive in restrictive plurality systems, small parties must be proactive dynamic actors making strategic decisions and interacting with other parties. They must balance their competing goals. On the one hand, pursuing a purely vote-driven strategy (Downs 1957) may weaken their policy pursuits, which typically provided the underlying motivation for the formation of these parties. On the other hand, a purely policy-driven strategy (Wittman 1973, 1983) may lead to the parties' disappearance, as they may be too far from the median voter or larger parties may simply adopt the small parties' policies and absorb their potential voters (Kirchheimer 1966; Adams et al. 2006).

In this concluding chapter, I first summarize the study's empirical findings and discuss their implications for the balancing-interests model of party competition. Second, I use these findings to offer some explanations for why the French and British Greens have had differing levels of success using these strategies. Finally, I discuss empirical extensions of this theoretical framework for understanding small-party survival in other contexts.

BALANCING INTERESTS THROUGH THREE STRATEGIES

Policy Strategies

The cross-national test of the balancing thesis in chapter 2 demonstrates how the greens balance their competing interests of policy differentiation and vote maximization. Using both expert survey and manifesto data, I show that an optimal amount of policy differentiation exists between the greens and the large mainstream-left party that will maximize green vote potential. Some policy differentiation is crucial; without it, the parties lose their raison d'être. But when too little or too much differentiation occurs, green party vote share is compromised. The small party faces the challenge of identifying this optimal point and adapting policy preferences to reach it. Moreover, the findings from this cross-national analysis demonstrate that the balancing of preferences is important for small parties in Western Europe, regardless of the electoral system.

Electoral Strategies

Chapters 3 and 4 examine the French and British Greens' different electoral strategies. In the 1997 and 2002 legislative elections, the French Greens entered into preelection coalitions (PECs) with the Socialists in which one party stood down and supported the candidate of the other party in some districts. This strategy resulted in Green representation in the National Assembly (eight members of Parliament [MPs] in 1997 and three in 2002). The threat from both the right and the extreme right predicts the electoral districts in which there is likely to be a PEC. In 2007, the Greens chose not to enter into a national-level PEC with the Socialists, but the Socialists did not run candidates against the Greens' three incumbents. In addition, a local agreement resulted in the election of a fourth Green MP. The decision to not enter into a PEC in 2007 demonstrates both the party's dynamic decision making and how its decisions are affected by political context.

Because PECs are not part of the party toolbox in the United Kingdom, the British Greens have utilized different strategies. Since the mid-1990s, they have had a clear two-level strategy that entails focusing on local elections and targeting specific constituencies in national elections. By concentrating its resources, the party has elected many members to local and county councils and has made major progress toward electing its first MP to Westminster. In 2005, the party won 22 percent in its top constituency and finished third, barely 2 percentage points behind the Conservatives.

Despite their differing strategies, both parties have sought to balance their electoral and policy goals within the constraints of their particular political system. A combination of strategy and political context has led the French Greens to be more electorally successful.

Communication Strategies

Parties can also balance their policy and vote preferences through their communication strategies, as chapter 5 shows. A communication strategy that balances these competing goals can go a long way toward establishing a party's credibility. While newspaper coverage is key, the issues covered and the tone of the articles are also important for voters. The French and British Greens take differing overall approaches to the media. While the French Green MPs and members of the European Parliament (MEPs) tend to create news through extraparliamentary events, such as protests and internal debates, the British Greens' coverage focuses on policy, both domestic and European. Furthermore, whereas France has little tradition of letters to the editor, most of the British MEPs' articles were self-written. Thus, each party has devised its media strategy by carefully considering the media culture in its particular country. Moreover, these strategies balance the parties' desires for a presence in national newspapers with the positive coverage that aids in establishing their credibility and attracting voters.

Through these strategies, small parties have stepped up to face their challenges and have taken a role in determining their own fates, performing a balancing act that has enabled them not only to survive but also to achieve some policy and electoral success. The degree of success small parties achieve, however, will be driven by their continued balancing of votes and policy through their policy, electoral, and communication strategies as well as by how the major parties react—that is, whether (and how) the major parties seek to chip away at, or choose to work with, the small parties.

STRATEGIC DECISIONS, SURVIVAL, AND SUCCESS FOR THE FRENCH AND BRITISH GREENS

Although both the British and French Greens have persevered, the French Greens have arguably had more success—most obviously in terms of electoral victories, particularly in the National Assembly. But the French Greens have also won seats on local and regional councils across the country, and in the 2009 European Parliament election, the party increased its delegation from six to fourteen. The British Greens' delegation, in contrast, remained at two. We also see the French Greens' success in their ability to attract media attention and have articles written about them (as opposed to having party members write the articles), even if journalists are not necessarily portraying the party in the most favorable way.

Much of what explains the differences in the two parties' strategies is exogenous to the parties themselves and is wrapped up in the two countries' political systems. Such factors include party systems, expectations for interparty interactions, and media culture and history. But these exogenous factors also inform the differences that are endogenous to the parties. The parties' willingness to compromise both with other parties and on their core ideals, for example, helps to explain the differing strategies. The British Greens have demonstrated an enduring commitment to "doing politics differently" by not "doing deals" with other parties and only recently moving to a single-leader model of party organization. For the French Greens, retaining their metaideology of *écologie* has been the paramount underlying motivation driving their policy decisions and willingness to work with (or not work with, as was the case in 2007) the Socialists.

IMPLICATIONS FOR SMALL-PARTY SURVIVAL

The results of this book have important implications for understanding small-party survival. While most previous studies have presented a less optimistic prognosis for the survival of small parties, especially in more restrictive electoral systems, my findings offer some hope. By balancing their often-competing goals, these parties can have more control over their fates and not be in a position only to react to existing parties, institutions, and attitudes.

Two important questions remain. First, is there is an optimal level of balancing preferences? Second, if so, how do we know when a party has achieved an optimal balance? Although survival is simply whether a party exists at all, a party's ability to balance its preferences may vary. Furthermore, a party's likelihood for survival is tied to this balancing. Too much policy differentiation, focusing on electing individuals to the national parliament (a goal that might not be attainable), or writing letters to the editor in a media culture that does not support that strategy may lead a small party to falter. The statistical analysis of manifestos and party expert surveys has enabled me to identify an optimal point of policy differentiation as it relates to maximizing vote share. However, for electoral and communication strategies, it is harder to identify a more generalized optimal level of balancing to ensure survival, because balancing is inextricably tied to political context.

We can say, however, that a party has achieved an optimal balance when it has survived. Survival is not based on only one election but is an over-time assessment of a political party's perseverance. Unlike survival, success is a more subjective term. How success is defined can vary across and within parties, across types of strategies, and political contexts. But it may be easier to identify the optimal level of balancing that is required to achieve success once that term is defined. This is a task for future research.

MOVING BEYOND WESTERN EUROPEAN GREEN PARTIES

While the analysis in this book has focused on Western European green parties as one example of an ideologically limited small party, the theoretical framework can also help us to understand small-party survival more generally. Applying the balancing theory to other parties, electoral systems, and countries is crucial for further assessing its generalizability and portability. In this section, I offer four of the many possible avenues for further research.

Party Type and Electoral System in Europe

In chapter 1, I presented an overview of three families of small parties in Western Europe that Meguid (2005, 2008) has identified as niche parties. In addition to green parties, there are far-right and ethnoterritorial or regional parties. Extending my balancing thesis to these two party families is a logical extension of the analysis, though perhaps somewhat challenging. The policy-balancing test would work with the far-right parties, as we could explore policy differentiation between the far-right and mainstream party in a given country. Regional parties may be more problematic, since some regional parties are left-wing (for example, the Party of Wales in the United Kingdom and Esquerra Republicana de Catalunya [Republican Left of Catalonia] in Spain) and others are right-wing (for example, the Italian Lega Nord [Northern League] and the Belgian Vlaams Blok/Belang [Flemish Block/Interest]). Thus, selecting the ideologically closest party from which a regional party is distinguishing its policy preferences and whether it is left, right, or far right will depend on the country. But making overall generalizable conclusions for the entire party family may not be possible for theoretical and empirical reasons. Analyzing the parties' electoral and communication strategies would not present the same challenge.

A second useful extension would be to examine the strategies of other types of small parties not constrained by the niche definition. These parties from across the ideological and party family spectrum have remained small in terms of their political influence, characterized as low numbers of vote and seat share and minimal influence in national governing coalitions. Examples of such parties include the Swedish Kristdemokraterna (Christian Democrats) and French Parti Radical de Gauche (Radical Party of the Left). Conducting similar set of analyses using these parties' strategies would add to the value of the balancing theory.

A third empirical extension of the analysis would explore how different electoral rules affect party strategies and contribute to the likelihood of survival and ultimate success of different types of small parties. My cross-national analysis of policy positions demonstrates that parties that balance their vote and policy preferences have more electoral success, regardless of electoral system. Moving forward, looking more specifically at how variations in electoral rules affect policy, electoral, and communication strategies will be both empirically and theoretically useful for further understanding the survival of small parties and the generalizability of the balancing theory.

Studies have demonstrated that parties behave differently under different electoral rules (for example, Kitschelt 1989; Tsebelis 1990; Lijphart 1994; Cox 1997; Norris 2004; Chhibber and Kollman 1998, 2004; Ezrow 2010). Moreover, electoral rules affect how parties craft their electoral strategies, interact and coordinate with other parties, and position their policy preferences. In her study of radical right party success, Norris (2005a) makes a similar argument. We know, for example, that France's restrictive plurality system has encouraged French parties to enter into PECs with other parties (Schlesinger and Schlesinger 1990, 2000; Tsebelis 1990). A desire to reap the economic benefits that accrue to the largest parties has resulted in parties coordinating across districts in national elections in first-past-the-post systems such as the United States and India (Chhibber and Kollman 1998, 2004).

Although all Western European countries except France and the United Kingdom use some form of a proportional representation (PR) system, important variations exist (among them: thresholds, district magnitudes, and electoral formulas) and might affect party strategy. Thresholds vary from a low of 0.67 percent in the Netherlands to 5 percent in Germany. District magnitudes range from 2 or 3 to 150 in the Netherlands. Various formulas are used, some favoring small parties (largest remainders), while others are more beneficial to larger parties (d'Hondt). Finally, whereas some PR systems are open-list or preferential (Finland, Ireland, Malta), others are closed-list (Spain, Portugal). Table 6.1 highlights some of these differences.

Analyzing party strategies across plurality and PR systems will determine whether balancing is a necessary condition for survival across both broad types of electoral systems as well as within the different types of PR systems and will help to answer several important questions. Have some parties in PR systems with high district magnitudes and low thresholds survived by devoting all of their resources to policy differentiation? Is there a tipping point of a threshold or district magnitude in which balancing between local and national electoral goals becomes more of a necessity for small parties? Finally, do the variations in electoral systems have more of an effect on certain types of balancing strategies or small parties?

Region and State Structure

A fourth instructive extension would be to explore the portability of the balancing theory to explain the survival of small parties in non-European plurality systems. One such extension would be a comparative study of the strategies of the American and Canadian Green parties. Both parties have had relatively little national success but have participated actively in their respective political systems for more than twenty years. In addition, both

TABLE 6.1. Electoral Systems in Western Europe

Country	Electoral System[a]	Average District Magnitude	Threshold (%)	Electoral Formula	Open/ Closed List
Austria	PR	4.26	4.0	LR-Hare	Open
Belgium	PR	7.5	—	d'Hondt	Open
Denmark	PR	7.94	2.0	Mod. St. Laguë	Open
Finland	PR	13.3	—	d'Hondt	Open
France	TRS	1	—	plurality	N.A.
Germany	MMP	1/328	5.0	LR-Hare	Closed
Greece	PR	5.14	3.0	LR-Hare	Open
Iceland	PR	6.25	—	LR-Hare	Closed
Ireland	PR-STV	4.0	—	LR-Droop	Open
Italy	PR	1/155	4.0	LR-Hare	Open
Luxembourg	PR	15	—	LR-Droop	Panachage
Malta	PR-STV	5	—	LR-Droop	N.A.
Netherlands	PR	150	0.7	d'Hondt	Closed
Norway	PR	8.26	4.0	Mod. St. Laguë	Closed
Portugal	PR	11.3	—	d'Hondt	Closed
Spain	PR	6.73	3.0	d'Hondt	Closed
Sweden	PR	10.69	4.0	Mod. St. Laguë	Open
Switzerland	PR	7.7	—	d'Hondt	Panachage
United Kingdom	FPTP	1	—	plurality	N.A.

Source: Farrell 2001; Blais and Massicotte 2002; M. Golder 2005; Norris 2004; Interparliamentary Union; International Institute for Democracy and Electoral Assistance.

Note: N.A. = not applicable.

[a] PR = proportional representation; TRS = two-round system; MMP = mixed-member proportional; PR-STV = single transferable vote; FPTP = first past the post; LR = largest remainder. The average district magnitude is for the lowest tier, except in MMP systems, where the single-member district and PR district magnitudes are both listed. Except for the PR seats in Germany and Italy, the source is M. Golder (2005) and the value is the average magnitude in 2000 for the lowest tier. For the PR seats in Germany and Italy, the sources are Norris 2000 and 2005a. The threshold is the legal threshold. Dashes indicate that there is no legal threshold. The electoral formula is for the lowest tier or the PR seats in the MMP systems. Italy's system from 1994 to 2005 is represented in this table. For the 2006 election, PR was reintroduced. Panachage allows voters to distribute their votes to individual candidates across parties.

the United States and Canada are federal systems, allowing for the study of the parties' strategic behavior at both the provincial/state level and the federal level. The existence of both national and subnational parties not only increases the number of cases for analysis but also functions as an important structural variable in the study of green party survival.

The Green Party of Canada was founded in 1983 and has run candidates in federal elections since 1984. At its founding, it was decentralized and had no single national leader or constitution to which all the provincial parties subscribed. By the 1990s, the party moved to a single national leader and dropped much of "its commitment to grass-roots democracy, consensus, and decentralization" (Sharp and Krajnc 2009, 235). In 2003, Jim Harris was elected party leader with a vision of the Greens as a professional party, running candidates in all ridings, or constituencies, and winning seats. To achieve these goals, he undertook a large fund-raising campaign, hired staff members with specific skill sets, rented permanent office space, and developed a professional Web site. In the 2004 election, the Greens became only the fourth federal party to run candidates in all 308 ridings. It ran 308 candidates again in the 2006 elections and 303 in 2008. The party's vote share has steadily increased over the past three elections, as figure 6.1 shows. The Greens reached their electoral peak in 2008, when they received 6.78 percent of the vote nationally. Following the 2004 election, the party crossed the 2 percent threshold for federal funding eligibility.[1]

Although election to the national parliament has thus far eluded the Canadian Greens, independent MP Blair Wilson joined the Green Party in August 2008. Just two months later, however, he was defeated in the October 2008 elections, before he had the opportunity to officially sit as a Green MP (Stueck 2008). In 2008, the party's current leader, Elizabeth May, won 32 percent of the vote in her Nova Scotia constituency, the highest vote share ever received by a Green Party candidate, although she still trailed the winner by 14 percent. The party's greatest federal electoral success to date may have occurred in 2006, when May won 26 percent of the vote in a by-election in London North-Centre, just 9 percentage points behind the Conservative candidate (Green Party of Canada; Elections Canada).

The Canadian Greens are making some progress at the provincial and local levels of government as well. Although the party has yet to achieve representation in provincial parliaments, Green parties are active in eight of Canada's ten provinces. The Green parties of Ontario and British Columbia have been the most successful. In British Columbia, the party has won an average of 10 percent of the vote in recent provincial elections

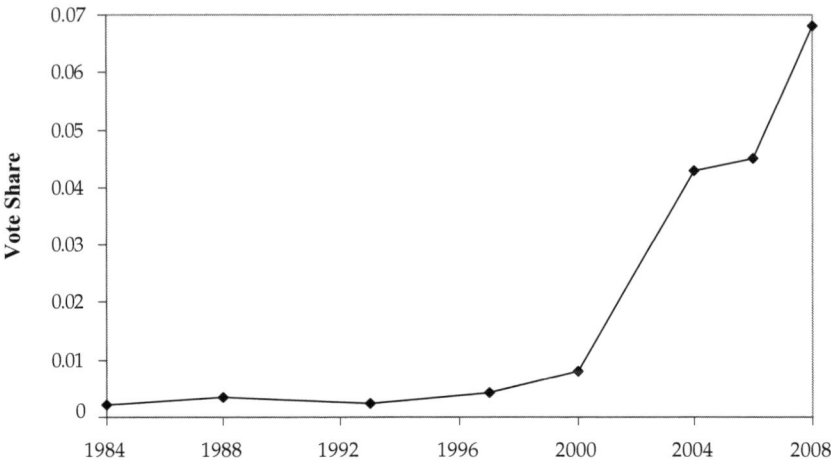

Fig. 6.1. Electoral history of Green Party of Canada. (Data from Center on Democratic Performance; Adam Carr's Election Archive.)

(Sharp and Krajnc 2009, 225). At the local level, most of the Greens' success has also been in British Columbia. The party elected its first city councillor in Vancouver in 1999, and a handful of Greens currently hold local offices in British Columbia, including the mayor of Whistler (Green Party of British Columbia).

The Green Party of Canada has begun to engage in electoral deals with other parties at the national level.[2] In 2008, in an effort to defeat the Conservative candidate, the Greens and the leader of the Liberal Party, Stéphane Dion, who was elected party leader on a proenvironmental platform, entered into a PEC in the district of Central Nova, where Green Party leader May was the candidate. May also approached the New Democratic Party leader, Jack Layton, about a similar arrangement, but he was not interested. The Liberals did not run a candidate against May; in exchange, the Greens did not run a candidate against Dion, though his riding was a safe Liberal seat. In the end, the Conservative candidate won in Central Nova with 46 percent of the vote (Taber 2007; Argell 2008). During the subsequent negotiations regarding the formation of a governing coalition, Dion left open the possibility that if he were to become prime minister, he would appoint May to the Senate, giving her the Greens' first seat. In the end,

Conservative Stephen Harper became prime minister, and he filled all of the open Senate seats with Conservatives (Curry 2008a, b).

In sum, the Canadian Green Party's history, development, and relationship with other parties mirror the experiences of both the French and British Greens. The Canadian Greens are now a more professional organization with electoral goals, but they are also very committed to their ideological agenda. An in-depth analysis of the strategic choices and behavior of the party at both the federal and provincial levels will be an illuminating application and test of the balancing thesis.

The U.S. Green Party was founded in 1984 as the Green Committees of Correspondence. It was a decentralized, grassroots organization run by volunteers. Over the next few years, the organization developed into the Greens and eventually the Greens/Green Party USA (G/GPUSA). The party ran only a handful of candidates through the 1980s—for example, three in 1985, four in 1986, and eight in 1987. By 1990, the Greens ran twenty-one candidates for various offices. In 1986, the Greens won their first elections in two county board of supervisors races in Wisconsin. These individuals, along with other Greens elected in the earlier years, however, won in nonpartisan elections, and the Green Party label did not appear on the ballot (Berg 2009, 247). The party first ran candidates for state senate in 1988, governor and U.S. House in 1990, state house and U.S. Senate in 1992, and president in 1996 (Green Party of the United States).

The majority of the Greens' success has been at the local level; however, three Greens have won election at the state level. In a 1999 special election to the California State Assembly, Audie Bock became the first Green elected at the state level, but she switched her registration to independent seven months later and lost in the 2000 election (Sanchez 1999). John Eder was elected to the Maine House of Representatives in 2002 and served two terms before his defeat in 2006 (Green Party of the United States). Finally, Richard Carroll was elected to the Arkansas House of Representatives as a Green in 2008 but switched to the Democratic Party five months after his election (Lyon 2009).

As in the British Green Party, the U.S. Greens experienced a great deal of internal debate by the 1990s: some party members were committed to running candidates at all levels of government, while others wanted to focus on the party's core ideological principles through grassroots, nonelectoral activities. The election-focused Greens split from the G/GPUSA and formed the Association of State Green Parties (ASGP) in 1992. The ASGP was behind Ralph Nader's 1996 presidential candidacy. In 2001, the ASGP renamed itself the Green Party of the United States (GPUS), and even though the G/GPUSA party continues to function, the GPUS is now the primary U.S. Green party. While it remains a federation of state parties, the GPUS has a small national structure, with a coordinating committee of state representatives, a steering committee, and a small number of paid staff (Berg 2009, 250).

Table 6.2 presents the Greens' experiences in U.S. presidential elections from 1996 to 2008. In 1996, Nader and his running mate, Winona LaDuke, were on the ballot in twenty-two states and won 0.7 percent of the vote nationally. In 2000, the high point of the Greens' success to date, the party received more than 2.7 percent of the vote in the forty-four states where Nader appeared on the ballot. In a handful of states, including Massachusetts, Rhode Island, and Vermont, Nader's results topped 6 percent, and he peaked with 10.1 percent of the vote in Alaska. In 2004, the Green-nominated ticket of David Cobb and Pat LaMarche won only 0.1 percent of the vote; Nader ran as an independent and won 0.4 percent. The Greens have not recovered electorally from the 2004 split, and the party's 2008 nominee received only 0.1 percent of the vote.

Small U.S. parties, like the Greens, arguably have some of the biggest challenges to surmount. Like most third parties in U.S. history, the Greens have to overcome the hurdle of the two-party tradition, restrictive ballot access laws, party financing, and the co-optation of their issues by the major parties (Rosenstone, Behr, and Lazarus 1996; Meguid 2008; Berg 2009). However, even with these hurdles, the Greens have had some success at the local and state levels. The party has evolved into an electorally focused

TABLE 6.2. Green Party Results in U.S. Presidential Elections

Year	Presidential/Vice-Presidential Candidate	States on Ballot[a]	Votes	Vote Share (%)
1996	Nader/LaDuke	22	685,128	0.71
2000	Nader/LaDuke	44	2,882,955	2.74
2004	Cobb/LaMarche	28	119,859	0.10
2008	McKinney/Clemente	32	161,797	0.12

Source: Federal Election Commission.
[a]Includes District of Columbia.

party, working to win elections, keep its elected officials in the party, and preserve its ideological distinction. Studying its strategic behavior and decisions, especially at the local and state levels, will be a crucial test of the balancing thesis. The United States may well be the most unlikely system in which to see the survival of a small party, but since the Greens' development into an electoral party in the 1990s, they have demonstrated their perseverance as more than a leader-driven presidential party, like many other third parties in U.S. history (Rosenstone, Behr, and Lazarus 1996). Moreover, if the balancing thesis holds in the "critical case" (Eckstein 1975) of the U.S. Green Party, then it demonstrates the model's theoretical portability.

CONCLUSION

This book is an important first step in understanding small-party behavior. It has offered a new model of party competition to explain small-party survival. This model gives small parties the agency they have lacked in previous empirical and theoretical studies. Only through the strategic balancing of preferences have the parties persevered despite adverse electoral conditions. These findings have significant practical and theoretical implications not only for small parties (as they develop strategies) but also for researchers seeking to understand party competition more generally and small-party survival in particular. How survival translates into success remains an open question, however. Both future research and further small-party experiences will enable us to determine the relationship between balancing preferences and ultimate success (however defined) in the policy, electoral, and communication spheres.

APPENDIX A

Cross-National Policy Dimensions

The following are the issue dimensions used from the Laver and Hunt 1992 and Benoit and Laver 2006 data:

Environment: 1 = supports protection of the environment even at the cost of economic growth; 20 = supports economic growth, even at the cost of damage to the environment.

Decentralization: 1 = promotes decentralization of all administrative and decision-making functions; 20 = opposes any decentralization of administrative and decision-making functions.

EU Authority: 1 = favors increasing the range of areas in which the EU can set policy; 20 = favors reducing the range of areas in which the EU can set policy. For Ireland, the question is about strengthening the EU; for France, the question refers to an expanded and stronger EU (only Benoit and Laver 2006).

The following are the issue dimensions used from the Budge et al. 2001 and Klingemann et al. 2006 data:

Per 108—European Integration: Positive, which includes "favourable mention of European integration in general; desirability of expanding the European Union and/or of increasing its competence; desirability of . . . joining (or remaining a member)" (Klingemann et al. 2006, 154).

Per 301—Decentralization: Positive, which includes "support for federalism or devolution; more regional autonomy for policy or economy; support for keeping up local and regional customs and symbols; favourable mention of special consideration for local areas" (155).

Per 416—Anti-Growth Economy: Positive, which includes "favourable mention of anti-growth politics and steady-state economy; ecologism/'Green Politics' especially as applied to economic policy; sustainable development" (157).

Per 501—Environmental Protection: Positive, which includes "preservation of countryside, forests, etc.; general preservation of natural resources against selfish interests; proper use of national parks ... environmental improvement. 'Ecologism'/'Green' politics as applied to environmental policy" (157).

Per 503—Social Justice: Positive, which includes "concept of equality; need for fair treatment of all people; special protection for underprivileged; need for fair distribution of resources; removal of class barriers; end to discrimination on the grounds of race, sex, gender, disability, age, sexual orientation, etc." (158).

Because of potential seepage in the coding of the multiculturalism dimension (Benoit, Laver, and Mikhaylov 2007, 13), I combine the following three dimensions for the multiculturalism measure, following the suggestion offered by Klingemann et al. 2006, 115.

Per 607—Multiculturalism: Positive, which includes "favourable mention of cultural diversity, communalism, cultural plurality and pillarization; preservation of autonomy of religious, linguistic heritages within a country including special educational provisions" (Klingemann et al. 2006, 159).

Per 705—Underprivileged Minority Groups: Positive, which includes "favourable reference to underprivileged minorities who are defined neither in economic nor in demographic terms, e.g. the handicapped, homosexuals, immigrants, etc." (159).

Per 706—Non-Economic Demographic Groups: Positive, which includes "favourable mention of, or need for, assistance to women, the elderly, young people, linguistic groups, etc; special interest groups of all kinds" (159).

TABLE A.1. Green and Socialist Parties in Party Dyad Analysis

Country	Green Party	Socialist Party	Data Set/Years
Austria	Die Grünen/Die Grüne Alternative	Sozialdemokratische Partei Österreichs (SPO)	CMP (1986–2002), LH, BL
Belgium (Wallonia)	Ecolo	Parti Socialiste (PS)	CMP (1981–2003), LH, BL
Belgium (Flanders)	AGALEV	Socialistische Partij (SP)	CMP (1981–99), LH, BL
Denmark	De Grønne	Socialdemokraterne (SD)	LH
Denmark	De Grønne	Socialistisk Folkeparti (SF)	LH
Finland	Vihreä Liitto	Suomen Sosialidemokraattinen Puolue (SDP)	CMP (1986–2003), LH, BL
France	Les Verts	Parti Socialiste (PS)	CMP (1993–2002), LH, BL
Germany	Bündnis 90/Die Grünen	Sozialdemokratische Partei Deutschlands (SPD)	CMP (1983–2002), LH, BL
Iceland	Vinstrihreyfingin-grænt framboð	Samfylkingin	CMP (1999–2003), BL
Ireland	Green Party/Comhaontas Glas	Labour Party/Páirtí an Lucht Oibre	CMP (1989–2002), BL
Italy	Federazione dei Verdi	Partito Socialista Italiano (PSI)	CMP (1987), LH
Italy	Federazione dei Verdi	Partito Democratico della Sinistra (PDS)	CMP (1992–96)
Italy	Il Girasole	Democratici di Sinistra (DS)	CMP (2001), BL
Luxembourg	Déi Gréng	Lëtzebuerger Sozialistesch Arbechterparte (LSAP)	CMP (1984, 1994, 1999), LH, BL
Luxembourg	Gréng Lëscht Ekologesch Initiativ (GLEI)	Lëtzebuerger Sozialistesch Arbechterparte (LSAP)	CMP (1989)
Luxembourg	Gréng Alternativ Partei (GAP)	Lëtzebuerger Sozialistesch Arbechterparte (LSAP)	CMP (1989)
Netherlands	GroenLinks	Partij van de Arbeid (PvdA)	CMP (1989–2003), BL
Netherlands	GroenLinks	Socialistische Partij (SP)	CMP (1994–2003), BL
Portugal	Partido Ecologista "Os Verdes"	Partido Socialista (PS)	CMP (1983–87), LH, BL
Sweden	Miljöpartiet de Gröna	Sveriges Socialdemokratiska Arbetareparti (SAP)	CMP (1988–2002), LH, BL
Switzerland	Grüne Partei der Schweiz	Sozialdemokratische Partei der Schweiz (SP)	CMP (1979–2003), BL

Note: CMP = Comparative Manifestos Project (Budge et al. 2001; Klingemann et al. 2006); LH = Laver and Hunt 1992; BL = Benoit and Laver 2006.

TABLE A.2. Additional Socialist/Social Democratic Parties

Country	Socialist Party	Data Set/Year
Denmark	Socialdemokraterne (SD)	CMP (1979–2001), BL
Denmark	Socialistisk Folkeparti (SF)	CMP (1990–2001), BL
Greece	Panellinio Sosialistikó Kínima (PASOK)	CMP (1981–2000), LH, BL
Iceland	Alþýðuflokkurinn	CMP (1979–95), LH
Ireland	Labour Party/ Páirtí an Lucht Oibre	CMP (1981–87), LH
Malta	Partit Laburista	CMP (1996–98), LH, BL
Netherlands	Partij van de Arbeid (PvdA)	CMP (1981–86), LH
Norway	Det Norske Arbeiderparti (DNA)	CMP (1981–2001), LH, BL
Spain	Partido Socialista Obrero Español (PsoE)	CMP (1979–2000), LH
United Kingdom	Labour Party	CMP (1979–2005), LH, BL

Note: Additional parties included in tables 2.1 and 2.3. These are socialist/social democratic parties in countries without a green party, where the green party is not in the data set, or before the green party formed/was included in the data set.

APPENDIX B

Multinomial Logit versus Nested Logit for Type of Alliance Analysis

Before choosing multinomial logit (MNL), I also considered using nested logit (NL) and multinomial probit (MNP). I chose MNL for theoretical reasons. NL implies that the two decisions—whether the district will be included in the PEC between the Greens or Socialists and, if yes, whether the candidate will be a Green or a Socialist—are independent of each other. Although this may be the ideal decision-making process and may occur in some districts, I am not confident that such a methodical two-part decision is made when deciding the strategy for each district. Politics gets in the way at times, and the decisions can become muddled. In addition, although factors may influence whether a Green or Socialist candidate is selected after a district is chosen for the PEC, these factors may also influence whether the district is chosen as part of the national alliance. In using MNL, I am claiming that the parties make one decision about which strategy to use—no alliance, Green alliance, or Socialist alliance. If the parties are making this decision, it does not violate the Independence of Irrelevant Alternatives (IIA) assumption. However, dependence exists across districts, in that choosing one strategy in a given district affects which strategy will be chosen in subsequent districts. If IIA were violated in this scenario, then a Green alliance versus a Socialist alliance would be informed by no alliance. If the decision was among districts, then the inclusion of District 1 rather than District 2 in the PEC would be informed by the decision about what to do with District 3, and so forth. In this scenario, IIA is violated. If IIA is violated, then MNP needs to be used. I posit that the decision occurs among strategies, not districts, so IIA is not violated; MNP therefore does not need to be used.

TABLE B.1. Descriptive Statistics for Models Predicting Alliance

Variable	N	Mean	Min	Max	S.D.
02Alliance	555	0.30	0	1	0.46
97Alliance	555	0.19	0	1	0.40
99European (%)	555	0.10	0.03	0.23	0.03
Mamère (%)	555	0.05	0.02	0.11	0.01
Right (%)	555	0.36	0.11	0.72	0.09
FN97 (%)	555	0.15	0	0.35	0.06
Le Pen (%)	555	0.17	0.07	0.30	0.05
Min. BAC+2 (%)	555	0.15	0.06	0.49	0.08
Unemployment (%)	555	0.13	0.06	0.37	0.04
20–39 (%)	555	0.28	0.17	0.45	0.04
Immigrants (%)	555	0.02	0.00	0.13	0.02
Left incumbent	555	0.56	0	1	0.50

TABLE B.2. Description of Variables for Models Predicting Alliance

Variable Name	Variable Description
02Alliance	2002 alliance in district
97Alliance	1997 alliance in district
99European	vote share of Cohn-Bendit (Verts) list in 1999 European elections by legislative district
Mamère	vote share of Mamère in 2002 presidential election by legislative district
Right	combined vote share of all right candidates (UDF, UDF-Diss, RPR, RPR-Diss, DVD/UPF, and LDI) in first round of 1997 legislative election
FN97	FN vote share in first round of 1997 legislative elections
Le Pen	vote share of Le Pen in 2002 presidential election by legislative district
Min. BAC+2	percentage of those with a minimum of BAC+2 in district
Unemployment	rate of unemployment in a given district
20–39	percentage of those ages 20–39 in district
Immigrants	percentage of those of Magrebin or Turkish nationality in district
Left incumbent	left incumbent in district

APPENDIX C

TABLE C.1. Descriptive Statistics for Models Predicting Green Candidate

Variable	N	Mean	Min	Max	S.D.
05 Green candidate	566	0.32	0	1	0.47
01 Green vote share	566	0.68	0	0.09	0.01
01 Labour vote share	566	0.43	0.06	0.78	0.17
01 Lib Dem vote share	565	0.18	0.05	0.60	0.11
01 Conservative vote share	566	0.33	0.05	0.59	0.12
Majority (%)	565	0.23	0.01	0.69	0.15
Renters (%)	564	0.31	0.11	0.77	0.11
Public transport (%)	564	0.14	0.01	0.60	0.13
Students (%)	531	0.07	0.04	0.27	0.04
Professionals (%)	531	0.05	0.01	0.15	0.02
Nonwhite (%)	564	0.08	0.01	0.66	0.12

TABLE C.2. Description of Variables for Models Predicting Green Candidate

Variable Name	Variable Description
05 Green Candidate	Green candidate in 2005
01 Green vote share	2001 Green vote share
01 Labour vote share	2001 Labour vote share
01 Lib Dem vote share	2001 Lib Dem vote share
01 Conservative vote share	2001 Conservative vote share
Majority (%)	percentage of winning candidate's majority
Renters (%)	percentage of renters
Public transport (%)	percentage of public-transport users
Students (%)	percentage of students
Professionals (%)	percentage of white-collar professionals
Nonwhite (%)	percentage of nonwhite residents

Notes

Chapter 1

1. British People is not to be confused with the far-right British People's Party, the most recent incarnation of which was founded in 2005.
2. Volatility is measured by the Pedersen Index (Pedersen 1979), which is the sum of the percentage vote gains/losses of all the parties from one election to the next divided by the number of parties.
3. The Austrian Greens' highest vote share was 11.05 percent in 2006, which resulted in twenty-one seats; the French FN's highest vote share was 11.34 percent in the 2002 legislative elections, which translated into zero seats (under proportional representation, it won 9.65 percent of the vote and thirty-five seats in 1986); Flemish Block/Interest's highest vote share was 11.99 percent in 2007, which resulted in seventeen seats; and the Finnish Greens' highest vote share was 8.5 percent in 2007, which gave the party fifteen seats.
4. The British Liberal Democrats are characterized as a small party only when considering seat share as a consequence of the first-past-the-post electoral system and the geographic concentration of its vote share.
5. Outside of Europe, studies have demonstrated that small parties also have more success in PR systems. Van Cott (2005) and Rice and Van Cott (2006), for example, find that indigenous parties in Latin America have been more successful in more permissive electoral systems. Similarly, in a cross-national study of electoral systems and democratization, Birch (2005) finds that if the party system is weak or highly decentralized, single-member districts can lead to the dominance of one large party.
6. This is a useful way of thinking about how rules can help small parties to succeed, though it is often discussed in the literature in terms of explaining new party formation (see Rüdig 1990; Hug 2001).
7. For further analysis of how the larger British parties' strategies undermined the Green Party, see Meguid 2008.
8. Since 1960, only the 1992 presidential debates included a third-party candidate, independent H. Ross Perot. In 1980, the FEC included independent John Anderson in the scheduled debates. However, because of disagreements over

Anderson's inclusion, the first debate took place between Republican Ronald Reagan and Anderson, while the second debate included Democrat Jimmy Carter and Reagan.

9. In their analysis of the underlying causes of political participation, Rosenstone and Hansen (1993, 139–40) refer to this turnover as the generational hypothesis. They hypothesize that differences across age groups are related to the differing socialization experiences of each generation.

10. I use the term *vote maximization* as a catchall term for all behavior that is vote- or seat-seeking.

11. Whereas Van Cott (2005, 18) defines a successful party as one that "meets the criteria of electoral viability and regularly elects its candidates to national office," Hug (2001, 65) suggests that the degree of success a party expects is related to the explanation for its emergence.

12. For further discussion of selecting on the dependent variable under conditions of necessity and sufficiency, see Geddes 1990; Dion 1998.

13. France and the United Kingdom have other small parties that fit into Meguid's (2008) classification of niche parties that have contested multiple national elections. These party pairs are the British National Front, the British National Party and the French National Front, and the Scottish National Party; Plaid Cymru (Party of Wales), the Union Démocratique Bretonne (Breton Democratic Union), and the U Partitu di a Nazione Corsa (Party of the Corsican Nation). Although data availability may make studying these parties more difficult, these comparisons would offer further observations about how small parties balance competing interests.

14. The parties that consolidated to form the Greens included Ecologie '78 (Ecology '78), Ecologie Aujourd'hui (Ecology Today), Confédération Ecologiste (Ecologist Confederation), and the Parti Ecologiste (Ecologist Party).

15. One of the Greens' incumbent deputies, Martine Billard, switched to the Parti de Gauche (Left Party) in July 2009.

16. Elections to the French presidency use a two-round system. Only the top two finishers in the first round qualify for the second round. This differs from the legislative elections, in which all candidates who receive at least 12.5 percent of the vote in the first round advance to the second round. In both elections, a candidate who wins a majority in the first round is declared the winner.

17. French senators are indirectly elected by an electoral college from each of the ninety-six departments that includes members of the National Assembly, department and regional councillors, mayors, and city councillors (http://www.senat.fr/lng/en/election_senateurs.html [accessed 15 July 2009]). Elections to the European Parliament use a PR system.

18. The party changed its name from People to the Ecology Party in 1975, to the Green Party in 1985, and finally to the Green Party of England and Wales in 1990, after the Scottish Greens left to form an independent party.

19. The first Green city councillor in the United Kingdom was John Marjoram, who was elected in 1986 from Stroud.

20. Information from author interviews with Peter Cranie, National Elections Coordinator, and Chris Rose, National Election Agent, conducted 23 and 26 June 2006, respectively, in London.

Chapter 2

1. A similar test would compare the positions of far-right parties with those of the largest mainstream center-right party. Testing the thesis on ethnoterritorial or regional parties would be more difficult because there is not necessarily a clear mainstream party family with which these parties are closest and to which they would lose voters. In some countries, the mainstream party might be a socialist party, while in others, it might be a right or far-right party.

2. Volkens's (2007) article is part of a special issue of *Electoral Studies* in which the contributors address the debates surrounding the use of the party manifestos and the expert survey methods, specifically in coding parties on the left-right dimension.

3. Although two additional expert surveys have been conducted (Castles and Mair 1984; Huber and Inglehart 1995), they only ask experts to place the parties on the left-right dimension and do not ask for issue-specific placements.

4. The environment and energy group of issues covers a range of policies, including the reduction of greenhouse gas emissions, development of renewable energy, promotion of sustainability, institution of ecotaxes, and protection of nature and biodiversity.

5. Germany uses a mixed system that incorporates both plurality and PR. Except for 1994–2006, in which it used a system similar to Germany's, Italy had a PR system throughout the period under analysis. Ireland and Malta use PR–single transferable vote.

6. Laver and Hunt (1992) did not ask experts a question on the European Community.

7. Benoit, Laver, and Mikhaylov's (2009, 503) correction is based on the assumption that "there are many different possible texts that could have been written to communicate the same underlying policy position." Thus, re-creating the stochastic process that resulted in each manifesto will correct for errors in the point estimates. Klingemann et al. (2006, xvi), however, firmly believe that each manifesto is "the only authoritative policy statement approved by an official convention or congress." Consequently, Budge (n.d.) questions the underlying assumption of Benoit, Laver, and Mikhaylov's correction.

8. Several alternative explanations for the greens' increasing vote share exist. The political context could have changed, making the greens' issues more acceptable to voters over time. (For further discussion of the growing influence of postmaterialism in European politics, see see Inglehart 1997; Dalton 2008.) It is also possible that as the greens have evolved as a party, they have become more successful at campaigning and conveying their message to voters. However, both of these factors could be considered endogenous to the parties' deci-

sions to shift their policies and thus are difficult to disentangle and consider as separate explanations for increasing green vote share. This analysis seeks to highlight the relationship between policy differentiation and vote maximization.

9. As a robustness check, I replicated my analysis of the 1990–2003 period using Benoit, Laver, and Mikhaylov's (2009) SIMEX correction for the CMP data. The bootstrapped estimates flattened out the curves, and while they showed some support for H2.2, they did not support H2.3, the balancing thesis. One of the reasons the corrected data did not confirm my expectations may be because of the small N. The new estimates greatly reduce the variation among observations, which has a more pronounced effect on small data sets. In addition, the uncertainty estimates can have more of an effect on single policies or scales based on a few policy categories, such as the green agenda scale, which includes eight issue dimensions.

Chapter 3

Parts of this chapter draw from two previously published articles in *French Politics* and *Party Politics*. The opening quotation is from the author's interview with Mamère, 3 June 2003, in Paris.

1. Since 1976, a candidate must receive 12.5 percent of the vote based on the number of registered voters. Because of declining voter turnout rates, candidates in some districts must receive as much as 17 percent of votes cast to move to the second round.

2. ENPP = $1/\Sigma s_i^2$, where s is the seat share of each party, i.

3. In the 1986 legislative elections, the FN won thirty-five seats because of a onetime switch to a proportional representation system based on department lists (Cole and Campbell 1989, 133–43).

4. The Communists' vote and seat share has been declining since the early 1990s. In 2007, the PCF won 4.6 percent of the first-round vote and fifteen seats, a decrease of six seats from 2002 and twenty-two seats from 1997.

5. Both S. N. Golder (2006a, 2006b) and Blais and Indridason (2007) consider the underlying logic of preelection alliance formation in detail.

6. Metropolitan France is distinguished from France's overseas departments and territories, which also elect members to the National Assembly. Since 1988, the Parliament has had 577 members, each representing a single-member district. A total of 555 districts are in metropolitan France and Corsica, while 22 are in France's overseas departments (Guadeloupe, Martinique, Réunion, and French Guyana) and territories (Mayotte [whose citizens voted in favor of transitioning to an overseas department in a 2009 referendum], New Caledonia, French Polynesia, St. Pierre and Miquelon, Wallis and Futuna, St. Martin, and St. Barthélemy). Citizens of St. Martin and St. Barthélemy voted to secede from Guadeloupe in 2003 and were granted territory status by the French Parliament in 2007. They are represented in the National Assembly by one of Guadeloupe's

deputies. Under the 1998 Noumea Accord, New Caledonians will vote on independence sometime between 2014 and 2019. Unless otherwise specified, all discussions of national election results refer only to metropolitan France.

7. A PEC has both short-term and longer-term outcomes. Through the PEC, the Greens can elect representatives to the National Assembly in the short term. Having deputies gives the Greens credibility as a party, so that in the long term, they may be able to elect deputies without PECs. However, from this longer-term perspective, FN success in the short term might be beneficial for the Greens if enough FN deputies were elected to form a parliamentary group that swung environmental policy so far to the right that voters would become frustrated and vote for the Greens in the next election. But this scenario assumes that the FN would win enough seats to impact policy and that voters both care enough about the environment as an issue and would vote for a small party such as the Greens (rather than for the Socialists) in the following election. Given the uncertainty of this set of outcomes, the Greens focus on the more short-term goal of minimizing the FN's electoral success.

8. Under slightly different electoral rules, in which only the top two candidates advance to the second round, the left's vote share was split among nine parties in the first round of the 2002 presidential elections. This resulted in a third-place finish for the Socialist candidate, Lionel Jospin, and a second-round contest between the right and the extreme right.

9. The Greens have also chosen to enter into alliances with the Socialists for local elections in some municipalities. These alliances often include joint manifestos. Even though the electoral system in municipalities with at least thirty-five hundred inhabitants is a two-round proportional representation system, the Greens have run joint lists with the Socialists as a way of maximizing vote share. In the 2001 municipal elections, the Greens ran an independent list in the first round and then joined with the Socialists in the second round in some municipalities; while in others, it ran on a joint list with other parties on the left from the first round. In 2008, it ran autonomous lists from the first round in all cities with more than fifty thousand inhabitants. Under election rules, parties or lists that obtain at least 5 percent of the vote in the first round can join with another party and present a unified list in the second round. A party may move to the second round on its own if it receives at least 10 percent of the first-round vote. Municipalities with fewer than thirty-five hundred residents use a system similar to that of the legislative elections to elect their city councillors, thus making PECs among the parties on the left and right even more likely (Martin 1994, 111–14; France, Interior Ministry 2001; personal intervew with Green's 2007 election coordinator, Michel Boch, 19 June 2007, in Paris).

10. Interview with MP Billard, 20 May 2003, in Paris.

11. Although France does not have a traditional parliamentary government in which the party that receives the largest number of seats must craft a governing coalition and government, the literature often talks about the French government as a coalition if more than one party holds ministerial posts, as was

the case under Jospin's PS government (1997–2002), which had a Green minister of the environment.

12. In the National Assembly, each deputy has a *suppléant* (alternate). The *suppléant* is elected simultaneously with the deputy and replaces him/her if s/he is appointed to the government or Constitutional Council, remains on a temporary mission for the government for longer than six months, or dies (W. Andrews 1962, 275–76). Typically, the *suppléant* is from the same party as the candidate for deputy. However, in Green-Socialist alliance districts, each candidate-*suppléant* pair contains a representative from each party. In Green-led districts, the *suppléants* are typically prominent Socialist politicians (city councillor, mayor, and so forth). As the ballot in figure 3.1 shows, Pierre Aidenbaum, a Socialist mayor in Paris, was the Green candidate's *suppléant* in this alliance district.

13. In 2002, in seven districts, the alliances included the Greens, Socialists, Communists, and Radicals, commonly known as the *gauche plurielle* (plural left). In two districts, the Greens entered into an alliance only with the Communists. In these nine districts, the other leftist parties supported the Green candidate. My analysis uses only the districts in which both the Greens and the Socialists were part of the alliance.

14. Information on the alliance decision-making process is from interviews with Serge Malloreau, 2002 Greens' election coordinator, conducted in Paris, 1 October 2002 and 23 June 2003, and Jean-Luc Bennahmias, chief negotiator for the Greens in 1997, conducted 6 June 2003 in Paris. Election results are from Centre d'Informatisation 2007a.

15. I am interested in the effect of a 1997 alliance on a 2002 alliance. The variable that measures the strength of the mainstream right includes the vote shares for candidates who ran with the RPR, UDF, or Divers Droite (Miscellaneous Right) labels as well as those who were dissident candidates of the RPR and UDF. The variable was constructed in this manner because from the perspective of a left voter, a candidate or representative from any of these parties or affiliations is less preferred than one on the left.

16. In the French census, nationality is often understood more broadly as citizenship. A respondent can check one of three categories: (1) native-born French; (2) naturalized French; or (3) foreign. Those who claim foreign nationality thus are not French citizens and are immigrants. Respondents are also asked their place of birth. The available census data do not break out by country the birthplace of those who have emigrated to France. The measure I use therefore groups only immigrants from the Maghreb and Turkey and not those who are naturalized citizens of Magrebin origin, for example (Institut National 2002). Under President Sarkozy, there has been an effort to start collecting data on ethnicity and nationality. In 2009, following a speech in which Sarkozy argued for the need for tools to measure diversity, a government commission was established to determine the best way to collect information on ethnic origin ("To Count or Not to Count," 2009).

17. The correlations between the vote share of the FN candidate in the 1997

legislative election and the percentage of the population who are immigrants and the percentage who are unemployed are 0.53 and 0.38, respectively. All correlations are significant at the 0.01 level.

18. Long and Freese's (2003) postestimation commands were used for the multivariate analysis.

19. The pseudo R^2 for all four models is fairly low because the majority of values for the dependent variable are 0 (387 of 555). However, of the four models, the pseudo R^2 is slightly higher for Model 1.

20. A Wald test shows that all four of the independent variables are distinct from 0 at the 0.01 significance level.

21. Alliances existed in only six districts in which Le Pen's vote share was less than 10 percent.

22. The standard deviations of three variables are as follows: Le Pen, 0.05; Right, 0.09; Mamère, 0.01.

23. This result could be related to the part of the population this variable captures. As discussed earlier, it includes only those individuals who are noncitizens, not naturalized or native-born French citizens from North Africa or Turkey. If these other groups were included, the numbers would be much greater and might have a more significant effect on the probability of an alliance as an even stronger proxy for Le Pen support. These naturalized citizens of Magrebin decent may also represent a strong countervote for Le Pen, which may decrease the probability of an alliance. The data do not permit me to determine which explanation is accurate.

24. An interaction of the age and education variables is also not significant. Thus, a district with a high percentage of both young and highly educated voters does not predict an alliance.

25. See appendix B for further discussion of the choice of MNL.

26. For a further discussion of how to interpret MNL, see Maddala 1983; Liao 1994.

27. Wald tests for the model show that I cannot reject the null hypothesis that education is not equal to 0 and that unemployment is distinct from 0 only at the 0.1 level. I can, however, reject the null hypothesis that left incumbent is equal to 0 at the 0.01 level of significance.

28. This analysis does not consider several other possible explanatory variables, including the role of local politicians, size of local party membership, number of activists, seats on municipal councils, and municipal election results. These variables should be included in future research on PECs.

29. Author interviews with two members of the Green Party's negotiating team, Michel Boch and Jérôme Gleizas, conducted 19 and 22 June 2007, in Paris, France.

30. Of the fourteen districts in the Socialists' counterproposal, the left won seven seats, three more than the Greens won without a formal PEC. Thus, had the Greens worked with the Socialists nationally, they could have won seven seats instead of four.

31. Le Pen won 16.9 percent of the first-round votes in 2002 and 10.4 percent in 2007. Socialist Lionel Jospin took 16.2 percent of the votes in 2002, largely because the left's votes were divided among nine parties. Together, the parties on the left, excluding the Socialists, won nearly 29 percent of the vote. In 2007, Royal's vote share was 25.9 percent in the first round, while seven other left-wing parties combined to win 10.6 percent of the vote.

32. For more on the 2007 legislative elections, see Sauger 2007; Spoon 2008.

33. In 2002, the two parties had no programmatic agreement. The preelection agreement addressed only the districts in which the parties would support each other's candidates, not issue positions (Boch, interview; Gleizas, interview).

34. *Ecologie* is an all-encompassing term that includes the key issues on the Greens' agenda—the environment, social justice, and grassroots democracy.

35. French parties have a long history of merging and forming new parties. In 1965, for example, François Mitterrand brought together several parties on the noncommunist left to form the new Fédération de la Gauche Démocrate et Socialiste (Federation of the Democratic and Socialist Left) as a counterbalance to the PCF. Mitterrand's party dissolved in 1968, only to reemerge as the current Socialist Party a year later. More recently, in 2002, Jacques Chirac founded the UMP, which joined the RPR and part of the UDF together into one party. In 2007, Bayrou dissolved the UDF to form the MoDem.

Chapter 4

Some of the background material discussed in this chapter draws from a previously published article in *Party Politics*.

1. The Manifesto for a Sustainable Society is "a statement of the policies needed to fulfill the Green Vision and create a society based on ecological sustainability and social justice. It is not a programme for a single term of government, but an expression of what is necessary to achieve these long term goals" (Green Party of England and Wales n.d.).

2. Interview with Member of the European Parliament (MEP) Jean Lambert, 16 June 2006, in London, England.

3. Interview with Peter Cranie, 23 June 2006, in London. GPEx chair Richard Mallender shared similar sentiments in an interview on 12 July 2006, in Brighton. In addition, this idea of a "different kind of politics" was conveyed by several other party leaders and elected officials.

4. The five-hundred-pound deposit required to stand in each constituency is refunded if the candidate's vote share is 5 percent or greater.

5. Local parties are typically found at the city and county level. Each of the ten English and Welsh regions (East Midlands, Eastern, London, North East, North West, South East, South West, Wales, West Midlands, Yorkshire and the Humber) also has a regional Green Party. These constituencies, plus Scotland and Northern Ireland, elect the United Kingdom's members of the European Parliament.

6. Cranie, interview.

7. Interview with David Williams, Oxford City Councillor, 5 June 2006, in Oxford.

8. Interviews with Jean Lambert, Peter Cranie, and Assembly Member Darren Johnson, 20 June 2006, in London.

9. Although governments in Europe tend to include several parties, notable exceptions occur. Greece, Norway, Spain, and Sweden have had single-party governments for long periods over the past thirty years.

10. Prior to 2010, the Lib-Lab pact was the closest to a coalition the British government had come since 1945. It began in March 1977, when Labour prime minister Jim Callaghan, facing a vote of no confidence, approached the Liberal Party to help save the government. In exchange for Labour's support for a handful of Liberal policies, the Liberal Party, led by David Steel, agreed to vote with the government against any motion of no confidence. The pact ended by mutual agreement in July 1978 (I. Marsh 1990).

11. Norwich and Norfolk are in the process of applying for this change in status. For more information, see www.norwich.gov.uk/site_files/pages/City _Council__Unitary_Council.html (accessed 10 December 2008).

12. Interview with Elise Benjamin, Oxford City Councillor, 5 June 2006, in Oxford; interview with Chris Rose, National Elections Agent, 26 June 2006, in London.

13. Johnson, interview; interview with Noel Lynch, Coordinator of the London Green Party, 26 June 2006, in London.

14. Lambert suggested this explanation of the difference. Beyond the Communists, Socialists, Radicals, and Greens, several other parties are active on the extreme left of the French ideological spectrum. These include Lutte Ouvrière (Workers' Struggle), the Ligue Communiste Révolutionnaire (Revolutionary Communist League), and the Parti des Travailleurs (Workers' Party). While these three parties have not won any seats in Parliament, their candidates' vote shares, combined with those of the Green and Radical candidates, prevented the Socialist candidate, Lionel Jospin, from advancing to the second round of the 2002 presidential election.

15. With some of the Liberal Democrats' recent positions on issues, such as opposition to British involvement in Iraq, some left-leaning voters have supported the party. However, the Liberal Democrats remain ideologically a liberal party. Other small, mostly single-issue, left-wing parties have representation on some local city and county councils. For example, the Independent Working Class Association had two seats on the Oxford City Council as of 2008, and RESPECT had nearly twenty councillors on various councils throughout the United Kingdom.

16. The "electoralist" wing of the party, long focused on electing MPs to Westminster, introduced the Green 2000 initiative. The "decentralists," conversely, wanted the party to focus on elections to city and county councils and other representative bodies not based on plurality elections and formulated the Basis for Renewal plan.

17. Both Labour and the Conservatives have done some targeting in recent elections; see Johnston and Pattie 2006, 204–12.
18. Lambert, interview.
19. The independent Scottish Green Party is focusing on the electing members to the devolved Scottish Parliament, which also uses a mixed-member PR system. The Scottish Greens have had representation in the parliament since its founding in 1999. Since 2007, the party has 2 of the 129 seats and has been in a governing coalition with the Scottish National Party.
20. Johnson, interview.
21. Johnson, interview; Lynch, interview.
22. Benjamin, interview.
23. Mallender, interview.
24. Interview with Norwich city councillor, 25 July 2006, Norwich.
25. Interview with Brighton and Hove city councillor, 5 July 2006, Brighton.
26. Rose, interview.
27. Cranie, interview; Rose, interview.
28. Local Green parties represent various geographic entities from single cities to entire counties. The jurisdiction of the Norwich Green Party (www.norwichgreenparty.org) is the city of Norwich. The Oxfordshire Greens (www.greenoxford.com) represent the entire county of Oxfordshire. The Brighton and Hove Green Party (www.brightonandhovegreenparty.org.uk) covers the cities of Brighton and Hove.
29. Lewisham Deptford was the third targeted constituency in 2005. I do not include an in-depth discussion of the local party's targeting and campaign strategy as it closely resembles that of the Norwich Greens. In addition, the party's candidate in 2001 and 2005, Darren Johnson, is also a well-known figure within the local and the London parties.
30. Ramsay, interview.
31. Ibid.
32. Interview with Norwich city councillors, 21 July 2006, Norwich.
33. Ibid., 25 July 2006.
34. Ibid., 19 and 21 July 2006.
35. During the spring and summer of 2006, Cameron demonstrated his "greenness" by choosing to bike to his office at Westminster. But he was heavily criticized because his hybrid Lexus followed behind with his suit and file boxes (BBC News Online 2006).
36. Interviews with Norwich city councillors, 19, 21, and 25 July 2006.
37. Interview with Oxford city councillor, 8 June 2006, Oxford. In Oxford East, the party has run a different candidate in every election since 1987. In Oxford West and Abingdon, Mike Woodin stood in the 1992, 1997, and 2001 elections.
38. Interview with Oxfordshire Green Party Elections Agent, 14 June 2006, Oxford.
39. The Labour–Co-operative label denotes those individuals who are joint

candidates of the Labour and Co-operative Parties at the local and national levels. The parties essentially have formed a PEC in some constituencies, but the Co-Operative party does not stand its own candidates; it only runs joint candidates with Labour. Although many Labour MPs, including Gordon Brown, are Co-op members, only those candidates who have been officially endorsed by both parties can use the Labour–Co-op designation. As of 2009, there were 29 Labour-Co-op MPs and about 350 local councillors. For more information on the Co-operative Party, see http://party.coop.

40. Whether targeting leads to the use of nationally known candidates or having nationally known candidates leads to targeting in a given constituency is difficult to untangle. The constituency's candidate or potential candidate is factored into the national party's considerations about which constituencies to target.

41. Interview with Brighton and Hove city councillors, 7 July 2006, in Brighton.

42. Ramsay, interview.

43. Cranie, interview.

44. In the 2009 European Parliament elections, the BNP won its first two seats. In both of the regions where it won seats, its vote shares were slightly larger than those of the Greens. In the North West region, the BNP finished fifth with 8.0 percent of the vote, and the Greens placed sixth with 7.7 percent of the vote. In the Yorkshire and Humber region, the parties again finished fifth and sixth, with the BNP winning 9.8 percent and the Greens receiving 8.5 percent of the vote. In both constituencies, the vote shares of the BNP and Greens increased from the previous election. In the North West region, the head of the Greens' list, Cranie, effectively ran against the BNP's Nick Griffin, the head of its list. Recognizing that it made little sense to run against one of the larger parties, the Greens sought to convince Green-leaning voters to vote for them as a way of stopping the racist anti-immigrant politics of Griffin and the BNP. They argued that Labour and the Liberal Democrats were guaranteed seats under the system, so there was little concern about throwing away one's vote and thereby helping one's least preferred party. Furthermore, the d'Hondt system of seat allocation means that the final seat may be allocated on the basis of a small margin of votes ("Peter Cranie" n.d.). Given the BNP's increased support in the European Parliament elections, it might also be useful to look at the relationship between BNP support in these elections and the constituencies in which the Greens stood candidates in the 2010 election.

45. Meguid (2008, 124) and Frankland (1990, 19) argue that the Greens drew voters largely from the Conservatives and centrist voters in the 1989 European Parliament elections, in which they won 14.9 percent of the vote. More recently, David Cameron's "Vote Green, Go Blue" campaign signaled the Conservatives' policy focus on the environment. Thus, the Conservative Party may receive a potential Green supporter's vote.

46. Adding data on representation on city, county, and unitary councils to a

regression analysis on where the Greens stand candidates still would not tell the entire story, since what would be most indicative of some national pattern is not only where there are candidates but also what determines which are paper candidates and which are provided more resources by the local party. Only case studies of individual local parties, such as those discussed previously, can answer this question.

Chapter 5

1. The 2009 debate between Angela Merkel, the leader of the Christlich Demokratische Union Deutschlands–Christlich-Soziale Union in Bayern (Christian Democratic Union–Christian Social Union of Bavaria), and Frank Walter Steinmeir, head of the Social Democratic Party, is a recent example of this trend.

2. Cranie, interview.

3. In France, parties have been required to file yearly financial statements only since 1988 (Law 88-227, 11 March 1988). In the United Kingdom, the Political Parties, Elections, and Referendums Act of 2000 created an independent electoral commission to regulate parties and their funding. The act also required parties to submit yearly financial statements. Thus, although the trends discussed may extend over a longer time period, data are only available from these dates.

4. All monetary amounts have been standardized to 2007 U.S. dollars.

5. Unlike the British Greens, the French Greens have always had a single party leader, the national secretary. The current secretary is Cécile Duflot, who was elected in November 2006.

6. The Executive College is the party executive, whereas the National Interregional Council is the legislative branch in the party structure. As of December 2008, the Executive College has comprised eleven members, down from fifteen (see Les Verts 2008). The Council is composed of 120 members and 120 alternates.

7. The United Kingdom Elections Act was implemented in anticipation of a forthcoming European Council decision. In 1998, the Treaty of Amsterdam added to the European Community Treaty a specification that the electoral procedure for elections to the EP had to be based on "common principles." Council Decision 8964/02 subsequently mandated that all elections to the EP must be based on PR and use either a list or single transferable vote (STV) system. Except for Malta and Ireland, which use STV, all EU countries used list-PR in 2009.

8. Because the United Kingdom has fewer elected officials, media coverage from 15 June 1999 (when the two Green MEPs were first elected) through 14 June 2004 was also collected and analyzed. Unless otherwise noted, all discussions and comparisons of the British MEPs refer to the 2004–7 period.

9. The data collection and coding were conducted by two research assistants from June 2008 to January 2009. To ensure consistency in coding, each assistant went back and coded a sample of the articles the other had coded every

couple of weeks. If there were discrepancies between the two codings, I reviewed and clarified the criteria with the assistants and then cross-coded other articles with them to ensure that the discrepancies were resolved.

10. I use the term *article* to refer to any distinct item in the newspaper. Thus, although letters to the editor and opinion pieces may not technically be articles, I include them in this term.

11. French law has permitted civil unions (*pacte civil de solidarité*) since 1999 but does not permit same-sex marriage (see Law 99-944, 15 November 1999). As of July 2008, France recognizes marriages between same-sex couples who have wed overseas.

12. Voynet is another longtime Green Party leader and was one of the party's founding members. She served as an MEP (1989–94) and an MP (1997) until she became Jospin's environment minister, a position she held until 2001, when she became the Greens' national secretary and Cochet became minister. Voynet was the party's presidential nominee in 1995 and 2007 and was elected senator in 2004; she currently holds both this position and the mayorship of Montreuil, a Paris suburb.

13. Cochet has always been a member of the pragmatic wing of the party, which saw the party as ideologically on the left and supported preelection coalitions with the Socialists. This group has worked to ensure that the party is not portrayed as singly focused on the environment.

14. The Greens-EFA group, founded in 1999, comprises green and regional party MEPs.

15. Hulot decided not to run for the presidency when a January 2007 poll showed that 58 percent of respondents would not support his candidacy ("Nicolas Hulot" 2007).

16. When Bennahmias first left the Greens, he was still seated with the Greens-EFA group in the EP. He now has joined the rest of the MoDem MEPs in the Alliance of Liberals and Democrats group. He is currently the vice president of the MoDem (Ecoiffier 2007).

Chapter 6

1. The 2 percent threshold was established by reforms in the Election Act of 2003 (Sharp and Krajnc 2009, 238; Green Party of Canada).

2. For a discussion of PECs at the municipal level with left-wing parties, see Sharp and Krajnc 2009, n. 2.

References

Following the main references is a section that includes data and other primary sources and a list of interviews conducted with party leaders and elected officials.

Adams, James, Michael Clark, Lawrence Ezrow, and Garrett Glasgow. 2006. "Are Niche Parties Fundamentally Different from Mainstream Parties? The Causes and the Electoral Consequences of Western European Parties' Policy Shifts, 1976–1998." *American Journal of Political Science* 50.3: 513–29.

Adams, James, and Samuel Merrill III. 2006. "Why Small, Centrist Third Parties Motivate Policy Divergence by Major Parties." *American Political Science Review* 100.3: 403–17.

Adams, James, Samuel Merrill III, and Bernard Grofman. 2005. *A Unified Theory of Party Competition: A Cross-National Analysis Integrating Spatial and Behavioral Factors.* Cambridge: Cambridge University Press.

Aldrich, John H. 1983. "A Downsian Spatial Model with Party Activism." *American Political Science Review* 77.4: 974–90.

Aldrich, John H. 1995. *Why Parties? The Origin and Transformation of Political Parties in America.* Chicago: University of Chicago Press.

Alvarez, R. Michael, and Jonathan Nagler. 2000. "A New Approach for Modelling Strategic Voting in Multiparty Elections." *British Journal of Political Science* 30.1: 57–75.

Amorim Neto, Octavio, and Gary W. Cox. 1997. "Electoral Institutions, Cleavage Structures, and the Number of Parties." *American Journal of Political Science* 41.1: 149–74.

Andrews, Josephine T., and Jeannette Money. N.d. "Champions and Challengers: Ideology and the Success of Political Parties in Established Party Systems." Unpublished manuscript.

Andrews, William. 1962. "The *Suppléant* System for the French National Assembly." *Parliamentary Affairs* 16.3: 274–78.

Argell, Siri. 2008. "Dion Gets No Lift from Raising Glass with Greens." *Toronto Globe and Mail*, 15 October, A1.

Auffray, Alain. 2004. "Cinq Motions en Concurrence." *Libération*. 16 October, Politique 12.
BBC News Online. 2006. "Hypocrisy Claim over Cameron Bike." 28 April. http://news.bbc.co.uk/2/hi/uk_news/politics/4953922.stm. Accessed 15 August 2006.
BBC News Online. 2007. "Greens Pull Out of City Coalition." 11 May. http://news.bbc.co.uk/2/hi/uk_news/england/west_yorkshire/6646159.stm. Accessed 12 November 2007.
Benoit, Kenneth, Michael Laver, and Slava Mikhaylov. 2007. "Mapping Policy Preferences with Uncertainty: Measuring and Correcting Error in Comparative Manifesto Project Estimates." Paper presented at the annual meeting of the Midwest Political Science Association, Chicago, 12–15 April.
Benoit, Kenneth, Michael Laver, and Slava Mikhaylov. 2009. "Treating Words as Data with Error: Uncertainty in Text Statements of Policy Positions." *American Journal of Political Science* 52.2: 495–513.
Berg, John C. 2003. "Spoiler or Builder? The Effect of Ralph Nader's 2000 Campaign on the U.S. Greens." In *The State of the Parties: The Changing Role of Contemporary American Parties*, 4th ed., ed. John C. Green and Rick Farmer. Lanham, MD: Rowman and Littlefield.
Berg, John C. 2009. "Greens in the USA." In *Green Parties in Transition: The End of Grass-Roots Democracy?* ed. E. Gene Frankland, Paul Lucardie, and Benoît Rihoux. Farnham: Ashgate.
Birch, Sarah. 2005. "Single-Member District Electoral Systems and Democratic Transition." *Electoral Studies* 24.2: 281–301.
Birch, Sarah. 2009. "Real Progress: Prospects for Green Party Support in Britain." *Parliamentary Affairs* 62.1: 53–71.
Blais, André, and Indridi Indridason. 2007. "Making Candidates Count: The Logic of Electoral Alliances in Two-Round Legislative Elections." *Journal of Politics* 69.1: 193–205.
Blais, André, Richard Nadeau, Elisabeth Gidengil, and Neil Nevitte. 2001. "Measuring Strategic Voting in Multiparty Plurality Elections." *Electoral Studies* 20.3: 343–52.
Blühdorn, Ingolfur, and Joseph Szarka. 2004. "Managing Strategic Positioning Choices: A Reappraisal of the Development Paths of the French and German Green Parties." *Journal of Contemporary European Studies* 12.3: 303–19.
Bomberg, Elizabeth. 1998. *Green Parties and Politics in the European Union*. New York: Routledge.
Bomberg, Elizabeth. 2002. "The Europeanization of Green Parties: Exploring the EU's Impact." *West European Politics* 25.3: 29–50.
Bomberg, Elizabeth, and Neil Carter. 2006. "The Greens in Brussels: Shaping or Shaped?" *European Journal of Political Research* 45: S99–S125.
Bowler, Shaun, and David M. Farrell. 1992. "The Study of Election Campaigning." In *Electoral Strategies and Political Marketing*, ed. Shaun Bowler and David Farrell. Basingstoke: Macmillan.

Boy, Daniel. 2002. "France." In *Green Parties in National Governments,* ed. Ferdinand Müller-Rommel and Thomas Poguntke. Portland, OR: Cass.

Budge, Ian. N.d. "Estimating Measurement Error and Uncertainty." Unpublished manuscript.

Budge, Ian. 1994. "A New Spatial Theory of Party Competition: Uncertainty, Ideology, and Party Equilibria Viewed Comparatively and Temporally." *British Journal of Political Science* 24.4: 443–67.

Burchell, Jon. 2000. "Here Come the Greens (Again): The Green Party in Britain during the 1990s." *Environmental Politics* 9.3: 145–50.

Burchell, Jon. 2002. *The Evolution of Green Politics: Development and Change within European Green Parties.* London: Earthscan.

Campbell, Angus, Phil Converse, Donald Stokes, and Warren Miller. 1960. *The American Voter.* Chicago: University of Chicago Press.

Carey, Sean, and Jonathan Burton. 2004. "Research Note: The Influence of the Press in Shaping Public Opinion towards the European Union in Britain." *Political Studies.* 52.3: 623–40.

Carrubba, Cliff, and Richard J. Timpone. 2005. "Explaining Vote Switching Across First and Second Order Elections: Evidence from Europe." *Comparative Political Studies* 38.3: 260-81.

Carter, Neil. 1992. "Whatever Happened to the Environment? The British General Election of 1992." *Environmental Politics* 1.3: 442–48.

Carter, Neil. 1997. "The 1997 British General Election." *Environmental Politics* 6.3: 156–61.

Carter, Neil. 2006. "Party Politicization of the Environment in Britain." *Party Politics* 12.6: 747–67.

Carter, Neil. 2008. "The Green Party: Emerging from the Political Wilderness?" *British Politics* 3.2: 223–40.

Carter, Neil, and Christopher Rootes. 2006. "The Environment and the Greens in the 2005 Elections in Britain." *Environmental Politics* 15.3: 473–78.

Castles, Francis G., and Peter Mair. 1984. "Left–Right Political Scales: Some Expert Judgments." *European Journal of Political Research* 12.1: 73–88.

Chandra, Kachan. 2007. *Why Ethnic Parties Succeed: Patronage and Ethnic Head Counts in India.* New York: Cambridge University Press.

Chhibber, Pradeep K., and Ken Kollman. 1998. "Party Aggregation and the Number of Parties in India and the United States." *American Political Science Review* 92.2: 329–42.

Chhibber, Pradeep K., and Ken Kollman. 2004. *The Formation of National Party Systems: Federalism and Party Competition in Canada, Great Britain, India, and the United States.* Princeton: Princeton University Press.

Clark, Alistair. 2004. "The Continued Relevance of Local Parties in Representative Democracies." *Politics* 24.1: 35–45.

Clark, William Roberts, and Matt Golder. 2006. "Rehabilitating Duverger's Theory: Testing the Mechanical and Strategic Modifying Effects of Electoral Laws." *Comparative Political Studies* 39.6: 679–708.

Cole, Alistair, and Peter Campbell. 1989. *French Electoral Systems and Elections since 1789*. Aldershot: Gower.
Cole, Alistair, and Brian Doherty. 1995. "Pas Comme les Autres: The French Greens at the Crossroads." In *The Green Challenge: The Development of Green Parties in Europe*, ed. Dick Richardson and Chris Rootes. New York: Routledge.
Cordier, Caroline. 2004. "Les Courants des Verts Préparent la Succession de Gilles Lemaire." *Le Monde*, 28 August, 7.
Cox, Gary W. 1997. *Making Votes Count: Strategic Coordination in the World's Electoral Systems*. Cambridge: Cambridge University Press.
Cox, Gary W. 1999. "Electoral Rules and Electoral Coordination." *Annual Review of Political Science* 2:145–61.
Curry, Bill. 2008a. "Elizabeth May Discusses Senate Seat with Dion." *Toronto Globe and Mail*, 3 December, A4.
Curry, Bill. 2008b. "Harper Vows to Name 18 New Senators." *Toronto Globe and Mail*, 12 December, A5.
Curtice, John, and Holli A. Semetko. 1994. "Does It Matter What the Papers Say?" In *Labour's Last Chance: The 1992 Election and Beyond*, ed. Roger Jowell, John Curtice, Anthony F. Heath, and Bridget Taylor. Aldershot: Dartmouth.
Cutts, David, and Nick Shryane. 2006. "Did Local Activism Really Matter? Liberal Democrat Campaigning and the 2001 British General Election." *British Journal of Politics and International Relations* 8.3: 427–44.
Dalton, Russell J. 1990. "The Challenge of New Movements." In *Challenging the Political Order: New Social and Political Movements in Western Democracies*, ed. Russell J. Dalton and Manfred Kuechler. New York: Oxford University Press.
Dalton, Russell J. 2008. *Citizen Politics: Public Opinion and Political Parties in Advanced Industrial Democracies*. 3d ed. New York: Seven Bridges.
Dalton, Russell J., Paul A. Beck, and Robert Huckfeldt. 1998. "Partisan Cues and the Media: Information Flows in the 1992 Presidential Election." *American Political Science Review* 92.1: 111–26.
Dalton, Russell J., Scott Flanagan, and Paul Beck, eds. 1984. *Electoral Change in Advanced Industrial Democracies*. Princeton: Princeton University Press.
Dalton, Russell J., Ian McAllister, and Martin P. Wattenberg. 2000. "The Consequences of Partisan Dealignment." In *Parties without Partisans: Political Change in Advanced Industrial Democracies*, ed. Russell J. Dalton and Martin P. Wattenberg. New York: Oxford University Press.
Dalton, Russell J., and Martin P. Wattenberg, eds. 2000. *Parties without Partisans: Political Change in Advanced Industrial Democracies*. New York: Oxford University Press.
Dao, James. 2000. "The 2000 Campaign: The Green Party; Democrats Hear Thunder on Left, and Try to Steal Some of Nader's." *New York Times*, 24 October, A1.
Denver, David. 2001. "The Liberal Democrat Campaign." In *Britain Votes*, ed. Pippa Norris. New York: Oxford University Press.

Denver, David, and Gordon Hands. 1997. *Modern Constituency Electioneering: Local Campaigning in the 1992 General Election.* London: Cass.

Denver, David, Gordon Hands, Justin Fisher, and Iain MacAllister. 2003. "Constituency Campaigning in Britain 1992–2001." *Party Politics* 9.5: 541–59.

Denver, David, Gordon Hands, and Simon Henig. 1998. "Triumph of Targeting? Constituency Campaigning in the 1997 Election." In *British Elections and Parties Review,* vol. 8, *The 1997 General Election,* ed. David Denver, Justin Fisher, Philip Cowley, and Charles Pattie. London: Cass.

Dion, Douglas. 1998. "Evidence and Inference in the Comparative Case Study." *Comparative Politics* 30.2: 127–45.

Downs, Anthony. 1957. *An Economic Theory of Democracy.* New York: Harper and Row.

Duverger, Maurice. 1954. *Political Parties.* New York: Wiley.

Druckman, James N. 2005. "Media Matter: How Newspapers and Television News Cover Campaigns and Influence Voters." *Political Communication* 22.4: 463–81.

Eckstein, Harry. 1975. "Case Study and Theory in Political Science." In *Strategies of Inquiry: Handbook of Political Science,* vol. 7, ed. Fred I. Greenstein and Nelson W. Polsby. Reading, MA: Addison-Wesley.

Ecoiffier, Matthieu. 2007. "'Je Suis Bayrou, mais Je ne Passe pas à Droite!': Mouvement Démocrate; Jean-Luc Bennahmias, Ex-Secrétaire Général des Verts, Quitte les Ecologistes et Rejoint le Nouveau Parti." *Libération,* 10 May, Evenement 5.

Ezrow, Lawrence. 2008. "On the Inverse Relationship between Votes and Proximity for Niche Parties." *European Journal of Political Research* 47.2 : 206–20.

Ezrow, Lawrence. 2010. *Linking Citizens and Parties: How Electoral Systems Matter for Political Representation.* Oxford: Oxford University Press.

Farrell, David M. 1996. "Campaign Strategies and Tactics." In *Comparing Democracies: Elections and Voting in a Comparative Perspective,* ed. Lawrence LeDuc, Richard Niemi, and Pippa Norris. Thousand Oaks, CA: Sage.

Farrell, David M., and Paul Webb. 2000. "Political Parties as Campaign Organizations." In *Parties without Partisans: Political Changes in Advanced Industrial Democracies,* ed. Russell J. Dalton and Martin Wattenberg. New York: Oxford University Press.

Faucher, Florence. 1998. "Is There Hope for the French Ecology Movement?" *Environmental Politics* 7.3: 42–65.

Faucher, Florence. 2004. "The Greens 2002: Coming Down to Earth." In *The French Presidential and Legislative Elections of 2002,* ed. John Gaffney. Aldershot: Ashgate.

Ferrara, Federico, and J. Timo Weishaupt. 2004. "Get Your Act Together: Party Performance in European Parliament Election." *European Union Politics* 5.3: 283–306.

Fowler, Carwyn, and Rhys Jones. 2006. "Can Environmentalism and Nationalism Be Reconciled? The Plaid Cymru/Green Party Alliance, 1991–95." *Regional and Federal Studies* 16.3: 315–31.

Frankland, E. Gene. 1990. "Does Green Politics Have a Future in Britain? An American Perspective." In *Green Politics One*, ed. Wolfgang Rüdig. Edinburgh: Edinburgh University Press.

Gallagher, Michael, Michael Laver, and Peter Mair. 2006. *Representative Government in Modern Europe.* 4th ed. New York: McGraw-Hill.

Geddes, Barbara. 1990. "How the Cases You Choose Affect the Answer You Get: Selection Bias in Comparative Politics." *Political Analysis* 2.1: 131–50.

Gerber, Alan, Dean Karlan, and Daniel Bergan. 2006. *Does the Media Matter? A Field Experiment Measuring the Effect of Newspapers on Voting Behavior and Political Opinions.* Yale Economic Applications and Policy Discussion Paper 12. New Haven: Yale University.

Glover, Julian. 2006. "Thatcher's Torch Extinguished as Cameron's Conservatives Carve New Logo Out of Oak." *Guardian*, 9 August, 6.

Golder, Sona Nadenichek. 2006a. *The Logic of Pre-Electoral Coalition Formation.* Columbus: Ohio State University Press.

Golder, Sona Nadenichek. 2006b. "Pre-Electoral Coalition Formation in Parliamentary Democracies." *British Journal of Political Science* 36.2: 193–212.

Harmel, Robert. 2002. "Party Organizational Change: Competing Explanations?" In *Political Parties in the New Europe: Political and Analytical Changes*, ed. Kurt Richard Luther and Ferdinand Müller-Rommel. New York: Oxford University Press.

Harmel, Robert, and Kenneth Janda. 1994. "An Integrated Theory of Party Goals and Party Change." *Journal of Theoretical Politics* 6.3: 259–87.

Harmel, Robert, and John D. Robertson. 1985. "Formation and Success of New Parties: A Cross-National Analysis." *International Political Science Review* 6.4: 501–23.

Hicken, Allen. 2009. *Building Party Systems in Developing Democracies.* New York: Cambridge University Press.

Hinich, Melvin, and Michael Munger. 1997. *Analytical Politics.* Cambridge: Cambridge University Press.

Hitchcock, William I. 2003. *The Struggle for Europe: The Turbulent History of a Divided Continent, 1945 to the Present.* New York: Anchor Books.

Hix, Simon, and Michael Marsh. 2007. "Punishment or Protest? Understanding European Parliament Elections." *Journal of Politics* 69.2: 495–510.

Hobolt, Sara Binzer, Jae-Jae Spoon, and James Tilly. 2009. "A Vote against Europe? Explaining Defection in the 1999 and 2004 European Parliament Elections." *British Journal of Political Science* 39.1: 93–115.

Holliday, Ian. 1994. "Dealing in Green Votes." *Government and Opposition* 29.1: 64–79.

Huber, John, and Ronald Inglehart. 1995. "Expert Interpretations of Party Space and Party Locations in 42 Societies." *Party Politics* 1.1: 73–111.

Hug, Simon. 2001. *Altering Party Systems: Strategic Behavior and the Emergence of New Political Parties in Western Democracies.* Ann Arbor: University of Michigan Press.

Ignazi, Piero. 1992. "The Silent Counter-Revolution: Hypotheses on the Emer-

gence of Extreme Right-Wing Parties in Europe." *European Journal of Political Research* 22.1: 3–34.
Inglehart, Ronald. 1995. "Public Support for Environmental Protection: Objective Problems and Subjective Values in 43 Societies." *PS: Political Science and Politics* 28.1: 57–72.
Inglehart, Ronald. 1997. *Modernization and Postmodernization: Cultural, Economic, and Political Change in 43 Societies.* Princeton: Princeton University Press.
Inglehart, Ronald, and Jacques-René Rabier. 1986. "Political Realignment in Advanced Industrial Society: From Class-Based Politics to Quality-of-Life Politics." *Government and Opposition* 21.4: 456–79.
Iyengar, Shanto. 1997. "Overview." In *Do the Media Govern: Politicians, Voters, and Reporters in America,* ed. Shanto Iyengar and Richard Reeves. Thousand Oaks, CA: Sage.
Iyengar, Shanto, and Donald Kinder. 1987. *News That Matters. Agenda-Setting and Priming in a Television Age.* Chicago: University of Chicago Press.
Jick, Todd D. 1979. "Mixing Qualitative and Quantitative Methods: Triangulation in Action." *Administrative Studies Quarterly* 24.4: 602–11.
Johnston, Ron, and Charles Pattie. 2006. *Putting Voters in Their Place: Geography and Elections in Great Britain.* New York: Oxford University Press.
Judge, David, and David Earnshaw. 2003. *The European Parliament.* New York: Palgrave Macmillan.
Katz, Richard, and Peter Mair. 1995. "Changing Models of Party Organization and Party Democracy." *Party Politics* 1.1: 5–28.
Keaten, Jamey. 2006. "Royal Wins French Socialists' Nomination." Associated Press Online. 17 November.
Kedar, Orit. 2005. "When Moderate Voters Prefer Extreme Parties: Policy Balancing in Parliamentary Elections." *American Political Science Review* 99.2: 185–99.
Kedar, Orit. 2009. *Voting for Policy, Not Parties: How Voters Compensate for Power Sharing.* New York: Cambridge University Press.
Key, V. O. 1958. *Politics, Parties, and Pressure Groups.* 4th ed. New York: Crowell.
King, Gary, Robert O. Keohane, and Sidney Verba. 1994. *Designing Social Inquiry: Scientific Inference in Qualitative Research.* Princeton: Princeton University Press.
Kirchheimer, Otto. 1966. "The Transformation of the Western European Party Systems." In *Political Parties and Political Development,* ed. Joseph LaPalombara and Martin Weiner. Princeton: Princeton University Press.
Kitschelt, Herbert. 1988. "Left-Libertarian Parties: Explaining Innovation in Competitive Party Systems." *World Politics* 40.2: 194–234.
Kitschelt, Herbert. 1989. *The Logics of Party Formation: Ecological Politics in Belgium and West Germany.* Ithaca: Cornell University Press.
Kitschelt, Herbert. 1995. *The Radical Right in Western Europe: A Comparative Analysis.* Ann Arbor: University of Michigan Press.
Koole, Ruud. 1996. "Cadre, Catch-all, or Cartel? A Comment on the Notion of the Cartel Party." *Party Politics* 2.4: 507–23.

Kuhn, Raymond. 1995. *The Media in France*. New York: Routledge.
Laakso, Markku, and Rein Taagepera. 1979. "Effective Number of Parties: A Measure with Application to West Europe." *Comparative Political Studies* 12.1: 3–27.
Laver, Michael. 2005. "Policy and the Dynamics of Political Competition." *American Political Science Review* 99.2: 263–81.
Laver, Michael, and John Garry. 2007. "Estimating Policy Positions from Political Texts." *American Journal of Political Science* 44.3: 619–34.
Laver, Michael, and Norman Schofield. 1998. *Multiparty Government: The Politics of Coalition in Europe*. Ann Arbor: University of Michigan Press.
Lewis-Beck, Michael S., William G. Jacoby, Helmut Norpoth, and Herbert F. Weisberg. 2008. *The American Voter Revisited*. Ann Arbor: University of Michigan Press.
Liao, Tim Futing. 1994. *Interpreting Probability Models: Logit, Probit, and Other Generalized Linear Models*. Thousand Oaks, CA: Sage.
Lijphart, Arend. 1994. *Electoral Systems and Party Systems: A Study of Twenty-seven Democracies, 1945–1990*. Oxford: Oxford University Press.
Long, J. Scott, and Jeremy Freese. 2003. *Regression Models for Categorical Dependent Variables Using Stata*. College Station, TX: Stata.
Lyon, John. 2009. "State's First Green Party Legislator to Switch Parties." *Arkansas News*, 29 April. www.arkansasnews.com. Accessed 14 June 2009.
Maddala, G. S. 1983. *Limited-Dependent Qualitative Variables in Econometrics*. New York: Cambridge University Press.
Markovits, Andrei S., and Philip S. Gorski. 1993. *The German Left: Red, Green, and Beyond*. Cambridge: Polity.
Marsh, Ian. 1990. "Liberal Priorities, the Lib-Lab Pact, and the Requirement for Policy Influence." *Parliamentary Affairs* 43.3: 292–321.
Marsh, Michael. 1998. "Testing the Second-Order Election Model after Four European Elections." *British Journal of Political Science* 28.4: 591-607.
Marsh, Michael. 2007. "European Parliament Elections and Loss of Governing Parties." In *European Elections and Domestic Politics*, ed. Wouter van der Brug and Cees van der Eijk. Notre Dame: University of Notre Dame Press.
Martin, Pierre. 1994. *Les Systèmes Electoraux et les Modes de Scrutin*. Paris: Montchrestien.
Mayer, Nonna. 2002. *Ces Français qui Votent FN*. Paris: Flammarion.
Mayer, Nonna, and Pascal Perrineau, eds. 1996. *Le Front National à Découvert*. Paris: Presses de la Fondation Nationale des Sciences Politiques.
Meguid, Bonnie M. 2005. "Competition between Unequals: The Role of Mainstream Party Strategy in Niche Party Success." *American Political Science Review* 99.3: 347–59.
Meguid, Bonnie M. 2008. *Party Competition between Unequals: Strategies and Electoral Fortunes in Western Europe*. New York: Cambridge University Press.
Miller, Gary, and Norman Schofield. 2003. "Activism and Partisan Realignment in the United States." *American Political Science Review* 97.2: 245–60.

Miller, Warren. 1991. "Party Identification, Realignment, and Party Voting: Back to the Basics." *American Political Science Review* 85.2: 557–68.

Moy, Patricia, and Michael Pfau. 2000. *With Malice towards All? The Media and Public Confidence in Democratic Institutions.* Westport, CT: Praeger.

Mozaffar, Shaheen, James R. Scarritt, and Glen Galaich. 2003. "Electoral Institutions, Ethnopolitical Cleavages, and Party Systems in Africa's Emerging Democracies." *American Political Science Review* 97.3: 379–90.

Müller, Wolfgang C., and Kaare Strøm. 1999. "Political Parties and Hard Choices." In *Policy, Office, or Votes: How Political Parties in Western Europe Make Hard Decisions,* ed. Kaare Strøm and Wolfgang C. Müller. New York: Cambridge University Press.

Newton, Kenneth, and Malcolm Brynin. 2001. "The National Press and Party Voting in the UK." *Political Studies* 49.2: 265–85.

"Nicolas Hulot Renonce à Se Présenter à l'Elysée, après Six Mois de Lobbying Écologique." 2007. *Le Monde,* 23 January, Politique 13.

Niemi, Richard G., Guy Whitten, and Mark N. Franklin. 1992. "Constituency Characteristics, Individual Characteristics, and Tactical Voting in the 1987 British General Election." *British Journal of Political Science* 22.2: 229–40.

Norris, Pippa. 2000. *A Virtuous Circle: Political Communications in Postindustrial Societies.* New York: Cambridge University Press.

Norris, Pippa. 2002. "Campaign Communications." In *Comparing Democracies 2: New Challenges in the Study of Elections and Voting,* ed. Lawrence LeDuc, Richard Niemi, and Pippa Norris. Thousand Oaks, CA: Sage.

Norris, Pippa. 2004. *Electoral Engineering: Voting Rules and Political Behavior.* New York: Cambridge University Press.

Norris, Pippa. 2005a. *Radical Right: Voters and Parties in the Electoral Market.* New York: Cambridge University Press.

Norris, Pippa, John Curtice, David Sanders, Margaret Scammell, and Holli A. Semetko. 1999. *On Message: Communicating the Campaign.* Thousand Oaks, CA: Sage.

O'Neill, Michael. 1997. *Green Parties and Political Change in Contemporary Europe: New Politics, Old Predicaments.* Aldershot: Ashgate.

Oppenhuis, Erik, Cees van der Eijk, and Mark N. Franklin. 1996. "The Party Context: Outcomes." In *Choosing Europe? The European Electorate and National Politics in the Face of Union,* ed. Cees van der Eijk, Mark N. Franklin, et al. Ann Arbor: University of Michigan Press.

Ordeshook, Peter, and Olga Shvetsova. 1994. "Ethnic Heterogeneity, District Magnitude, and the Number of Parties." *American Journal of Political Science* 38.1: 101–23.

Panebianco, Angelo. 1988. *Political Parties: Organization and Power.* Cambridge: Cambridge University Press.

Pedersen, Mogens N. 1979. "The Dynamics of European Party Systems: Changing Patterns of Electoral Volatility." *European Journal of Political Research* 7.1: 1–26.

Perrineau, Pascal. 1998. *Le Symptôme Le Pen: Radiographie des Électeurs du Front National*. Paris: Fayard.
Pierce, Roy. 1995. *Choosing the Chief: Presidential Elections in France and the United States*. Ann Arbor: University of Michigan Press.
Poguntke, Thomas, and Paul Webb. 2005. "The Presidentialization of Politics in Democratic Societies: A Framework for Analysis." In *The Presidentialization of Politics: A Comparative Study of Modern Democracies*, ed. Thomas Poguntke and Paul Webb. New York: Oxford University Press.
Przeworski, Adam, and John Sprague. 1986. *Paper Stones: A History of Electoral Socialism*. Chicago: University of Chicago Press.
Przeworski, Adam, and Henry Teune. 1970. *The Logic of Comparative Social Inquiry*. New York: Wiley-Interscience.
Rabinowitz, George, and Stuart Macdonald. 1989. "A Directional Theory of Issue Voting." *American Political Science Review* 83.1: 93–121.
Rae, Douglas W. 1967. *The Political Consequences of Electoral Laws*. New Haven: Yale University Press.
"Réfugiés Italiens: Que la France Honore sa Parole." 2004. *Libération*, 15 September, Courrier 7.
Reif, Karlheinz, and Hermann Schmitt. 1980. "Nine Second-Order National Elections: A Conceptual Framework for the Analysis of European Election Results." *European Journal for Political Research* 8.1: 3–44.
Renard, Xavier. 2007. "Dépasser les Verts, Nouvel Horizon de Cohn-Bendit; L'Elu Européen Etait Samedi à Tours pour Tenter de Refonder l'Ecologie Politique." *Libération*, 2 July, Politiques 9.
Rice, Roberta, and Donna Lee Van Cott. 2006. "The Emergence and Performance of Indigenous Peoples' Parties in South America." *Comparative Political Studies* 39.6: 709–32.
Riker, William H. 1982. "Rethinking Duverger's Law: An Essay on the History of Political Science." *American Political Science Review* 76.4: 753–66.
Rohrschneider, Robert. 1993. "New Party versus Old Left Realignments: Environmental Attitudes, Party Policies, and Partisan Affiliations in Four West European Countries." *Journal of Politics* 55.3: 682–701.
Rootes, Chris. 1995. "Britain: Greens in a Cold Climate." In *The Green Challenge: The Development of Green Parties in Europe*, ed. Dick Richardson and Chris Rootes. New York: Routledge.
Rosenstone, Steven J., Roy L. Behr, and Edward H. Lazarus. 1996. *Third Parties in America: Citizen Response to Major Party Failure*. 2nd ed. Princeton: Princeton University Press.
Rosenstone, Steven J., and John Mark Hansen. 1993. *Mobilization, Participation, and Democracy in America*. New York: Macmillan.
Rüdig, Wolfgang. 1990. *Explaining Green Party Development: Reflections on a Theoretical Framework*. Glasgow: University of Strathclyde.
Rüdig, Wolfgang. 2008. "Green Party Organization in Britain: Change and Con-

tinuity." In *Green Parties in Transition: The End of Grass-Roots Democracy?*, ed. E. Gene Frankland, Paul Lucardie, and Benoît Rihoux. Farnham: Ashgate.

Russell, Andrew, and Edward Fieldhouse. 2005. *Neither Left nor Right? The Liberal Democrats and the Electorate.* Manchester: Manchester University Press.

Sanchez, Rene. 1999. "Greens Turn Red over Defection." *Washington Post*, 30 October, A04.

Sauger, Nicholas. 2007. "The French Legislative and Presidential Elections of 2007." *West European Politics* 30.5: 1166–75.

Scarrow, Susan. 2000. "Parties without Members? Party Organization in a Changing Electoral Environment." In *Parties without Partisans: Political Changes in Advanced Industrial Democracies*, ed. Russell J. Dalton and Martin Wattenberg. New York: Oxford University Press.

Schain, Martin. 2000. "The National Front and the Legislative Elections of 1997." In *How France Votes*, ed. Michael S. Lewis-Beck. New York: Seven Bridges.

Schlesinger, Joseph A. 1991. *Political Parties and the Winning of Office.* Ann Arbor: University of Michigan Press.

Schlesinger, Joseph A., and Mildred S. Schlesinger. 1990. "The Reaffirmation of a Multiparty System in France." *American Political Science Review* 84.4: 1077–1101.

Schlesinger, Joseph A., and Mildred S. Schlesinger. 2000. "The Stability of the French Party System: The Enduring Impact of the Two-Ballot Electoral Rules." In *How France Votes*, ed. Michael S. Lewis-Beck. New York: Seven Bridges.

Schofield, Norman, and Itai Sened. 2006. *Multiparty Democracy: Elections and Legislative Politics.* New York: Cambridge University Press.

Schuessler, Alexander A. 2000. *A Logic of Expressive Choice.* Princeton: Princeton University Press.

Sciolino, Elaine. 2006. "Socialist Party Backs Woman in French Vote." *New York Times*, 17 November, A1.

Sciolino, Elaine. 2007. "French Interior Minister Sails to Presidential Nomination." *New York Times*, 15 January, A3.

Semetko, Holli A. 1996. "The Media." In *Comparing Democracies: Elections and Voting in Global Perspective*, ed. Lawrence Le Duc, Richard G. Niemi, and Pippa Norris. Thousand Oaks, CA: Sage.

Sharp, Jacqueline, and Anita Krajnc. 2009. "The Canadian Greens: Veering away from Grass-Roots Democracy So Soon?" In *Green Parties in Transition: The End of Grass-Roots Democracy?*, ed. E. Gene Frankland, Paul Lucardie, and Benoît Rihoux. Farnham: Ashgate.

Shull, Tad. 1999. *Redefining Red and Green: Ideology and Strategy in European Political Ecology.* Albany: State University of New York Press.

Sjöblom, Gunnar. 1968. *Party Strategies in Multiparty Systems.* Lund: Studentlitteratur.

Spoon, Jae-Jae. 2007. "Evolution of New Parties: From Electoral Outsiders to Downsian Players—Evidence from France." *French Politics* 5.2: 121–43.

Spoon, Jae-Jae. 2008. "Presidential and Legislative Elections in France, April–June 2007." *Electoral Studies* 27.1: 155–60.

Spoon, Jae-Jae. 2009. "Holding Their Own: The Persistence of the Green Parties in France and the UK." *Party Politics* 15.5: 615–34.

Strøm, Kaare. 1990. "A Behavioral Theory of Competitive Political Parties." *American Journal of Political Science* 34.2: 565–98.

Stueck, Wendy. 2008. "Tories Stifle Green Presence in House." *Toronto Globe and Mail*, 15 October, S2.

Swanson, David L., and Paolo Mancini. 1996. "Patterns of Modern Electoral Campaigning and Their Consequences." In *Politics, Media, and Modern Democracy: An International Study of Innovations in Electoral Campaigning and Their Consequences*, ed. David L. Swanson and Paolo Mancini. Westport, CT: Praeger.

Szarka, Joseph. 1994. "Green Politics in France: The Impasse of Non-Alignment." *Parliamentary Affairs* 47.3: 446–55.

Taagepera, Rein, and Matthew Sogberg Shugart. 1989. *Seats and Votes: The Effects and Determinants of Electoral Systems*. New Haven: Yale University Press.

Taber, Jane. 2007. "Insiders Shocked by Green-Grit Deal." *Toronto Globe and Mail*, 14 April, A4.

Tarrow, Sidney. 1998. *Power in Movement: Social Movements and Contentious Politics*. 2nd ed. New York: Cambridge University Press.

Tempest, Matthew. 2003. "Leader Question Dominates Green Conference." *Guardian*, 12 September, 11.

"To Count or Not to Count: France's Ethnic Minorities." 2009. *The Economist*, 28 March. www.economist.com. Accessed 5 January 2011.

Tsebelis, George. 1990. *Nested Games: Rational Choice in Comparative Politics*. Berkeley: University of California Press.

Van Cott, Donna Lee. 2005. *From Parties to Movements in Latin America: The Evolution of Ethnic Politics*. New York: Cambridge University Press.

van der Brug, Wouter, and Cees van der Eijk, eds. 2007. *European Elections and Domestic Politics: Lessons from the Past and Scenarios for the Future*. Notre Dame: University of Notre Dame Press.

van der Eijk, Cees, and Mark N. Franklin. 1996. *Choosing Europe? The European Electorate and National Politics in the Face of Union*. Ann Arbor: University of Michigan Press.

van der Eijk, Cees, Mark N. Franklin, and Michael Marsh. 1996. "What Voters Teach Us about Europe-Wide Elections: What Europe-Wide Elections Teach Us about Voters." *Electoral Studies* 15.2: 149–66.

van Eeckhout, Laetitia. 2004. "Noël Mamère Rompt Son Alliance avec Dominique Voynet; A Six Mois de Leur Congrès, les Verts Sont Toujours à la Recherche d'une 'Majorité Stable.'" *Le Monde*, 6 July, 7.

"Verts: Yves Cochet Propose de 'Dissoudre les Verts.'" 2005. *Le Monde*, 14 January.

Villalba, Bruno. 2008. "The French Greens: Changes in Activist Culture and Practices in a Constraining Environment." In *Green Parties in Transition: The End of Grass-Roots Democracy?*, ed. E. Gene Frankland, Paul Lucardie, and Benoît Rihoux. Farnham: Ashgate.

Virot, Pascal. 2007. "La Gauche en Mal d'Appareils." *Libération*, 25 June, Evenement 3.

Volkens, Andrea. 2007. "Strengths and Weaknesses of Approaches to Measuring Policy Positions of Parties." *Electoral Studies* 26.1: 108–20.

Wahl-Jorgensen, Karin. 2002. "Understanding the Conditions for Public Discourse: Four Rules for Selecting Letters to the Editor." *Journalism Studies* 3.1: 69–81.

Wahl-Jorgensen, Karin. 2004. "Playground of the Pundits or Voice of the People? Comparing British and Danish Opinion Pages." *Journalism Studies* 5.1: 59–70.

Wahl-Jorgensen, Karin. 2007. *Journalists and the Public: Newsroom Culture, Letters to the Editor, and Democracy*. Cresskill, NJ: Hampton.

Whitely, Paul, and Patrick Seyd. 1994. "Local Party Campaigning and Electoral Mobilisation in Britain." *Journal of Politics* 56.1: 242–52.

Widfeldt, Anders. 1999. *Linking Parties with People? Party Membership in Sweden, 1960–1997*. Aldershot: Ashgate.

Wittman, Donald A. 1973. "Parties as Utility Maximizers." *American Political Science Review* 67.2: 490–98.

Wittman, Donald A. 1983. "Candidate Motivation: A Synthesis of Alternative Theories." *American Political Science Review* 77.1: 142–57.

Ysmal, Colette. 1995. "Political Data Yearbook: France." *European Journal of Political Research* 28.3–4: 333–9.

Zappi, Sylvia. 2007a. "Ecologie Les Verts Sont dans une Crise Profonde après Leurs Mauvais Scores à la Présidentielle et aux Législatives; Yves Cochet Propose, sans Succès, aux Verts de Dissoudre pour se Refonder." *Le Monde*, 26 June, Politique 12.

Zappi, Sylvia. 2007b. "Jean-Luc Bennahmias: Au Centre l'Herbe Est Plus Verte." *Le Monde*, 23 May, Focus 17.

Data and Other Primary Sources

Adam Carr's Election Archive. http://psephos.adam-carr.net. Accessed 20 May 2009.

Benoit, Kenneth, and Michael Laver. 2006. *Party Policy in Modern Democracies*. London: Routledge.

Billard, Martine. 2007a. Posters and leaflets from legislative campaign.

Billard, Martine. 2007b. Letter to constituents in District 75-1. 6 June.

Blais, André, and Louis Massicotte. 2002. "Electoral Systems." In *Comparing Democracies 2: New Challenges in the Study of Elections and Voting*, ed. Lawrence LeDuc, Richard G. Niemi, and Pippa Norris. Thousand Oaks, CA: Sage.

British Labour Party. 2001. *Labour Party 2001 Manifesto.*
British Labour Party. 2005. *Labour Party 2005 Manifesto.*
Budge, Ian, Hans-Dieter Klingemann, Andrea Volkens, Judith Bara, and Eric Tanenbaum. 2001. *Mapping Policy Preferences: Estimates for Parties, Electors, and Governments, 1945–1988.* New York: Oxford University Press.
Center on Democratic Performance. Elections Results Archive. http://cdp.bing hamton.edu/era. Accessed 20 May 2009.
Centre d'Etude de la Vie Politique Française, Centre d'Informatisation des Données Socio-Politiques, and Centre d'Etudes et de Connaissances sur l'Opinion Publique. 2003. *Panel Electoral des Français 2002: Présidentielle et Législatives.* Grenoble, France: BDSP.
Centre d'Etude de la Vie Politique Française, Centre d'Informatisation des Données Socio-Politiques, and Centre de Recherches Administratives, Politiques, et Sociales. 2001. *French National Election Study, 1997* (Inter-University Consortium for Political Research version). Ann Arbor, MI: ICPSR.
Centre d'Informatisation des Données Socio-Politiques. 2007a. *Résultats des Elections Législatives par Circonscription, 1993–2007.* Grenoble: BDSP.
Centre d'Informatisation des Données Socio-Politiques. 2007b. *Résultats des Elections Présidentielles par Circonscription, 1995–2007.* Grenoble: BDSP.
Cochet, Yves. 2007. Posters and leaflets from legislative campaign.
Commission Nationale des Comptes de Campagne et des Financements Politiques. 1996. Publication Générale des Comptes des Partis et Groupements Politiques Afférents à l'Exercice 1995. *Journal Officiel.* 11–13 November. Annex to no. 262. p. 39153. Paris.
Commission Nationale des Comptes de Campagne et des Financements Politiques. 1997. Publication Générale des Comptes des Partis et Groupements Politiques Afférents à l'Exercice 1996. *Journal Officiel,* 29 October. Annex to no. 252, p. 45153. Paris.
Commission Nationale des Comptes de Campagne et des Financements Politiques. 2002. Publication Générale des Comptes des Partis et Groupements Politiques Afférents à l'Exercice 2000. *Journal Officiel,* 4 April. Annex to no. 79, p. 36205. Paris.
Commission Nationale des Comptes de Campagne et des Financements Politiques. 2004. Publication Générale des Comptes des Partis et Groupements Politiques au Titre de l'Exercice 2002. *Journal Officiel,* 18 September. Annex to no. 218, pp. 36218–19. Paris.
Commission Nationale des Comptes de Campagne et des Financements Politiques. 2005. Publication Générale des Comptes des Partis et Groupements Politiques au Titre de l'Exercice 2003. *Journal Officiel,* 8 September. Annex to no. 209, pp. 36212–13. Paris. http://www.cnccfp.fr/docs/partis/comptes/cnc cfp_comptes_2003.pdf. Accessed 16 March 2009.
Commission Nationale des Comptes de Campagne et des Financements Politiques. 2006. Publication Générale des Comptes des Partis et Groupements Politiques au Titre de l'Exercice 2004. *Journal Officiel,* 29 June. Annex to no.

149, pp. 36197–98. Paris. http://www.cnccfp.fr/docs/partis/comptes/cnc cfp_comptes_2004.pdf. Accessed 16 March 2009.
Commission Nationale des Comptes de Campagne et des Financements Politiques. 2007a. Publication. Générale des Comptes des Partis et Groupements Politiques au Titre de l'Exercice 2005. *Journal Officiel,* 25 January. Annex to no. 21, pp. 36205–6. Paris. http://www.cnccfp.fr/docs/partis/comptes/cnc cfp_comptes_2005.pdf. Accessed 16 March 2009.
Commission Nationale des Comptes de Campagne et des Financements Politiques. 2007b. Publication Générale des Comptes des Partis et Groupements Politiques au Titre de l'Exercice 2006. *Journal Officiel,* 27 December. Annex to no. 300, pp. 36687–88. Paris. http://www.cnccfp.fr/docs/partis/comptes/cnccfp_comptes_2006.pdf. Accessed 16 March 2009.
Commission Nationale des Comptes de Campagne et des Financements Politiques. 2008. Publication Générale des Comptes des Partis et Groupements Politiques au Titre de l'Exercice 2007. *Journal Officiel,* 17 December. Annex to no. 297, pp. 228–29. Paris. http://www.cnccfp.fr/docs/partis/comptes/cnc cfp_comptes_2007.pdf. Accessed 16 March 2009.
Elections Canada. www.elections.ca. Accessed 21 May 2009.
Election World. www.electionworld.org. Accessed 10 August 2007.
European Commission. 1999. *Eurobarometer* 51 (July). http://ec.europa.eu/pub lic_opinion/archives/eb/eb51/eb51_en.pdf. Accessed 19 May 2009.
European Election Study. 2004. *European Parliament Election Study 2004.* www.ees-homepage.net. Accessed 15 May 2009.
European Election Study. 2009. *European Parliament Election Study 2009, Voter Study.* Advance Release, 16 April 2010. www.piredeu.eu. Accessed 1 May 2010.
Farrell, David M. 2001. *Electoral Systems: A Comparative Introduction.* New York: Palgrave.
Federal Election Commission. www.fec.gov. Accessed 22 May 2009.
France. Interior Ministry. 2001. *Election Brochure.* Paris: Service d'Information du Gouvernement.
France. Interior Ministry. 2007. "Résultats des Elections Législatives 17 June 2007." www.interieur.gouv.fr/secions/a_votre_service/resultats-elections/LG2007/FE.html. Accessed 6 July 2007.
Golder, Matt. 2005. "Democratic Electoral Systems around the World, 1946–2000." *Electoral Studies* 24.1: 103–21.
Green Party of British Columbia. www.greenparty.bc.ca. Accessed 20 May 2009.
Green Party of Canada. www.greenparty.ca. Accessed 20 May 2009.
Green Party of England and Wales. N.d. *Manifesto for a Sustainable Society.* http://policy.greenparty.org.uk/mfss. Accessed 12 June 2006.
Green Party of England and Wales. 2001. *Green Party Manifesto: Reach for the Future.*
Green Party of England and Wales. 2002–8. *Report and Financial Statements.* http://www.electoralcommission.org.uk/party-finance/database-of-regis ters/statements-of-account. Accessed 12 March 2009.

Green Party of England and Wales. 2005. *Green Party Manifesto: The Real Choice for Real Change*.
Green Party of England and Wales. 2006. Constitution. Spring.
Green Party of England and Wales. 2007. "Results of Green Leadership Vote." http://www.greenparty.org.uk/news-archive/3249.html. Accessed 1 February 2009.
Green Party of England and Wales. 2008. "Caroline Lucas Is First Green Party Leader." http://www.greenparty.org.uk/news/caroline-lucas-is-first-green-party-leader.html. Accessed 3 February 2009.
Green Party of the United States. Election Database. www.gp.org/elections/candidates. Accessed 21 May 2009.
Guardian. 15 June 2004–31 December 2007.
Independent. 15 June 2004–31 December 2007.
Institut National de la Statistique et des Etudes Economiques. 2002. *Circonscriptions Législatives: Tableaux Analyses du Recensement de la Population, 1999*. (CD-ROM). Paris: INSEE.
Inter-Parliamentary Union. www.ipu.org. Accessed 10 June 2009.
International Institute for Democracy and Electoral Assistance. www.idea.int. Accessed 10 June 2009.
Klingemann, Hans-Dieter, Andrea Volkens, Judith Bara, Ian Budge, and Michael McDonald. 2006. *Mapping Policy Preferences II: Estimates for Parties, Electors, and Governments in Eastern Europe, European Union, and OECD, 1990–2003*. New York: Oxford University Press.
Kohlhaas, Jean-Charles. 2002. Letter to constituents in district 69-10. http://www.kohlhaas.lesverts.fr. Accessed 14 March 2003.
Laver, Michael, and W. Ben Hunt. 1992. *Policy and Party Competition*. London: Routledge.
Libération. 15 June 2004–31 December 2007.
Mackie, Thomas T. 1989. "General Elections in Western Nations during 1988." *European Journal of Political Research*. 17.6: 747-52.
Mackie, Thomas T. 1993. "United Kingdom." *European Journal of Political Research*. 24.4: 555–62.
Le Monde. 15 June 2004–31 December 2007.
Le Monde Dossiers et Documents. 1993. *Les Elections Législatives de Mars 1993*. Paris: Le Monde.
Le Monde Dossiers et Documents. 1997. *Les Elections Législatives 1997*. Paris: Le Monde.
National Assembly. 2002. "Elections Législatives 9 et 16 2002." www.assemble-nationale.com/elections/resultats.asp. Accessed 19 June 2002.
Norris, Pippa. 2005b. *British Parliamentary Constituency Database, 1992–2005*. http://ksghome.harvard.edu/~pnorris/Data/Data.htm. Accessed 5 January 2007.
Pagès, Olivier. 2007. Leaflet from legislative campaign.
Parti Socialiste. 2002. *La Vie en Mieux, La Vie Ensemble*.

Parti Socialiste. 2007. *Réussir Ensemble le Changement: Le Projet Socialiste pour la France.*
"Peter Cranie: An Anti-Racist Green Euro-MP for the North West of England." n.d. http://www.stopnickgriffin.org.uk. Accessed 15 June 2009.
United Kingdom Election Results. 1997. http://www.election.demon.co.uk/ge1997.html. Accessed 16 February 2010.
van der Eijk, Cees, et al. 2002. *1999 European Election Study* (Steinmetz Archive version). Amsterdam: Steinmetz Archive.
Les Verts. 1974–2007. Official Television Campaign Spots. Archived at the Institut National de l'Audiovisuel.
Les Verts. 2002. *Propositions pour le Programme des Verts: Législatives 2002.*
Les Verts. 2007a. *Le Monde Change, avec Les Verts Changeons le Monde: Programme des Elections Législatives 2007.*
Les Verts. 2007b. *Déclaration du Collège Exécutif des Verts du 11 Juin 2007.* 11 June. http://lesverts.fr/article.php3?id_article=3319. Accessed 20 June 2007.
Les Verts. 2008. *Communiqué de Presse: Le Collège Exécutif des Verts 2008–2011.* 9 December. http://lesverts.fr/article.php3?id_article=4309. Accessed 3 February 2009.

Party Leader and Elected Official Interviews

A1. United Kingdom—Cited in Text

Benjamin, Elise (Oxford City Councillor). 5 June 2006, Oxford.
Cranie, Peter (Green Party Executive Elections Coordinator). 23 June 2006, London.
Johnson, Darren (Green Party Member, Greater London Assembly). 20 June 2006, London.
Lambert, Jean (Green Party Member, European Parliament). 16 June 2006, London.
Lynch, Noel (Coordinator, London Green Party). 26 June 2006, London.
Mallender, Richard (Green Party Executive Chair). 12 July 2006, Brighton.
Oxfordshire Green Party Elections Agent. 14 June 2006, Oxford.
Ramsay, Adrian (Norwich City Councillor). 21 July 2006, Norwich.
Rose, Chris (Green Party National Elections Agent). 26 June 2006, London.
Taylor, Keith (Green Party Co-Principal Speaker). 13 July 2006, Brighton.
Williams, David (Oxford City Councillor). 5 June 2006, Oxford.

A2. United Kingdom—Not Cited by Name in Text

Members of Brighton and Hove City Council. July 2006.
Members of Lewisham Borough Council. June 2006.
Members of Norfolk County Council. July 2006.
Members of Norwich City Council. July 2006.

Members of Oxford City Council. June 2006.
Members of Oxfordshire County Council. June 2006.

B1. France—Cited in Text

Bennahmias, Jean-Luc (Green Chief Negotiator, 1997 Legislative Elections). 6 June 2003, Paris.
Billard, Martine (Green Party Deputy). 20 May 2003, Paris.
Boch, Michel (Green Party Elections Coordinator, 2007 Legislative Elections). 19 June 2007, Paris.
Cochet, Yves (Green Party Deputy). 20 May 2003, Paris.
Gleizas, Jérôme (Green Party Paris City Councillor and Member of Negotiating Team for 2007 Legislative Elections). 22 June 2007, Paris.
Malloreau, Serge (Green Party Elections Coordinator, 2002 Legislative Elections). 1 October 2002, 23 June 2003, Paris.
Mamère, Nöel (Green Party Deputy). 3 June 2003, Paris.

B2. France —Not Cited in Text

Boutault, Jacques (Green Party Mayor of Second Arrondissement, Paris). 20 May 2003, Paris.
Contassot, Yves (Deputy Mayor for Green Spaces, Paris). 3 June 2003, Paris.
Desessard, Jean (Green Party Senator). 21 June 2007, Paris.
Dubarry, Véronique (Tenth Arrondissement Councillor and Paris City Councillor). 16 May 2003, Paris.
Feraud, Rémi (Socialist Party Leader, Tenth Arrondissement, Paris). 26 May 2003, Paris.
Hufschmitt, Philippe (Green Party Leader, Tenth Arrondissement, Paris). 31 May 2003, Paris.
Knowles, Xavier (Spokesperson, Paris Green Party). 22 May 2003, Paris.
Kohlhaas, Jean-Charles (Green Party Rhône Departmental Secretary). 18 February 2003, Lyon.
Lebret, Marc (Socialist Party Leader, Third Arrondissement, Paris). 7 November 2002, Paris.
Lemaire, Gilles (Green Party National Secretary, 2002–3). 7 October 2002, 23 May 2003, Paris.
Marron, Gilles (Socialist Party Leader, Fourth Arrondissement, Paris). 4 November 2002, Paris.
Robert, Marc (Member, 2001 Green Municipal Negotiating Team). 31 May 2003, Paris.

Index

Adams, James, 6, 14, 29–30, 140
AGALEV. *See* To Start Living Differently
Aidenbaum, Pierre, 166n12
ALDE. *See* Alliance of Liberal Democrats
Aldrich, John H., 31
Alliance Ecologiste Indépendant. *See* Independent Ecologist Alliance
Alliance 90/The Greens, 7
Alliance of Ecologists, 20
Alliance of Liberals and Democrats, 173n16
Alvarez, R. Michael, 28, 95
Amorim Neto, Ocatvio, 9
Anders Gaan Leven. *See* To Start Living Differently
Anderson, John, 161n8
Andrews, Josephine T., 30
Andrews, William, 166n12
Argell, Siri, 148
ASGP. *See* Green Party of the United States
Assemblée Nationale. *See* National Assembly, parties in
Association of State Green Parties. *See* Green Party of the United States
Aubert, Marie-Hélène, 115–16, 131
Auffray, Alain, 127
Austria, parties in, 2–5, 7, 36, 42, 49, 51, 155, 161n3
Austrian Freedom Party, 5
Austrian Social Democratic Party, 51
Avodah. *See* Labor Party, Israeli

Balancing-interests hypothesis, 33, 35, 52
Basis for Renewal initiative, 22, 85, 87, 97, 169n16

Basque Solidarity, 1
Bayrou, François, 76, 116, 132, 168n35
Behr, Roy L., 9, 11, 150–51
Belgium, parties in, 2–4, 35, 36, 42, 155
Benjamin, Elise, 89, 169n12, 170n22
Bennahmias, Jean-Luc, 76, 115–16, 131–32, 166n14, 173n16
Benoit, Kenneth, 18, 24, 33–41, 43, 153, 154, 155, 163n7, 164n9
Berg, John C., 149–50
Bergan, Daniel, 110
Billard, Martine, 57, 74–75, 115–16, 129–32, 162n15, 165n10
Birch, Sarah, 104, 161n5
Blais, André, 28, 146, 164n5
BNP. *See* British National Party
Bock, Audie, 149
Bomberg, Elizabeth, 34
Bowler, Shaun, 112
Boy, Daniel, 58
Breton Democratic Union, 162n13
Brighton Pavilion, British Parliamentary constituency of, x, 23, 81, 85, 89–92, 99–101, 115
British Conservative Party, ix, 2, 10, 82–84, 86–88, 90, 93, 95, 97–98, 100, 104–6, 141, 159, 170n17, 171n45
British general election, 1992, 22–23, 80–81, 86, 137, 170n37
British general election, 1997, 23, 80–81, 86–87, 91, 99, 100, 170n37
British general election, 2001, 23, 31, 32, 80–81, 87, 91–93, 98–99, 103–5, 113, 170n29, 170n37

193

British general election, 2005, ix, x, 6, 8, 19, 23, 26, 32, 34, 80–82, 87, 90–93, 95, 98–105, 107, 119, 121, 135, 141, 170n29
British general election, 2010, ix, x, 8, 23, 91, 99, 103, 107, 115, 169n10, 171n44
British Green Party
  in Brighton and Hove, 100–102
  campaign strategies of, 102–3
  and coalitions, 81–84
  communication strategies of, 141–42
  and constituency selection, 103–6
  constraints of electoral system on, 19, 80–81
  and decentralist strategies, 85, 102–3
  electoral success of, 80, 107
  and electoralist strategies, 24, 85–91
  in the European Union, x, 22–23, 97, 107, 114, 118, 141–42, 168n5
  goals of, 22–23
  and grassroots activities, x, 22, 80, 85–86, 90, 92–97, 100, 107
  history of, 22–23
  in House of Commons, x, 23, 99
  internal party politics of, 22–23, 87, 102, 122, 125–27, 134–36
  in local government, 23, 83–84, 91–102, 107
  in London, 32, 81, 83, 87–88, 90, 113, 115, 118, 136, 168n5, 170n29
  media coverage of, 121–30, 133–38
  in national politics, 79–80, 82–87, 90
  in Norwich, 92–97
  in Oxford, 98–100
  and party conference, 1989, 79
  and policy differentiation, 31–32
  policy positions of, 18, 26, 31–32, 34, 36, 79, 82, 94, 96, 168n1
  policy strategies of, 93, 99, 102
  and professionalization, 113–14
  and relationships with other parties, 79–84
  and state structure, 8–9
  support for, 87, 94, 96
  in Wales, 32, 79–80, 82–83, 85, 91, 103, 111, 113–14, 118, 124, 137, 144, 162n18, 168n5
  and Welsh Assembly, 32
British local elections, 2005, 82, 98
British local elections, 2009, 92, 96

British National Front, 162n13
British National Party, 103, 162n13, 171n44
British Parliamentary Constituency Database, 80–81, 105
Brynin, Malcolm, 110
Budge, Ian, 24, 29, 33–34, 42, 45, 47–48, 153, 154, 163n7
Bundestag, 88
Bündnis 90/Die Grünen. *See* Alliance 90/The Greens
Burchell, John, 15, 20, 22–23, 79, 87
Burton, Jonathan, 110

Callaghan, Jim, 169n10
Cameron, David, ix, 97, 170n35, 171n45
Campbell, Angus, 11
Campbell, Peter, 164n3
Canada, parties in, 8, 146–49, 173n1
Carey, Sean, 110
Carroll, Richard, 149
Carrubba, Cliff, 117
Cartel parties, 10
Carter, Jimmy, 161–62n8
Carter, Neil, 26–27, 34, 80–81, 85, 114, 125, 133
Casa delle Liberta. *See* House of Freedoms
Castagnou, Pierre, 74–75
Castles, Francis G., 163n3
Catchall parties, 5, 9–10, 13, 15, 29
CDU. *See* German Christian Democratic Union
Challenger parties, 30
Champion parties, 30
Chhibber, Pradeep K., 8, 145
Chirac, Jacques, 21, 49, 75, 168n35
Christian Democrats, Swedish, 6, 144
Christian Social Union of Bavaria, 172n1
Christlich Demokratische Union Deutschlands. *See* German Christian Democratic Union
Christlich-Soziale Union in Bayern. *See* Christian Social Union of Bavaria
Civil solidarity pact, 173n11
Clark, Alistair, 94
Clark, Michael, 6, 14, 29–30, 140
Clark, William Roberts, 9
Cobb, David, 150

Cochet, Yves, 8, 74–75, 77, 115–16, 127, 129–32, 173n12, 173n13
Cohn-Bendit, Daniel, 77, 158
Cole, Alistair, 20, 164n3
Coligação Democrática Unitária. *See* Democratic Unity Coalition
Comhaontas Glas. *See* Green Alliance
Commission Nationale de Comptes de Campagne et de Financements Politiques, 113
Communication strategies, and newspaper culture, 16, 137
Comparative Manifestos Project, 33, 35, 40, 41, 43, 49, 51–52, 155–56, 164n9
Compensatory voting, 12
Confederation Ecologiste. *See* Ecologist Confederation
Conservative Party of Canada, 147–49
Context, definition of, 16–17
Cordier, Caroline, 127
Cox, Gary W., 7, 9, 28, 95, 145
Cranie, Peter, 80, 82–83, 102, 112, 163n20, 168n3, 168n6, 169n8, 170n27, 171n43, 171n44, 172n2
Credibility, definition of, 17
CSU. *See* Christian Socialist Union of Bavaria
Curry, Bill, 148
Curtice, John, 110
Cutts, David, 87, 94

Dafis, Cynog, 79
Dalton, Russell J., 2, 6, 11, 34, 54, 62, 104, 110, 163n8
Dao, James, 10
de Rugy, François, 74, 116
Delanoë, Bertrand, 74
Delors, Jacques, 74
Democratic Movement, 76–77, 116, 168n35, 173n16
Democratic Party, 10, 149
Democratic Unity Coalition, 49
Denmark, parties in, 3, 4, 36, 42, 45, 146, 155–56
Denver, David, 86–87, 94
d'Hondt system, 145–46, 171n44
Dion, Douglas, 162n12
Dion, Stéphane, 148
District magnitude, 7–8, 145–46
Divers Droite. *See* Miscellaneous Right
Doherty, Brian, 20

Dominique Voynet, 1, 8, 21, 75, 127, 130
Downs, Anthony, 10, 12–14, 26–27, 29, 140
Duflot, Cécile, 78, 172n5
Durability, definition of, 16
Dutch List Pim Fortuyn, 11
Duverger, Maurice, 7, 58, 95
Duverger's Law, 8–9, 18
DVD. *See* Miscellaneous Right

EA. *See* Basque Solidarity
Earnshaw, David, 117, 120
Eckstein, Harry, 151
Ecoiffier, Matthieu, 173n16
Ecolo. *See* Ecologist
Ecologie, French ideology of, 26, 34, 76, 78, 142, 168n34
Ecologie Aujourd'hui. *See* Ecology Today
Ecologie '78. *See* Ecology '78
Ecologist, 7, 154
Ecologist Confederation, 162n14
Ecologist Party, 162n14
Ecology Party. *See* British Green Party
Ecology '78, 162n14
Ecology Today, 162n14
Eder, John, 149
Electoral competition, 13
Electoral thresholds, 7–8, 16–17, 54, 57, 118, 145–47, 173n1
Electoral volatility, 2, 161n2
Entente des Ecologistes. *See* Alliance of Ecologists
Environmental Party, the, Greens, the, 37
ERC. *See* Republican Left of Catalonia
Esquerra Republicana de Catalunya. *See* Republican Left of Catalonia
Ethnoterritorial parties, 2, 6–7, 26, 144, 163n1
Europe Ecologie list, 119
European Constitution, 119, 121–22, 125, 127, 130–32
European Council Decision 8964/02, 172n7
European Election Study 2004, 111
European Election Study 2009, 111
European Parliament, parties in, 1, 4, 77, 168n5, 171n44, 171n45, 173n16
European parliamentary elections, 1984, 19
European parliamentary elections, 1989, 20, 22, 116, 118, 137, 171n45

European parliamentary elections, 1994, 116–18, 137
European parliamentary elections, 1999, 62–63, 114, 116, 118, 133–34, 172n8
European parliamentary elections, 2004, 76, 97, 113–16, 118–19, 130, 134
European parliamentary elections, 2009, 23, 142, 171n44
European parliamentary elections, in Britain, 97, 113–15, 137, 172n8
European parliamentary elections, in France, 19, 22, 62–63, 76, 115–17, 118–19, 137
Eusko Alkartasuna. *See* Basque Solidarity
Expert survey data, 17, 24, 33–37, 40–41, 43, 51–52, 140, 143, 163n2, 163n3
Ezrow, Lawrence, 7, 29–30, 50, 145

Fabius, Laurent, 75
Farrell, David M., 9, 94, 112, 146
Faucher, Florence, 20–21
Federal Election Commission, 9, 150
Federalism, 8, 153
Fédération de la Gauche Démocrate et Socialiste. *See* Federation of the Democratic and Socialist Left
Federation of the Democratic and Socialist Left, 168n35
Federation of the Greens, 37
Federazione dei Verdi. *See* Federation of the Greens
Ferrara, Federico, 64, 117
Fieldhouse, Edward, 86–87
Finland, parties in, 2–4, 7, 30, 36, 42, 51, 155, 161n3
Finnish Social Democratic Party, 51
Finnish Swedish People's Party, 7, 30
Flanagan, Scott, 11
Flash parties, 11
Flautre, Hélène, 115–16, 131
Flemish Block/Interest, 2, 144, 161n3
Flemish Green Party, 36, 43
FN. *See* National Front
Fowler, Carwyn, 79
FPÖ. *See* Austrian Freedom Party
Frankland, E. Gene, 79, 171n45
Franklin, Mark, 28, 64, 95, 117, 128
Freese, Jeremy, 167n18
Freiheitliche Partei Österreichs. *See* Austrian Freedom Party

French Communist Party, 9
French Green Party
  and 1997 legislative election, 8, 21, 49–50, 53–56, 59–60, 62, 69–71, 73, 76, 113, 140–41, 166n14
  and 2002 legislative election, 8, 21–22, 24, 49–50, 53–56, 58–71, 75, 113, 140–41, 166nn13–14, 168n33
  and 2007 legislative election, 19–22, 24, 26, 53–56, 73–78, 113, 126, 132, 141–42
  campaign strategies of, 57–59, 73–74
  communication strategies of, 24–25
  and electoral constraints, 71–72, 145
  and electoral reform, 51, 54–56, 78
  electoral success of, 25, 55, 60
  and EU Constitution, 125–26
  in the European Union, 77, 117–19
  goals of, 78
  history of, 19–22
  internal party politics of, 22, 62, 75–77, 83, 114, 126, 132, 141–42, 162nn14–15
  leadership of, 131–32
  media coverage of, 119–38, 141–42
  in the National Assembly, 21, 57, 72, 74–76, 129, 141–42, 165n7, 166n12
  and policy differentiation, 74
  policy positions of, 34, 37, 49–51, 76, 78
  policy strategies of, 58, 72–73
  and preelection coalitions, 8, 24, 49–50, 53, 56–72, 136–37, 140–41, 166nn13–15
  and professionalization, 113
  and relationship to other parties, 24, 60–61, 74–75
  support for, 56–58, 61–62
  and voters, 61–62, 77
French legislative elections, 1988, 55, 164n6, 172n3
French legislative elections, 1993, 20–22, 49, 55
French legislative elections, 1997, 8, 21, 49–50, 53–56, 59–60, 62–63, 67, 69–71, 73, 113, 140–41, 164n4, 166nn14–15, 166n17
French legislative elections, 2002, 8, 21–22, 24, 49–51, 53–56, 58–71, 75–76, 113, 140–41, 164n4, 166nn13–15, 168n31, 169n14
French legislative elections, 2007, 24, 26, 53–56, 73–78, 113, 116, 121, 126, 132, 141–42, 164n4

INDEX 197

French presidential elections, 1988, 20
French presidential elections, 2002, 21, 76, 117, 131, 165n8
French presidential elections, 2007, 24, 113, 130–31, 168n31, 173n12, 173n15
French regional elections, 1992, 20
Front National. *See* National Front

Gallagher, Michael, 2, 54
Garry, John, 40
Gauche plurielle. *See* Plural left
GE. *See* Generation Ecology
Geddes, Barbara, 162n12
Génération Ecologie. *See* Generation Ecology
Generation Ecology, 20, 116
Generational hypothesis, 162n9
Gerber, Alan, 110
German Christian Democratic Union, 172n1
German Social Democratic Party, 2, 155
Germany, parties in, 2–4, 7–8, 15, 20, 30, 36, 42, 51, 76, 88, 155
G/GPUSA. *See* Green Party of the United States
GL. *See* Green Left
Glasgow, Garrett, 6, 14, 29, 30, 140
Glover, Julian, 10
Golder, Matt, 9, 146
Golder, Sona Nadenichek, 56, 164n5
Gorski, Philip S., 26
GPEx. *See* Green Party Executive
GPUS. *See* Green Party of the United States
Grassroots politics, in Britain, x, 22, 34, 80, 85–86, 90, 92, 94, 97, 100, 107
Grassroots politics, in France, 78, 168n34
Grassroots politics, revisionist school of, 94
Greater London Assembly, 19, 23, 83, 87–88
Greece, parties in, 3–4, 36, 42, 45, 156, 169n9
Green!, 7
Green agenda
 definition of, 34
 saliency of, 40–46
Green Alliance, 7, 155
Green Committees of Correspondence. *See* Green Party of the United States
Green League, Finnish, 2, 7, 30, 161n3
Green Left, 30, 155

Green parties
 and European integration, 34, 36, 40, 42, 44–46, 153
 in the European Union, 1, 77, 131, 173n12, 173n14
 and multiculturalism, 34–35, 40–42, 44–46, 154
 as niche parties, 2, 4, 6, 144
 origins of, 2, 19, 124–25
 policy preferences of, 34–50
 and social justice, 21, 34–35, 40, 42–45, 78, 155, 168n34, 168n1 (chap. 4)
 successes of, 2, 7, 41, 50, 146–51
Green Party Executive, 80, 89, 103, 112, 168n3
Green Party of British Columbia, 148
Green Party of Canada, 147–49, 173n1
Green Party of England and Wales. *See* British Green Party
Green Party of the United States, 149–51
Green 2000 initiative, 22, 85, 169n16
Green Wash, 96–97
Greenleaf, 89
Greens, the, Austrian, 2, 155–56
Greens, the, Luxembourgish, 39, 155
Greens-European Free Alliance, 1, 77, 131, 173n14, 173n16
Greens/Green Party USA. *See* Green Party of the United States
Gréng, Déi. *See* Greens, the Luxembourgish
Griffin, Nick, 171n44
Groen!. *See* Green!
GroenLinks. *See* Green Left
Guardian, The, 120, 124, 134, 137
Grünen, Die. *See* Greens, the, Austrian

Hands, Gordon, 86, 94
Hansen, John Mark, 162n9
Harmel, Robert, 9, 14, 16
Harper, Steven, 149
Harris, Evan, 99
Harris, Jim, 147
Hicken, Allen, 8
Hinich, Melvin, 14
Hitchcock, William I., 139
Hix, Simon, 64, 117
Hobolt, Sara Binzer, 64, 117
Hollande, François, 56
Holliday, Ian, 20
House of Freedoms, 53
Huber, John, 163n3

Hug, Simon, 9, 11, 161n6, 162n11
Hulot, Nicolas, 132, 173n15
Hunt, W. Ben, 17, 24, 34–38, 153–54, 163n6

Iceland, parties in, 2–4, 36, 38, 42, 155–56
Ignazi, Piero, 11
Independent, The, 120, 124, 128, 134
Independent Ecologist Alliance, 119, 126
Independent Ecologist Movement, 119, 126
Independent Working Class Association, 169n15
India, parties in, 8, 16, 145
Indridason, Indridi, 164n5
Inglehart, Ronald, 6, 11, 34, 62, 104, 163n3
Institutional reform, French party positions, 51
Ireland, parties in, 2–4, 7–8, 30, 32, 36–37, 42, 118, 155–56
Isler Béguin, Marie-Anne, 115–16, 131–32
Israel, parties in, 53
Issue salience, 14, 35–36, 38–39, 41, 43
Italian Communist Party, 2
Italy, parties in, 3–4, 8, 36, 42, 53, 155
IWCA. *See* Independent Working Class Association
Iyengar, Shanto, 110

Janda, Kenneth, 14
Jick, Todd D., 18
Johnson, Darren, 83, 88, 136, 169n8, 169n13, 170nn20–21, 170n29
Johnston, Ron, 87, 170n17
Jones, Jenny, 136
Jones, Rhys, 79
Jospin, Lionel, 8, 21, 59, 65, 116, 165–66n11, 168n31, 169n14, 173n12
Judge, David, 117, 120

Karlan, Dean, 110
Katz, Richard, 10
Keaten, Jamey, 75
Kedar, Orit, 12
Keohane, Robert O., 18
Key, V. O., 109
Key Seats Initiative, 86–87, 90

Kinder, Donald, 110
King, Gary, 18
Kirchheimer, Otto, 5, 9, 13, 29, 140
Kitschelt, Herbert, 10–11, 13, 26, 145
Klingemann, Hans-Dieter, 17, 24, 33–34, 41–42, 45, 48, 153–55, 156, 163n7
Kohlhaas, Jean-Charles, 56–57
Kollman, Ken, 8, 145
Koole, Ruud, 9
Krajnc, Anita, 147–48, 173nn1–2
Kristdemokraterna. *See* Christian Democrats, Swedish
Kuhn, Raymond, 111

Laakso, Markku, 53
Labor Party, Israeli, 52–53
Labour Party, British, 34, 45, 82–85, 97, 100, 155–56
Labour Party, Maltese, 37
Labour Party Co-operative, 100, 170n39
LaDuke, Winona, 150
Lalonde, Brice, 20
LaMarche, Pat, 150
Lambert, Jean
  and activities in the European Parliament, 83, 85, 114–15, 118, 125, 133–34, 168n2
  and activities in the United Kingdom, 22, 87, 169n8
Latin America, parties in, 17, 161
Laver, Michael, 2, 17, 24, 27, 33–41, 43, 54, 83, 153–55, 156, 163nn6–7, 164n9
Law 88-227, 172n3
Law 99-944, 173n11
Layton, Jack, 148
Lazarus, Edward H., 9, 11, 150–51
LCR. *See* Revolutionary Communist League
Le Pen, Jean-Marie, 21, 61–68, 70, 72, 75, 158, 167nn21–23, 168n31
Left Party, 162n15
Lega Nord. *See* Northern League
Lewis-Beck, Michael S., 11
Lewisham Deptford, British parliamentary constituency, ix, 23, 81, 90–91, 170n29
Liao, Tim Futing, 167n26
Liberal Democrats, ix, 6, 8–9, 19, 79, 83–84, 86–87, 90–93, 95, 99–100, 104, 106–7, 118, 161n4, 169n15, 171n44
Liberal Party of Canada, 148

Libération (Libé), 120, 123–24, 128
Lib-Lab pact, 83, 169n10
Ligue Communiste Revolutionnaire.
  See Revolutionary Communist
  League
Lijphart, Arend, 145
Lijst Pim Fortuyn. *See* List Pim Fortuyn
Likud, 53
Lipietz, Alain, 115–16, 129–32
List Pim Fortuyn, 11
LN. *See* Northern League
Local Government Act of 1992, 83
Long, J. Scott, 167n18
Lucas, Caroline
  and activities in the European Parliament, 85, 99, 118
  and activities in the United Kingdom, x, 23, 85, 91, 99, 100, 114–15
  and media coverage, 125, 129–30, 133–35, 137
L'Ulivo. *See* Olive Tree, the
Lutte Ouvrière. *See* Workers' Struggle
Luxembourg, parties in, 3–4, 7, 36, 39, 42, 46, 155
Lynch, Noel, 169n13, 170n21

M + 1 rule, 7
Maddala, G. S., 167n26
Mainstream parties, 1–2, 12, 14, 20, 24, 27, 29–33, 50, 52, 57, 60, 69, 72, 140, 144, 163n1, 166n15
Mair, Peter, 2, 10, 54, 163n3
Majoritarian electoral systems, 8, 12, 18, 117
Mallender, Richard, 89, 168n3, 170n23
Malta, parties in, 8, 36, 42, 45, 156
Mamère, Noël, 164 unnumbered note, 167n22
  and elections, 21, 53, 62–68, 70–72, 74, 76, 116, 158
  and media coverage, 115–17, 124, 126, 129–32
Mancini, Paolo, 112
Manifesto for a Sustainable Society, 79, 96, 168n1
Marjoram, John, 162n19
Marker parties, 29
Markovits, Andrei S., 26
Marsh, Ian, 169n10
Marsh, Michael, 64, 117
Martin, Pierre, 165n9

Maslow's hierarchy of needs, 11
Materialism, 2, 11
May, Elizabeth, 147–48
Mayer, Nonna, 12, 61
Mayes, Ian, 137
McAllister, Ian, 2
Meguid, Bonnie M., 2, 6, 12, 14, 106, 144, 150, 161n7, 162n13, 171n45
MEI. *See* Independent Ecologist Movement
Members of the European Parliament
  in Britain, 19, 83, 85, 99, 107, 114–15, 118–20
  in France, 19, 115–20
  media coverage of, 114, 120–36
  strategies of, 119–20, 127, 129, 136–38
Merkel, Angela, 172n1
Merrill, Samuel, 14
Mikhaylov, Slava, 40–41, 154, 163n7, 164n9
Miljöpartiet de Gröna. *See* The Environmental Party, the Greens
Miller, Gary, 31
Miller, Warren, 11
Miscellaneous Right, 166
Mitterrand, François, 20, 119, 168n35
MoDem. *See* Democratic Movement
Monde, Le, 26, 55, 120, 123, 124
Money, Jeannette, 30
Mouvement Démocrate. *See* Democratic Movement
Mouvement des Radicaux de Gauche. *See* Movement of Radicals of the Left
Mouvement Ecologiste Indépendant. *See* Independent Ecologist Movement
Movement of Radicals of the Left, 119
Moy, Patricia, 110
Mozaffar, Shaheen, 9
MRG. *See* Movement of Radicals of the Left
Müller, Wolfgang, 13, 83
Munger, Michael, 14

Nader, Ralph, 10, 150
Nagler, Jonathan, 28, 95
National Assembly, parties in, 51, 55, 76–77, 166n12
National Front, 2, 54, 60, 103, 162n13
NDP. *See* New Democratic Party
Netherlands, parties in, 3–4, 7, 9, 36, 42, 45, 155–56

New Democratic Party, 148
New Left parties. *See* Niche parties
New Politics parties. *See* Niche parties
Newton, Kenneth, 110
Niche parties
　definition of, 1–2, 6
　and environment, 7, 30, 144
　and ethnoterritorialism, 7, 144
　and extreme right, 7, 12, 26, 144
　formation of, 11
　policy positions of, 29–30
　as small parties, 6, 139, 162n13
　strategies of, 13–14, 29–30
　success of, 2–4, 7, 12–14, 139
Niemi, Richard G., 28, 95
Norris, Pippa, 9, 80–81, 91, 94, 105, 110–12, 145–46
North West, British European Parliament constituency of, 171n44
Northern League, 1, 7, 30, 144
Norway, parties in, 3–4, 7, 36, 42, 45, 156, 169n9
Norwich City Council Elections, 87, 93
Norwich South, British constituency of, ix, 23, 81, 90–93, 95–96, 101–2
Nuclear energy, French party positions, 50–51, 76

Old Politics, 2, 6, 26
Olive Tree, the, 53
O'Neill, Michael, 20, 22, 79–80
Onesta, Gerard, 115–16, 131
Oppenhuis, Erik, 64
Ordeshook, Peter, 9

Pacte civil de solidarité. *See* Civil solidarity pact
Pagès, Olivier, 76
Panebianco, Angelo, 14, 94, 111
Parkin, Sara, 22
Parti Communiste Français. *See* French Communist Party
Parti de Gauche. *See* Left Party
Parti des Travailleurs. *See* Workers' Party
Parti Ecologiste. *See* Ecologist Party
Parti Radical de Gauche. *See* Radical Left Party
Parti Socialiste. *See* Socialist Party, French
Partido Social Democrata. *See* Social Democratic Party, Portuguese
Partido Socialista. *See* Socialist Party, Portuguese
Partit Laburista. *See* Labour Party, Maltese
Partito Comunista Italiano. *See* Italian Communist Party
Party leaders, strategies of, 22, 30–31, 52, 57, 77, 84, 87–89, 96, 106
Party leaders, types of, 27–28, 112
Party of the Corsican Nation, 162n13
Party of Wales, 79, 82, 144, 162n13
Pattie, Charles, 87, 170n17
PCF. *See* French Communist Party
PCI. *See* Italian Communist Party
Pedersen, Mogens N., 161n2
Pedersen Index, 161n2
People, 1, 161n1
People's Party, 161n1
Perot, H. Ross, 161n8
Perrineau, Pascal, 12, 61
Pfau, Michael, 110
PG. *See* Left Party
Pierce, Roy, 54
Plaid Cymru. *See* Party of Wales
Plural left, 49, 60, 166n13
PNC. *See* Party of the Corsican Nation
Poguntke, Thomas, 112
Political Parties, Elections and Referendums Act of 2000, 172n3
Portugal, parties in, 3–4, 36, 42, 45, 46, 49, 155
Postmaterialism, 11, 34, 163n8
Preelection alliances. *See* Preelection coalitions
Preelection coalitions
　in 1997 French legislative elections, 8, 21, 49–50, 56, 59–60
　in 2002 French legislative elections, 8, 24, 49–50, 53, 56–72
　in 2007 French legislative elections, 24, 53, 73–78
　in Britain, 79, 82
　conditions for, 60–73
　definition of, 49, 53
　Green-Socialist, 56–78, 173n13
Presidentialization, of parties, 112
PRG. *See* Radical Left Party
Professionalization, of parties, 111–13
Przeworski, Adam, 13–14, 31
PS. *See* Socialist Party, French; Socialist Party, Portuguese
PSD. *See* Social Democratic Party, Portuguese

PT. *See* Workers' Party
Pure policy-differentiation hypothesis, 32
Pure vote-maximization hypothesis, 33

Rabier, Jacques-René, 6, 11
Radical Left Party, 56
Radical right parties, 6–7, 145
Rae, Douglas W., 7
Rally for the Republic, 2, 54
Ramsay, Adrian, 85, 92–94, 101–2, 170n30, 171n42
Rassemblement pour la République. *See* Rally for the Republic
Reagan, Ronald, 161–62n8
Reif, Karlheinz, 64, 117, 128
Renard, Xavier, 77
Republican Left of Catalonia, 144
Republican Party, 10, 161–62n8
RESPECT, 82, 169n15
Revolutionary Communist League, 169n14
Rice, Roberta, 161n5
Riker, William H., 7
Robertson, John D., 9, 16
Rocard, Michel, 20, 119
Rootes, Christopher, 80
Rose, Chris, 90, 163n20, 169n12, 170nn26–27
Rosenstone, Steven J., 9, 11, 150–51, 162n9
Royal, Ségolène, 74–75, 168n31
RPR. *See* Rally for the Republic
Rüdig, Wolfgang, 9, 11, 22, 85, 114, 125, 161n6
Russell, Andrew, 86–87

Sanchez, Rene, 149
Sarkozy, Nicholas, 75, 77, 166n16
Sauger, Nicholas, 168n32
Scarrow, Susan, 94
Schain, Martin, 61
Schlesinger, Joseph A., 13, 54–56, 85, 145
Schlesinger, Mildred S., 54–56, 85, 145
Schmitt, Hermann, 64, 117, 128
Schofield, Norman, 31, 83
Schuessler, Alexander A., 28, 58
Schweizerische Volkspartei. *See* Swiss People's Party
Sciolino, Elaine, 75
Scotland, parties in, 9, 32, 80

Scottish National Party, 162n13, 170n19
Scottish Parliament, 170n19
SDP. *See* Social Democratic Party of Finland
Semetko, Holli A., 110
Sened, Itai, 31
Seyd, Patrick, 94
Sharp, Jacqueline, 147–48, 173nn1–2
Sheffield Central, British parliamentary constituency of, 81
Shryane, Nick, 87, 94
Shugart, Matthew Sogberg, 8
Shull, Tad, 34
Shvetsova, Olga, 9
Sjöblom, Gunnar, 13
Small parties
  communication strategies of, 2, 4, 12, 15, 18–19, 141–42
  and electoral constraints, 15, 24, 26, 53, 71–72, 80, 107, 141
  electoral strategies of, 2, 4, 12, 14–15, 18–19, 140–41
  leadership of, 14
  and media coverage, 107
  and plurality, 4, 8, 15, 17–18, 24, 27–28, 55, 78, 80, 87, 90–91, 95, 97, 107, 136, 139–40, 145–46
  and policy differentiation, 4, 15–16, 24–25, 28, 31–33, 38–40, 43, 46, 50–51, 139–40, 145
  policy strategy of, 2, 10, 12–15, 17, 24, 26–30, 49–50, 52, 140
  and presidentialization, 112
  and professionalization, 111–13
  and proportional representation, 4, 8, 28, 35, 51, 76, 117, 145, 161n5, 164n3, 165n9
  and second-order elections, 63–64, 107, 117, 128–29
  and state structure, 146–51
  success and failure of, 7, 9–10, 16
  and vote maximization, 4, 15–17, 23, 25, 27–28, 33, 46, 53, 138–40, 162n10, 163–64n8
Small party agency, definition of, 4, 12
Social cleavages, 9
Social Democratic Party, Portuguese, 46
Social Democratic Party of Finland, 51, 155
Socialist Party, French, 8, 34, 54, 76, 119, 155
Socialist Party, Portuguese, 46

Sozialdemokratische Partei der Schweiz. *See* Swiss Social Democratic Party
Sozialdemokratische Partei Deutschlands. *See* German Social Democratic Party
Sozialdemokratische Partei Österreichs. *See* Austrian Social Democratic Party
SP. *See* Swiss Social Democratic Party
Spain, parties in, 3–4, 36, 42, 45, 144, 156, 169n9
SPD. *See* German Social Democratic Party
SPÖ. *See* Austrian Social Democratic Party
Spoon, Jae-Jae, 64, 117, 168n32
Sprague, John, 13–14, 31
Steel, David, 169n10
Steinmeir, Frank Walter, 172n1
Stoke Newington, British constituency of, 81
Strategic, definition of, 16
Strauss-Kahn, Dominique, 75
Strøm, Kaare, 13, 83
Stueck, Wendy, 147
Success, definition of, 16
Suomen Sosialidemokraattinen Puolue. *See* Social Democratic Party of Finland
Suppléant, 56, 74, 166n12
Survivability, definition of, 16. *See* also durability
Survival, definition of, 16
Svenska Folkpartiet. *See* Swedish People's Party
SVP. *See* Swiss People's Party
Swanson, David L., 112
Sweden, parties in, 3–4, 7, 36, 42, 50, 155, 169n9
Swedish People's Party, 7, 30
Swiss People's Party, 1, 5
Swiss Social Democratic Party, 37
Switzerland, parties in, 3–4, 7, 36, 42, 155
Szarka, Joseph, 21

Taagepera, Rein, 8, 54
Taber, Jane, 148
Target Voters in Target Seats Initiative, 86
Tarrow, Sidney, 125
Taylor, Keith, x, 23, 90, 92, 99–101
Tempest, Matthew, 135
Teune, Henry, 18
Thatcher, Margaret, 87
Tilley, James, 117

Timpone, Richard J., 117
To Start Living Differently, 43, 155
Treaty of Amsterdam, 172n7
Tsebelis, George, 55, 85, 145

U Partitu di a Nazione Corsa. *See* Party of the Corsican Nation
UDB. *See* Breton Democratic Union
UDF. *See* Union for French Democracy
U.K. Electoral Commission, 113, 172n3
U.K. European Parliament Elections Act, 118
UKIP. *See* United Kingdom Independence Party
UMP. *See* Union for a Popular Movement
Union Démocratique Bretonne. *See* Breton Democratic Union
Union for a Popular Movement, 54
Union for French Democracy, 54
Union pour la Démocratie Française. *See* Union for French Democracy
Union pour un Mouvement Populaire. *See* Union for a Popular Movement
United Kingdom Independence Party, 118
United Kingdom Political Parties, Elections and Referendums Act of 2000, 172n3
United States, parties in, 8, 9, 137, 145–46, 149–51
U.S. Democratic Party, 10, 149

Van Cott, Donna Lee, 17, 161n5, 162n11
van der Brug, Wouter, 64, 117, 128
van der Eijk, Cees, 64, 117, 128
van Eeckhout, Laetitia, 127
Verba, Sidney, 18
Verts, Les. *See* French Green Party
Viability, definition of, 17
Villalba, Bruno, 112
Virheä Liitto. *See* Green League, Finnish
Virot, Pascal, 77
Vlaams Block/Belang. *See* Flemish Block/Interest
Volkens, Andrea, 33, 163n2
Vote Green, Go Blue, 10, 171n45
Vote maximization, 4, 15–17, 23, 25, 27–28, 33, 46, 53, 138–40, 162n10, 163–64n8
Voters, types of, 28–29
Voynet, Dominique, 1, 8, 21, 75, 126–27, 130–31, 173n12

Waechter, Antoine, 20–21
Wahl-Jorgensen, Karin, 137
Wales, parties in, 32, 79, 80, 82, 144
Wasted vote, 11, 95, 109
Wattenberg, Martin P., 2, 11
Webb, Paul, 9, 94, 112
Weishaupt, J. Timo, 64, 117
Whitely, Paul, 94
Whitten, Guy, 28, 95
Widfeldt, Anders, 94

Williams, David, 169n7
Wilson, Blair, 147
Wittman, Donald A., 14, 27, 73, 140
Woodin, Mike, 170n37
Workers' Party, 169n14
Workers' Struggle, 169n14

Ysmal, Colette, 119

Zappi, Sylvia, 76–77